THE PHILIPPINES EXPAT ADVISOR

HOW TO MOVE TO THE PHILIPPINES EASIER, FASTER AND CHEAPER!

by Dave DeWall

DEDICATED TO MY BEAUTIFUL ASAWA OF OF 13 YEARS, THE SAINTED PATIENT WIFE, MELINDA.

She's never given up on me despite my complaining, grumpiness and my occasional habit of drinking too many bottles of chilled San Miguel Pale Pilsen. God Bless Her. She's the best! How she puts up with me, I'll never know!

Table of Contents

INTRODUCTION

You've probably read a lot already about the Philippines if you've gone to the trouble to shell out some hard-earned money to buy this E-book. No doubt you have checked out some blogs and websites and perhaps have purchased other E-books extolling the praises of the "paradise" called the Philippines.

While I thoroughly enjoy living in the Philippines (aside from the occasional brown outs), it would be a disservice for me, or any one else, to classify this archipelago of 7,107 in Southeast Asia as a "paradise." Friend, if you think the PH is a "paradise," you've been smoking way too much shabu (meth.)

What I've constantly heard from readers of my website, **"PhilippinesPlus.com,"** is that I give a *realistic, unvarnished look* at life in the Philippines from the viewpoint of an old geezer, redneck, 60-year-old American expat.

I don't sugarcoat *anything*. I cut through the B.S. and give you an ***honest*** evaluation of what it's like for a foreigner to survive here.

Here's a comment I received on my website which helped prompt me to write this E-book: **"I started looking for articles and blogs by foreigners, particularly Americans, living in the Philippines after reading some brightly colored website banners touting the virtues of living in the Philippines, 'paradise', some called it. I never take those lofty marketing descriptions at face value, and reading your blog gives the place a sense of 'the real' for me. There are pros and cons to living everywhere, I guess.**

That remark got me thinking. While my new home is certainly ***NOT*** paradise, I'll give you my reasons in this E-book to explain my desire to live out the rest of my years here.

I will attempt to address some of the pros and cons of living in the PH and give you as realistic view as I can about. Believe me, spending a couple of weeks on vacation is *far* different once you step off that jet at NAIA in Manila. In fact, once you read this book, you might decide to stay put. I'm going to be brutally honest.

And what should you do once you decide you want to stay in the Philippines? What kind of visa should you get? I'll give you instructions and advice for what I think would be the best and cheapest option for you.

I'm going to give you a *no-holds-barred-look* at Filipinas (and Filipinos.) The scammers. The users. The sweet and innocent. The loyal and faithful (like my own spouse.) This information will be especially useful to you guys out there, single or married.

MY STORY

I'm a 60 year-old-redneck geezer from Central Illinois. Soon to be 61. Here's a picture from a trip my asawa (spouse, can refer to either male or female) and I took to Raymen Beach in Guimaras along with some of our nieces and nephews. Guimaras, a province in the Western Visayas region of the Philippines, is known throughout the world for their sweet mangoes.

I'm not smiling in this photo. I have no frickin' idea why. Every online article says that the author should have always have a nice photo of them smiling like a dumb ass. I wasn't up to it today.

As you can tell, I don't take myself too seriously but I've met some extremely pompous American expats in over three years of living in the Philippines. But I've met some good guys, also.

My wife has stayed with me for 13 years now. How on earth she has survived over 13 years of marriage to me is a testament to the love and loyalty you will find from most Filipinas.

I retired after almost 30 years of "working" for AT&T, the telephone communications giant. The last few years were sheer boredom. I was never so glad to see that day when my lump sum retirement account more than doubled after I turned the age of 55. At 57, I was out the door. Three months after my retirement we were living in the Philippines.

Talk about culture shock. Here's an **article** that my local newspaper, **The State-Journal Register,** back in Springfield, Illinois, ran on us September 13, 2009, only about two months after moving to the Philippines. It was written by one of the newspaper's gifted columnists, **Dave Bakke**:

Retiree's 'good life' includes Spam, lizards, cold baths

You hear people vow that someday they're going to chuck it all, move to an island in the ocean and live the good life. Dave DeWall has done it.

Dave retired at age 57 after almost 30 years at AT&T in Springfield, moved away from his home in Auburn and relocated in the Philippines, his wife Melinda's native country.
In Dave's case, the good life includes beautiful scenery and warm, sunny days spent kicking back with no commute and no deadlines, as well as sleeping under a mosquito net, eating a lot of Spam, dodging lizards, bathing with a bucket of cold water over his head and taking care of the pig in the back yard.

But it's all good.

Dave says he was bored with the central Illinois workaday world and craved adventure. Having visited the Philippines three times before, he was captivated by its white sand beaches and turquoise water. The cost of living there is not high. At about $450 a month, his retirement fund will cover it nicely for a long, long time. Dodging lizard droppings is a small price to pay.

"My wife just told me that her mom (she lives with us) killed the BIG lizard that was in our house the other night with her bolo knife (machete)," Dave wrote in an e-mail to me from the edge of a jungle in the Philippines. "Grandma (77 years old) is about five feet tall in heels and weighs 85 pounds."

Parts of the Philippines are modern, but Dave and Melinda live in a rural area that is fairly primitive. Lizards scamper over their walls and ceiling, hence the mosquito netting over the bed. It keeps the lizard droppings away, as well as blocking mosquitoes.
I reached Dave by phone at his home in the Philippines.

"It's pretty crazy," he says. "It's quite a change from Auburn and going to work in Springfield every day for AT&T."

Dave and Melinda live with her mother, twin nieces, and another niece and nephew. They are a 15-minute boat ride from Iloilo City, a city of 400,000, where they shop, buy groceries and go to concerts and dances. There, Dave can eat at McDonald's for a respite from his daily Spam. He has lost 25 pounds since mid-July, so watch for "The Spam Diet" someday on the New York Times best-seller list.

"I could do a commercial for Spam," he says. "I usually eat eggs in the morning, Campbell's soup and then Spam. Once in a while I'll get fish. They have good tilapia here."

He had a 60-foot communication tower built in his front yard so he can get a good Internet connection.

"I don't know what to do with all my time," he says. "That's why I'm on the computer all the time. I hear from one of my old co-workers. He e-mails me now and then."

The computer connection allows Dave to update his Facebook page, read this newspaper and write on his blog about his life on the edge of the jungle. His blog is The Rooster Crows at 4 a.m., (rooster4am.com), which it does, by the way.

The blog includes Dave's stories about lizards, the time his neighbor shot at the laundry lady's husband because she thought the guy had stolen their chickens and possibly eaten their dog, about the armed guards at the supermarket and his current effort to have a flush toilet installed in the house.

Dave's life isn't boring anymore.

Almost four years after that story, I've gained most of the weight back. But I walk an hour early every morning and have been eating healthier. My asawa buys fresh fish for me at the local wet market and I've cut down on my fast food and red meat. My spouse told me last night that my belly was getting smaller. That's always good news.

We don't live in Guimaras anymore but reside in a subdivision straight out of the Fifties.

"The Rooster Crows at 4am" was put to rest a couple of years ago. Most of the stories from that first effort have been imported to my new website.

We have screened windows in our rental home and don't have nearly the amount of lizard poop we had in Guimaras.

Don't use a mosquito net anymore but haven't gotten dengue fever, fortunately. You don't want that mosquito-borne disease. It's a potential killer.

And that part about living on $450 a month? Nope, that's not the case anymore as I soon found out. Try $1,000 a month if you're a single guy not living in the Metro Manila area and you don't any girlfriend's relatives sucking the life out of you.

MOVING TO THE PHILIPPINES CHECKLIST:

Here are some *basic things* to do that I recommend before making your move to the Philippines. You can print this page and add your own items.

These suggestions will be covered in detail next.

- GET A PLAN ORGANIZED. START WITH THIS CHECKLIST.

- GET YOUR PASSPORT.

- GET YOUR SHOTS.

- GET ALL OF YOUR UTILITIES PAID IN FULL & SHUT OFF.

- RESEARCH WHERE TO LIVE.

- PAY OFF ALL DEBTS BEFORE YOU MOVE.

- DECIDE WHAT TO BRING. DECIDE WHAT TO SELL.

- BUY A MAGICJACK BEFORE YOU MOVE.

- SET UP HOW TO RECIEVE YOUR MONEY.

- SET UP MAIL FORWARDING SERVICE.

- STOCK UP.

- SHIP YOUR STUFF.

- IF MARRIED OR HAVE A GIRLFRIEND MAKE SURE YOU DISCUSS WHAT SUPPORT IS EXPECTED FROM YOU.

- HAVE A CASH RESERVE TO BRING WITH YOU.

- HAVE AN EXIT STRATEGY.

MOVING TO THE PHILIPPINES

Here's detailed information on each checklist item I've suggested.

GET A PLAN ORGANIZED.

First off, don't think you'll come to the Philippines and get a **job**.

I *personally* would not move to the PH unless I had a **guaranteed monthly income   source.** I have an IRA account that was funded by a lump sum payment I received after almost 30 years with AT&T. I receive a fixed monthly amount from that account. In two years I hope to draw Social Security. Our income will more than double at that time. I have not talked to an expat yet that would recommend moving to the Philippines without some source of guaranteed income.

Our local SM Department Store and Robinsons Place employees in Iloilo City make 265 pesos a **DAY.** Around six US Dollars. That's a *DAY, NOT* per hour. The majority of them are college graduates and have to meet certain age and height requirements *AND* **be physically attractive.** This *IS NOT* America, there is rampant job discrimination throughout the Philippines.

But Dave, I'm a plumber or carpenter back in my home country. I'm *sure* I can get a job in the Philippines with my job skills. Wait a minute. I have to pick myself up from the floor. I was laughing so hard at that statement.

Do you actually *think* a Filipino is going to hire, *YOU*, a foreigner over a fellow Filipino? And if by some miracle you DO get hired, are you prepared to live on the daily wages of skilled laborers which is 150-170 pesos a **DAY?** 265 pesos a **DAY** for a carpenter or plumber in our region of Western Visayas, Panay Island near Iloilo City.

So get a plan which includes a guaranteed source of monthly *LEGAL* income. Don't be like the stupid American expat who landed in jail in the Philippines because he was exploiting under-aged Filipinas and filming them half-naked in staged "catfights." The moron was able to get out of jail and return to the United States, but if you are so desperate that you have to resort to such tactics, *STAY PUT!* We don't want you here. You give the rest of us expats a bad name.

Use my simple checklist as a guide. Add your own additional items. Do some **RESEARCH** online. Check out websites like mine, **"PhilippinesPlus.com."** Leave comments on the sites and ask questions. Most of us will be glad to offer our opinion. Listen, I'm trying to tell you the unvarnished truth. If you want pure B.S. and think you're moving to "paradise," then *don't* move here.

Sure it's a great place to live. I have no intentions of *EVER* moving back to America. I have no regrets about moving to the Philippines. **But get yourself some kind of plan and follow it.** To be honest, you've made a great start in that direction by purchasing this eBook. The more advance preparation and planning you can do beforehand, the better off you will be once you arrive here.

GET YOUR PASSPORT

I know, it sounds like a basic thing that most folks would know about or do before leaving their home country, but I'm including the following information regarding obtaining a passport from the United States because I want to cover as many bases as possible.

Before you need a visa to travel to another country such as the Philippines you'll need a **passport**. According to the American Heritage Dictionary, a **passport** is an official government document that certifies one's identity and citizenship and permits a citizen to travel abroad. So obviously securing a passport from your home country is necessary before planning any trip to a foreign country.

You'll also need to get pictures made for your passport. I went to my local Walgreen's, but there are many other outlets available.

Here's some information about First Time Applicants that must apply in person(from the **U.S. Department of State** Website):

- You are applying for your **first** U.S. passport
- You are **under age 16**
- Your previous U.S. passport was issued when you were **under age 16**
- Your previous U.S. passport was **lost, stolen, or damaged**
- Your previous U.S. passport was issued **more than 15 years ago**
- Your name has changed since your U.S. passport was issued and you are **unable** to **legally document your name change**

You can also renew by Mail if all of the following are true:

Your Most Recent U.S. Passport:

- ☑ Is **undamaged** and can be **submitted** with your application
- ☑ Was issued when you were **age 16 or older**
- ☑ Was issued within the last **15 years**
- ☑ Was issued in your **current name** or you can legally document your name change

If any of the above statements do not apply to you, you must <u>Apply in Person</u>

Need a U.S. Passport Immediately?

You should make an appointment to be seen at a Regional Passport Agency **only** if:

- The U.S. passport is needed in **less than 2 weeks** for international travel
- The U.S. passport is needed **within 4 weeks** to obtain a foreign visa

Contact the <u>National Passport Information Center</u> to make an appointment or locate a Passport Agency.

GET YOUR SHOTS (OR NOT?)

Here is some information regarding travel to the Philippines and recommended shots and vaccinations from the **Centers for Disease Control website.**

Have you scheduled a visit to your doctor or a travel medicine provider?

Ideally, set one up 4 to 6 weeks before your trip.

Most vaccines take time to become effective in your body and some vaccines must be given in a series over a period of days or sometimes weeks.

If it is less than 4 weeks before you leave, you should still see your doctor. You might still benefit from shots or medications and other information about how to protect yourself from illness and injury while traveling.

Are you aware of which types of vaccinations you or those traveling with you may need?

CDC divides vaccines for travel into three categories: routine, recommended, and required. While your doctor will tell you which ones you should have, it's best to be aware of them ahead of time.Before visiting the Philippines, you may need to get the following vaccinations and medications for vaccine-preventable diseases and other diseases you might be at risk for at your destination: (Note: Your doctor or health-care provider will determine what you will need, depending on factors such as your health and immunization history, areas of the country you will be visiting, and planned activities.)

Vaccine-Preventable Diseases

Vaccine recommendations are based on the best available risk information. Please note that the level of risk for vaccine-preventable diseases can change at any time.

Vaccination or Disease	Recommendations or Requirements for Vaccine-Preventable Diseases
Routine	Recommended if you are not up-to-date with routine shots, such as measles/mumps/rubella (MMR) vaccine, diphtheria/pertussis/tetanus (DPT) vaccine, poliovirus vaccine, etc.
Hepatitis A or immune globulin (IG)	Recommended for all unvaccinated people traveling to or working in countries with an intermediate or high level of hepatitis A virus infection (see map) where exposure might occur through food or water. Cases of travel-related hepatitis A can also occur in travelers to developing countries with "standard" tourist itineraries, accommodations, and food consumption behaviors.
Hepatitis B	Recommended for all unvaccinated persons traveling to or working in countries with intermediate to high levels of endemic HBV transmission (see map), especially those who might be exposed to blood or body fluids, have sexual contact with the local population, or be exposed through medical treatment (e.g., for an accident).
Typhoid	Recommended for all unvaccinated people traveling to or working in Southeast Asia, especially if staying with friends or relatives or visiting smaller cities, villages, or rural areas where exposure might occur through food or water.
Japanese encephalitis	Recommended if you plan to visit rural farming areas and under special circumstances, such as a known outbreak of Japanese encephalitis, see country-specific information.
Rabies	Recommended for travelers spending a lot of time outdoors, especially in rural areas, involved in activities such as bicycling, camping, or hiking. Also recommended for travelers with significant occupational risks (such as veterinarians), for long-term travelers and expatriates living in areas with a significant risk of exposure, and for travelers involved in any activities that might bring them into direct contact with bats, carnivores, and other mammals. Children are considered at higher risk because they tend to play with animals, may receive more severe bites, or may not report bites.

How many shots did my wife and I get before moving to the Philippines? *None.* We *did* visit our local hospital in America before we left for our new home, and inquired about the different vaccinations. Since our health insurance did not cover the cost of the shots we decided to pass on them. I believe the cost was going to be around 600 US Dollars total for both of us.

I *did* get some of the vaccinations during my initial visit to the Philippines in January 2000, but cannot even remember which ones, and the doctor I had gone to has since closed his practice, and I had no records of what I had received. You do not need proof of *ANY* immunizations to gain entry into the Philippine except by travelers entering the Philippines from an area infected with yellow fever. When we arrived in July 2009 we *did* have to fill out a brief questionnaire at the Manila airport which asked if we had been in contact with the swine flu virus but that was all.

You **might** want to consider having **rabies shots** before you move to the Philippines. Many dog owners here do not get rabies vaccinations for their animals (remember, many people are just struggling to find a daily meal) although the Melinda Gates Foundation has been sponsored free rabies vaccinations for dogs in my wife's home province of Guimaras.

Many stray dogs roam our current subdivision in Iloilo, and I've encountered packs of them on my daily morning walks. I also manage to toss a few stones at them which chases them away, but I'm always aware of the danger of getting bit by one of these canines, but have had no real scares from any of the mutts to speak of.

My asawa and I have now lived in the Philippines for over three years. We have been fortunate to have never needed any of the immunizations or shots recommended by the CDC. Should you get yours before you move here? That's entirely up to you. We personally have not found it necessary at this point.

GET ALL YOUR UTILITIES PAID IN FULL AND SHUT OFF

Now that might sound like obvious advice, but you really don't know if you will be returning to your home country again to live or not, and you need to make sure you leave in good standing. Unlike the Philippines, credit ratings and FICO scores *do* exist, of course, in the States. There's no guarantee that you will want to stay in the Philippines. It's not for everyone. Some expats make the adjustment. Some don't. But better to leave with those utility bills paid in full and avoid any possible huge deposits in case you do return.

Don't forget to call all of your utility companies and your cable or satellite provider and internet provider before you make your move. Keep all of your final bills in the records you are taking with you to the Philippines.

RESEARCH WHERE TO LIVE

Many expats recommend visiting a certain area in the Philippines and living there for awhile to see if you like your surroundings or not. I'll cover various cost of living expenses later and suggested places to live later in this E-book. In general it is cheaper to live in the province, outside of a big city, than it is to live in Metro Manila itself. Some folks living in Metro Manila might disagree with that, but all of my personal experiences and online research suggests that the provincial lifestyle is cheaper than life in the big city.

But please be forewarned that if you have been chatting with a Filipina online beforehand, don't plan on her city, town or barangay (local village) being your final destination. You might discover that your "she" is a "he," or is married or has a boyfriend. Also, her relatives may also present some problems, and that particular subject will also be covered later in this checklist.

Most guys are going to live in the region where their wife or girlfriend resides. That's what we did when we moved to Guimaras. Here's some other suggested places to live:

At the top of my list, is **Iloilo City** or the subdivision immediately surrounding it. Big city with a small town feel to it. Friendly people. Reasonable housing costs, only 145 US Dollars a month for the modern home in our subdivision. Lots of big shopping malls nearby. I'll be covering this topic in a later chapter of this E-book.

Go online. Check out some other good websites and forums that deal with the Philippines. Of course I recommend checking out my own

PhilippinesPlus.com, but here's a short list of some other sources of information online that I would suggest checking out.

- **LivingInThePhilippines** is the oldest and original forum dealing with life in the Philippines from the view of an expat. You can apply for membership (it's free), and the information I gleaned from this site proved to be *extremely useful* in planning our own move.
- **Expat Blog** covers expatriates from all across the globe, but has some useful advice from expats in the Philippines.
- **PhilFAQs** is a website operated by my friend, **Dave Starr**, who has been living in the PH for over five years. Dave's site has got a ton of information about jobs, operating a business and other helpful advice covering a wide range of topics.

View of the mountains from our subdivision outside of Iloilo City

PAY OFF ALL DEBTS BEFORE YOU MOVE

Pay off all your debts? Am I crazy? Yes, I've been told that more than once. But perhaps you think you can leave the United States along with a huge mountain of debt and unpaid bills behind you. Sure you *can* do that. There's no "Big Three" credit reporting agencies in the Philippines like there is in the States. No FICO scores. But again, what if things don't work out for you and you find yourself returning to your home country?

Bankruptcy is an option. Maybe with the "New Bankruptcy Law" that was passed in 2005, you might think you could not qualify if your income is too high. Guess again. I personally know people that made over $75,000 a year and were able to fully discharge all of their debts which were over $100,000. If you find the right lawyer it can be done. Do I recommend bankruptcy? Yes, in some cases people find it is necessary due to their circumstances. A person could come to the Philippines with a clean slate. We personally do not have ANY credit cards now, and I plan to keep it that way.

But aware that if you have debts you leave behind and did not file for bankruptcy, if you have a bank account, a hold could very well be put on that account for any outstanding debts.

If you're living on a fixed income as we are now, it is extremely advantageous for us not to have any outstanding debts. We have bought absolutely nothing on credit in the Philippines, but I can assure you that if you get behind in your payments on the new television or car, someone WILL be paying you a visit. And don't think they will not be able to get past the armed security guards of your subdivision. They will. I've seen it happen in our own guarded and gated community to a neighbor.

DECIDE WHAT TO BRING. DECIDE WHAT TO SELL.

If you're a pack rat and plan to move to the Philippines you might have some difficulty in getting rid of junk you have accumulated over the years. It was fairly easy for me, even though I'm married to someone who collects any empty bottles and jars she can. But I pared down the items I felt absolutely necessary to pack in the five balikbayan boxes (more on those later in this section) that we used to haul our stuff to the Philippines without *too much* protest from my asawa (spouse.)

Here are some items we decided to **hand carry with us to the Philippines:**

- **Passports** (make sure they are current and do not expire in the next six months before going to the Philippines.)
- **Airline tickets/ itinerary** from our travel agency
- **Cash and Debit Card**
- **Driver's license** from Illinois (good to have this with you since identification other than your passport is sometimes needed.)
- **Personal records** such as our **National Statistics Office of the Philippines, NSO,** certified copy of our Marriage Certificate in the Philippines. If you are married to a Filipina and want to obtain a balikbayan visa (more on that later) than the NSO copy is a necessity. I also carried my Birth Certificate with me along with my wife's NSO certified birth certificate from the Philippines.
- **Three suitcases** of clothes and personal grooming items. My wife had two suitcases, and I had one.

Since we sold our home and left the appliances for the new buyer, we sold our furniture to friends and had several garage sales to sell the remainder of our items. We shipped all of our remaining items in the aforementioned five **Balikbayan** boxes from the **Forex** company which delivered our boxes *directly* to our home in the Philippines for a cost of 100 USD each. Our items arrived in good condition.

A balikbayan box (literally, "Repatriate box") is an corrugated cardboard containing any number of items sent by an overseas Filipino known as a "balikbayan" (Philippine nationals who are permanently residing abroad including their spouses and children regardless of nationality or country of birth. It also refers to those of Filipino descent who acquired foreign citizenship and permanent status abroad.)

Though often shipped by freight forwarders specializing in balikbayan boxes by sea, such boxes can be brought by Filipinos returning to the Philippines by air. I'll be covering this topic in the checklist regarding **"Ship Your Stuff."**

BUY A MAGICJACK BEFORE YOU MOVE

If you want to make and receive unlimited international calls from the Philippines to the United States and Canada for just 20 dollars a year, then I highly recommend buying a **magicJack** telephone system before making your move. This is undoubtedly one of the best purchases I have ever made. The **magicJack** *does* require a high speed connection to work, and I had a 50 foot tower installed in our front yard at our home in Guimaras when we first moved to the Philippines (at a cost of $350 USD) in order to get a signal from **Smart Bro** for a monthly charge of just over 20 USD.

I have had my Broadband service for over two years and have been very satisfied with it. We now have a small rooftop antenna installed at the home we rent outside of Iloilo City.

Of course there are other options for making calls such as Skype, Vonage or Yahoo, but with magicJack offering a 5-year subscription plan for 69.95 why would I want to pay more for other services? Yes, Yahoo is free, and I've tried it, but I'm much more happier with the service I receive from magicJack.

Now don't get me wrong, the standard magicJack, which I have, is not perfect. The computer always has to be on in order to use it and when I'm online talking to my Dad in Vegas, I can't access any other screens I may be checking out without causing an extreme echo effect. The new magicJack PLUS is supposed to eliminate those problems, and it doesn't need to be plugged into a computer to work. My Dad purchased one and had some difficulty in setting it up at first, but seems to have the bugs worked out. I'm content to use my stand magicJack being a believer in the old adage, **"If it ain't broke, don't fix it."**

Make sure you purchase your unit before moving which is what I did. I also shipped my computer and thus, the magicJack program was installed when I got my Internet hooked up here. Otherwise the magicJack program will ask you to register the unit in the Philippines and thus you would have to pay International rates which defeats the purpose of buying the system in the first place.

I do not receive any compensation from magicJack. I am just letting you know what I think is the best option in the Philippines and what has worked for me these past three years. We did have a cordless phone that we had hooked up first, but had difficulty finding a replacement battery. We've since gone to a standard phone that works just fine with our magicJack.

SET UP HOW TO RECEIVE YOUR MONEY

Before my wife and I moved to the Philippines, I arranged with my local bank in Illinois to provide us with a debit card. I did not have one before. I advised the bank official in charge of debit cards of our pending move to the Philippines, and the bank arranged it so we would be able to access our funds once we did move.

The first thing you should do is have your pension, such as Social Security, or any monthly payment you receive set up as a direct deposit into your United States bank account. That just makes good common sense. If you don't know how to do that, your financial institution will help you. That's want my investment company does for us.

I did a search online before the move to find out what ATMs would be available to us. Found a list of plenty of ATMs in the nearby big city of Iloilo where we do the bulk of our shopping, but there were no ATMs that we could use in the province of Guimaras where we first moved to.

The majority of the time the ATMs we use are in service, but occasionally when they are down, we have to use an alternate ATM. At times brown outs, or power outages, occur which are very common in the Philippines, but again, we've always managed to find another working ATM in another part of the city. Keep in mind that not all ATMs accept international cards, but we've managed to find many banks such as BPI, BDO and China Bank that do.

My investment company makes a monthly direct deposit to our local bank, and I can access my accounts online in the Philippines. My account deposits our money in US Dollars, but I can only withdraw my funds in Philippine Pesos. All of the bank ATMs we use now started charging an extra transaction fee of P200 per transaction in 2010 for international cards.

Since we can only take out P10,000 at a time with a maximum of P20,000 a day, two withdrawals per day, which amounts to five times a month, we have an additional expense of P1,000 plus the normal fees we incur from our bank.

Another option that some expats use is to open an account once they arrive, and deposit a check from their home country bank and receive their funds that way. The only drawback to that is that it takes about 30 days for the transaction to complete. But the big advantage, of course, is that you avoid the P200 ATM bank fees for each withdrawal previously mentioned.

You could also use a remittance service such as XOOM or Western Union. We currently use XOOM and it has a very reasonable fee (5.99 US Dollars up to $2,000. You have may have to take a reduced USD to Peso exchange rate in exchange for the cheaper fee. XOOM is equal to what we were paying with our international ATM card fees from our bank in the States. More on this topic later.

SET UP A MAIL FORWARDING SERVICE

My wife and I had our mail delivery in the United States stopped and did not have it forwarded anywhere. Of course the US Post Office will not forward your mail to a foreign address, so I went to our local post office, filled out the necessary form, explained to the lady that worked at the counter what we were doing (and since we lived in a small town, the helpful postal employee knew me), and that was that.

She told me that they have had mail delivery stopped before for some people, and many years later, they were still getting mail at the post office. Since we had already received our final bills from all of our utility companies, I really was not concerned with any future mail we might be receiving.

We did not have a post office in the small town in Guimaras, where we used to live and did not have mail delivery as such. However, an official in our local barangay office delivered any mail addressed to us that we absolutely needed.

I had received some mail from my former company, AT&T, but never received any W-2 forms from them until months after the forms had been mailed from the States, and too late to file with my taxes. My W-2 was sent to me eventually in April via email (which I had originally requested.) Seems that my original W-2 was mailed to a wrong subdivision in our province.

I always gave the person from our barangay office a P50 tip if I was home when the delivery was made to make sure any future mail would be delivered promptly. Our utility bills were delivered by motorcycle messengers for the companies, and I did not tip them.

There is no mail delivery in the subdivision we live in outside of Iloilo City. But like in Guimaras, messengers deliver the various utility bills.

I have received correspondence from the IRS which was mailed on February 21st, 2011, and was not received at our home in Guimaras until that May. The mail was delivered to a company in Manila, and thankfully the business was kind enough to place the papers from the IRS in a new envelope and mailed them to our location in Guimaras.

How in the world that happened is beyond me, but at least it finally reached us. To add to my confusion, the IRS letter notified us that they had made a mistake on our calculations, and we were due a refund that they were going to mail in 4-6 weeks. However, we had already received our refund months before via direct deposit. I think the IRS must be as confused as our mail delivery service in the Philippines is.

That said, I *have* had mail successfully delivered from the United States to our home in Guimaras which we have kept as our main mailing address, and it *usually* has taken about two to three weeks to arrive. I have found an excellent **PhilPost** outlet in SM City Mall in nearby Iloilo where we do most of our shopping, and use their office to mail any necessary items to the United States. One international air mail letter costs a little over 50 cents (USD), and the Express Mail service, which I have used on two occasions, has delivered my necessary documents in as little as three days. They say it may take up to five days, and the service costs close to 20 USD now.

My wife did not advise using the post office located on our island of Guimaras since she informed me it would take weeks longer for any mail sent from there to arrive in America. We had tried the main post office in Iloilo City which is near the wharf our pump boat from Guimaras docks at, but found the lines long and the customer service from the postal clerk unacceptable.

If you *do* use want to use a mail forwarding service and avoid possibly missing important mail, I highly recommend **USA2Me**. You can receive mail, packages, faxes and purchases in your own USA Address. With USA2Me's International Mail Forwarding Service they bring you closer to the USA regardless if you're living on the edge of a jungle in the Philippines as we once did when we resided in Guimaras.

USA2Me provides you with a physical mailing address in the USA that you can manage online. You can just log in to your Mailbox Manager to see your mailbox inventory, forward shipments to you, or even discard junk mail. If you need to read your documents right away, they can even scan your documents to view online. All done with the utmost confidentiality.

You can use your USA2Me address to shop online. Just visit your favorite page and use your USA2Me address as your shipping address. They specialize in handling expatriate mail forward service. Please note that I am an affiliate of this company but I do not recommend any product or service on my website or E-books that I do not have 100% confidence in.

STOCK UP

I've discovered that since moving to the Philippines, there are some items I wish I would have purchased in bulk beforehand and shopped over in balikbayan boxes. Here's a list of some recommended items to stock up on:

Antibiotic creams: Neosporin or any similar generic products are hard to find, at least in our location. My wife uses a ointment called **"BL cream."** She uses it for any cuts or wounds that we might suffer, and is imported from China. Since moving to the Philippines we have used it extensively. I've had a severe infection on my foot from what started out as a small scratch and the application of this cheap product reduced the swelling and infection. I was able to fully recover from the wound without any visit to the doctor. At 25-50 pesos per container, it's a bargain and quite effective.

Diarrhea medications: Kaopectate or Imodium A-D are some popular brands available in the States. Your system has to get used to your new living conditions, and absolutely under *no circumstances drink tap water*. You'll find low pressure is quite common throughout the Philippines and health standards are not as vigorously enforced as they might be back in your home country. Drink bottled water or purified water delivered from a local *trusted* distributor. We pay 50 pesos for two large containers of purified water from our next door neighbor, Jesus, which generally lasts us a week.

Strong Pain Relievers: Tylenol, Advil, or high dosage aspirin along with 81 mg dosages which are recommended for those over 50 and are good for the heart. You can buy aspirin without a prescription, but it's more convenient and cheaper to buy it in the States

Sleep Aids: I tried to buy some sleeping pills once I arrived in the Philippines, but the pharmacy tech looked at me like I was from a different world (which, so to speak, I am.) However, I didn't find a need for them once I was here for several months. I'm retired. Doesn't matter what time I go to bed or what time I get up. But if you have extreme insomnia or other medical conditions making it difficult to fall asleep at night, I highly recommend purchasing some OTC medications beforehand.

Vitamins and Supplements: If you take any kind of vitamins or supplements such as folic acid or fish oil tablets, I would also suggest buying those in bulk beforehand and shipping them to the Philippines. While stores such as GNC can be found, their products are expensive as are local drugstore chains such as Mercury Drug and Watsons. I was able to find a bottle of 100 Alaska Deep Sea Fish Oil softgels, 1000 mg, at a kiosk at SM City for P300, a reasonable price.

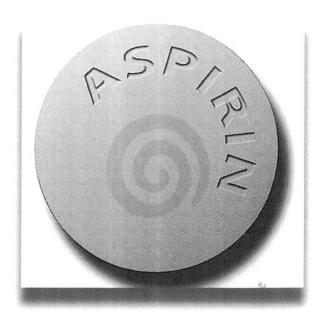

SHIP YOUR STUFF

Two of my *biggest* regrets are not sending my tools over and packing more electronic items, such as an extra television. I had a Craftsmen portable drill that I did not ship because it needed to be recharged but *could* have been recharged with an automatic voltage regulator available here. While there are many hardware stores in the Philippines, such as Ace Hardware outlets in nearby Iloilo City, and some tools *can* be purchased cheaper than in the United States, I still wish I would have shipped my tools over.

It would have been far wiser for me to have spent another $100 for an additional Balikbayan box and have the tools from my garage shipped to the Philippines. I did not think that I would be using tools that much in the Philippines, but found that they would have been extremely useful in the construction of our new restroom, Comfort Room, CR, back in Guimaras. And since our move to our rental home outside of Iloilo City, there have some tools I *could* have used that I formerly owned since many repairs done at a property you rent in the Philippines are done by the person renting the property and *NOT* the owner.

I did, however, have my computer and printer shipped to the Philippines and have it connected to a automatic voltage regulator which I purchased here for a little over 40 USD. I am extremely happy that I did make that decision since the price of computers in the Philippines is much more costly than the United States. However, I should have shipped a 32' LCD television that we had hanging on our wall in our bedroom, since LCD (and now LED) televisions are *quite* pricey in the Philippines. So my advice would be to spend some extra money and ship the tools and electronics you can and save yourself a great deal of money on future purchases of those items in the Philippines.

On a more positive note, I mentioned I had taken only one suitcase which contained all of my clothes I had decided to bring. I did not have any additional clothes shipped. I knew I would not need any coats or sweaters in my new home, and wanted a wardrobe change anyway. In the Philippines I wear cargo shorts, t-shirts and flip-flops called "slippers" here.

I have purchased about two dozen t-shirts from various SM Malls in the Philippines and usually buy the larger sized "Max" brand which can be bought for as little as a dollar up to a little over six dollars for the most expensive Max t-shirt. Bought some new cargo shorts and my wardrobe is complete.

IF MARRIED OR HAVE A GIRLFRIEND MAKE SURE YOU DISCUSS WHAT SUPPORT IS EXPECTED FROM YOU.

"I'm *not* going to support her, and I've made it clear to her that I will *NOT* support her family."

I chuckled to myself as I heard these words from a new expat friend of mine who recently had met a pretty pinay he had been introduced to. Within a month, she had her quit her job and had moved back to her home in rural Guimaras. Guess what? He's *now* supporting the girlfriend *AND* the family. All the cute Filipina had to do was tell her new boyfriend that she had to work too hard on her job as a domestic helper for a family in nearby Iloilo City. That's all it took. He told her to quit her job and move back home. He would take care of her.

If you are under the illusion that you're going to put your foot down and *not* support any of your wife or girlfriend's relatives, you have either been drinking *way too much* or taking *too many* mind-altering drugs.

My Filipina wife and I supported my mother-in-law and four nieces and nephews in her home in Guimaras for 11 years. My wife was working as an Overseas Contract Worker, OCW, (Overseas Filipino Worker, OFW, is the term used today) in Taiwan as a caretaker and domestic helper when we started writing as pen pals. I made a promise to her to support her mom when she ended her employment contract at the end of December 1999.

We married in January 2000 and until October 2011 I lived up to that promise. We sent 400 US Dollars every month until our arrival in the

Philippines in July 2009. My mother-in-law's medications, utility bills, and all of her food, along with the aforementioned nieces and nephew were paid entirely by us except for a few months when one of her sisters working in Kuwait sent P1,000 a month, about 23 US Dollars, to help us in supporting her son and daughter that lived with us.

We are now the talk of my mother-in-law's church as she goes around telling other parishioners and relatives that we have *"abandoned her"* and *"treat her like a dog."* Our pictures were placed in frames alongside Catholic saints my mother-in-law prayed to every day. We were once held in very high regard.

But after a disagreement with my wife's youngest sister, whose family lived in a nipa hut in our front yard, and whose children we were helping out, my wife wanted to move and get out of her house that she paid for in full and go to Iloilo where we now reside.

Will you be like an American expat that spent over 30,000 US Dollars on his four girlfriend's relatives in just four months? The man's own daughter had to put a hold on his account back in the States as his funds dramatically drained.

Will you be like an expat friend that lives in the Metro Manila area and is also being sucked dry financially by his girlfriend's relatives? These two examples are just the tip of the iceberg. Don't end up like both of these guys who later told me; **"Dave, I wish I would have listened to you."**

HAVE A CASH RESERVE TO BRING WITH YOU.

When we moved to the Philippines in July 2009, we took along 6,000 US Dollars in cash. Half of that was used to do some construction at our home in the Philippines when we first moved here. My advice would be to bring along *as much cash as you can.* Once in the Philippines I was able to go to a reliable money changer and was escorted by my sister-in-law that lives in Manila. While bringing cash might not be the wisest thing to do, I did not want to bother with finding ATMs at the time, even though I had a list of ATMs I could use with me, but wanted the convenience of cash. I had a bad experience with American Express Traveler's Checks in the Philippines over 12 years ago, took over two hours to get them cashed at my wife's bank, so that is another reason I decided on cash.

Just use *common sense* once you arrive in the Philippines. Obviously, don't flash your money around. If you go to a money changer, make sure the transaction is done in a private room and not observed by anyone else. The money changer my sister-in-law escorted me to had such a room. I have not had any problems with security issues in almost three years of living in the Philippines and having the cash on hand was not an issue. I always carry my wallet in my front pocket wherever I go. A money belt tucked inside your shirt is another option.

HAVE AN EXIT STRATEGY.

I didn't. My wife and I arrived in the Philippines in July 2009, but had no firm back-up plans or exit strategy before we arrived here. Honestly, I was ready to go back to the United States after just a few weeks. The initial euphoria and novelty of riding the jeepneys and pump boats and mingling with a different culture that I had felt on previous vacation visits to the Philippines soon dissipates as reality sets in.

I was totally unhappy with the conditions of our new home, the lack of privacy and the lack of our own bathroom, or **"comfort room", CR,** as it is called here. I was in a state of depression for weeks, but the installation of our 50 foot broad ban tower in our front yard, which provided me with high speed Internet access, gave me something to do during the day and enabled me to start my first website, **"The Rooster Crows at 4am!,"** which was the stepping stone for my current site, **"PhilippinesPlus.com."**

Being away from my normal routine and comfort zone in the United States had really disturbed me emotionally and was difficult to handle. Fortunately we found a local architect and contractor who started work on getting permits to construct a new private comfort room for us along with other improvements such as a new roof.

But I stuck it out and have made it past the two-and-half-year mark. Our new home in our subdivision outside of Iloilo City is a welcome change. No more relatives, especially my mother-in-law, to deal with, and we're so much closer to big shopping malls and cinemas that give us a break from the rural lifestyle we lived in Guimaras.

Not everyone loves the Philippines. Some people go back to their home country. But do you have an exit strategy? A back-up plan? Do you have the funds available to purchase a return ticket back home? Keep that in mind. Don't think you'll be able to go your home country's embassy and borrow some money from them. The US Embassy probably isn't going to loan you any money, and many other Western embassies have similar policies. Here's what the U.S. Embassy in Manila's website states:

Americans traveling abroad sometimes run out of funds either because of imprudence, robbery or other unforeseen circumstances. Destitute citizens may be entitled to financial assistance, but they must demonstrate that they have no other sources of income and are unable to receive financial assistance from friends or relatives.

In the limited circumstances under which the Embassy can entertain a loan application, the repayment guidelines are strict and applicants cannot obtain a US passport again until the loan is repaid. Frequently, individuals may feel they are destitute when in fact they are simply low on cash. Remember that credit cards, debit cards and ATM cards may also be used to obtain cash or pay bills. Family or friends in the U.S. can send funds through the procedures described below. The role of the Embassy in such cases is to help the person contact others in the U.S. who will be able to send funds to the person in distress.

The Embassy is not able to loan cash to individuals except under certain conditions. Americans seeking financial assistance must exhaust all other options first. We will ask an American to first make collect telephone calls to relatives or friends in the United States requesting funds to be transferred to Manila. Money transfers may be accomplished through the following means:

Funds may be transferred directly to the destitute person through Western Union.

Better get working on that exit strategy ASAP.

WHY MOVE TO THE PHILIPPINES?

Why move to the Philippines in the first place? What would possess a 57-year-old guy from a small town in Central Illinois to retire to a Third World Country back in July 2009 after spending a lifetime in the United States? Why in the world would someone give up their comfortable lifestyle to move literally on the edge of a jungle and live in some of the most primitive conditions I've ever seen? Surrounded by poverty where it is a daily struggle for our own relatives and neighbors to even find one meal for the day. Everyone will have different reasons for leaving their own home country to become an expat, or expatriate in the PH. Here are *my* Top Five **Reasons** why I moved to the Philippines:

1. **Cheaper Cost of Living.**
2. **It Was Time for a Change!**
3. **My Filipina Wife's Relatives Were All in the Philippines**
4. **I Wanted to Retire NOW!**
5. **My Wife Already Owned Her Own House and Property in the Philippines.**

The next section will go into more detail for each of my reasons. The "Cheaper Cost of Living" segment will contain information such as housing, utility, and food costs. It also has our monthly budget to give you an idea of how much it might cost you to live in the Philippines.

CHEAPER COST OF LIVING

Without a cheaper cost of living than what we were experiencing in the United States, my wife and I would not have been able to make our move when we did.

Along with visa questions, many future expats to the Philippines want information about the cost of living. I know that's something I researched heavily before my Filipina wife we retired to the Philippines. It's only natural that you would be curious about how much it will cost to rent a home, buy food, or pay those monthly utility bills.

Housing Costs

"Location. Location. Location." Isn't that the mantra of real estate agents worldwide? It applies to the Philippines, also. Where you choose to live will directly impact your cost of living in the PH. Do you plan to live in some high rise luxury condo in Makati in the Metro Manila area? I've known some expats who have such condos and pay 12,000 pesos a month. That's about 275 USD.

Or do you plan to live in a nipa hut in the province, a rural area, of the Philippines and adopt a "native lifestyle"? As mentioned earlier, my wife and I supported five people, including ourselves, on approximately 800 USD a month, but her property and house were paid for. Worried about tax bills? Don't be. My wife paid about 20 USD a year for her house and property.

I personally spoke to members of the United States Peace Corps in Guimaras. They live on $250 US Dollars a month! How do they do it? They have gone native. Eat a lot of rice and fish. No air con. No fan. They do, however, live in a sponsor's home and do not have rent. But they have been living this way for two years now. It's not easy, but it can be done. They are living proof.

Maybe you will end up in a subdivision outside a big city like my spouse and I now do. We moved from her home in a rural province, Guimaras, and now pay $145 US Dollars for a modern four room house, plus comfort room (restroom) near Iloilo City in the Western Visayas region. We don't have to haul groceries on a pump boat to go shopping or see a first run movie (which costs 2.50 USD.)

Entrance to our subdivision's pool outside of Iloilo City

Our monthly maintenance fees in our new home, which amount to only nine US Dollars, includes garbage pick-up three times a week, lawn maintenance, 24/7 security with three armed guards posted at the main gate to our subdivision, roaming patrol guards, and two guards stationed at the entrance to our particular section of this large subdivision.

We have paved streets, sidewalks, immaculately landscaped parks, and streetlights that work (and our subdivision owners are currently working on a project to greatly expand the number of streetlights we already have.) We feel like rich people. I'm treated like a celebrity by the guards. There is no way that we could have afforded such amenities back in the States.

Food Costs

Our food budget is certainly much lower now that we no longer support the relatives that we did while living in Guimaras. I usually eat Western-style food with a mixture of Filipino cuisine, while my Filipina wife eats the more traditional food of the Philippines such as pancit, adobo and sinigang which are always served with generous portions of rice.

Estimated food costs for my wife, her mother, and our niece (13) and nephew (11) were around 12,000 pesos a month (280 US Dollars.) My estimated monthly food costs are about 5,000 pesos a month (116 USD), but that doesn't include any trips to any fast food outlets at our local SM City such as McDonalds or KFC.

What's a "bare bones" minimum figure for an expat's monthly food budget? I *could* do it on P2,500. I wouldn't be living extravagantly by any means, but I could survive. You can eat at local talabahans that serve smoked oysters for as cheap as P30 for a heaping bowlful, and cheap BBQ pork sticks for 12P or less (see next photo.)

You can also usually find better bargains at the local wet markets which offer fresh fruits and vegetable and meat, fish and poultry. My wife shops at the local markets for her fruits and vegetables. She can buy a kilo of rice as cheap as 35 pesos. We only buy our meat from the local SM Supermarkets because we do not care for the conditions at some of the markets where meat is sold. Never have had any issues with any fish that we have purchased at the local outlets and find their prices on a par with the big chain supermarkets.

You're probably going to pay higher prices for food in the Metro Manila area. In Mindanao the price of food will be cheaper. We're in the mid-range of food costs in our region, the Western Visayas. Location will certainly have some impact on your monthly food budget.

Utility Costs

The Philippines has some of the *highest* costs for electricity in all of Southeast Asia. Brownout, power outages are frequent (depending on location.) In our area outside of Iloilo City we pay 10.65 pesos per kilowatt hour, and our monthly bill averages to about 3,200 pesos a month, approximately 72 USD. That's close to what our bill back in the States was during the summer months. We had an all-electric home, and the bill shot up to 400 USD a month during the cold Illinois winter months.

Water is cheap. We pay 179 pesos a month for our running water (which is currently only on in our subdivision three times a week for eight hours each of those days.) We stock up on water using three water barrels, and get our drinking water from our neighbor Jesus who sells a container for P25. You can get refills at different places for P15, but we don't feel like hauling our containers around, so we just trade our two containers each week in to our neighbor (see next photo which depicts our neighbor in his delivery truck as he makes the rounds in our subdivision.) We spend 200 pesos a month for the drinking water, and that brings our total water cost to 400 pesos.

DO NOT DRINK ANY TAP WATER! In our area around Iloilo City, as is the case in many municipalities of the Philippines, it is absolutely *not safe* to drink the water from the local city water system. Also be careful of any well water you may drink. While living in Guimaras we had a well on our property which had excellent drinking water. Neighbors from all around would go to the well to stock up on their water needs. But some wells in the Iloilo area *do not* have safe drinking water, and have even resulted in death for those that have consumed it.

We do not have a well at our present location, and the water we get smells horrible and certainly cannot be consumed. We use the aforementioned water barrels to stock up on water that we use primarily to flush the toilet in our CR, Comfort Room and wash with.

We pay 999 pesos a month for our Smart Bro unlimited Internet usage plan, and 445 pesos a month for our television cable service provided by Cable Star. We get HBO and Fox Premium Movie channels along with programs from the United States such as American Idol, Sons of Anarchy, The Big Bang Theory, Discovery Channel, TLC, National Geographic, etc., along with local Filipino channels.

Transportation Costs

We don't own a vehicle. Why should we? With public transportation so plentiful and cheap, why go through all the headaches? Some expats in the Philippines **do** own their own vehicle, but since I do not operate a business in which I might need my own set of wheels and have no children or relatives to haul around, opt to not own one at this time. No fuel costs. No maintenance. No insurance premiums. No stress driving around in traffic. It works for me.

Want to be a target in the Philippines? Drive around in that big SUV and see what kind of attention you attract even with darkly tinted windows. I have expat friends that have been targeted by local police when a "kano" is spotted as the driver. You might just find yourself opening your wallet to take care of that ticket on the spot or to even avoid a ride to the local jail. Think about it. This is *NOT* the United States or Canada or whatever country you might be from. You have no rights. But if you have 30,000 pesos a month to plunk down for a SUV payment, more power to you.

I have one American friend that was involved in two accidents when he first started driving in the Philippines. Who do you think paid for those at a cost of 40,000 pesos each? Doesn't matter if you're at fault or not. **YOU ARE A FOREIGNER!** There are no rules here. Take my word for it. My American friend doesn't drive anymore. His Filipina wife or Filipino driver does. But if you *do* get a vehicle, play it smart.

Iloilo, the province we live in, has nearby Iloilo City, with a population of over 400,000 people (not including roosters and dogs.) There are plenty of jeepneys, tricycles and pedicabs to haul you around.

It's about a 25 minute walk to our main gate to catch a jeepney (but you can take a subdivision shuttle for only eight pesos), and the jeepney fare to SM City, about 20-25 minutes away is 16 pesos (it's a two jeepney ride to SM.)

Rates for public utility vehicles such as jeepneys are set by the Land Transportation Office (LTO) of the Philippines and **MUST** be posted in full view of any passengers in each vehicle. Do not let a driver try to take advantage of you just because you are a foreigner. It's happened to me, but only once. I got off the jeepney when the driver replied *"How much do you want to pay?"* after my wife asked how much a fare was to a local beach. Just hop on another jeepney with an honest driver that is going to follow the posted fare. Most do.

Is it safe? I've never had a problem. But I have a "don't-take-any-crap" attitude, also. I talk to people on the jeepneys in Iloilo all the time. I'm respectful. But I also don't tolerate any nonsense. Ask my wife. Never have had my pockets picked (carry my money in my front pocket, always secured) but have known expats that **have** had their wallets stolen while in a jeepney. Just be aware of your surroundings, and you shouldn't have any difficulty.

Some people use money belts. I wouldn't advise carrying a backpack because those are easy targets for thieves who can cut your pack with a razor and steal from you. You won't be aware of it until it's too late.

Most of our jeepney travel is done in the Iloilo area where we live. I've also traveled in jeepneys in Manila. We've also used the LRT, Light Rail Transit System in Metro Manila. Just have to keep your eyes open. Again, I've never had any difficulty with public transportation even in Manila. I also would recommend FX vans which are found throughout the Metro area if you do not want to travel on a crowded jeepney. FX vans usually have air con, and though crowded, are a very reasonably priced alternative to taxis. We used to catch a van to SM Fairview in Quezon City, a 25-minute ride, for 20 pesos each.

Tricycles, basically a motorcycle with a sidecar attached, are good for short trips where walking to your destination might be too long and depends on how hot the sun might be beating down on you or how hard it was raining. They have reasonable fares like the jeepneys. However, if you're riding a tricycle whose rates you are not sure of, make sure you *ask beforehand.*

We occasionally use taxis if we are doing a big grocery shopping trip at our local SM City or SM Hypermarket. The flag down rate for the cabs is 40 pesos, and we can generally find a taxi that goes to our subdivision for 250 pesos, 5.80 US Dollars. We always have to go off-meter due to the distance involved, but since we usually only have to use a cab once or twice a month, the expense is not too great. Our estimated monthly transportation costs are about 1,000 pesos, about 23 USD, a month.

OUR ESTIMATED MONTHLY BUDGET

Here's a look at our estimated monthly budget at our new residence in our subdivision outside of Iloilo City which is located in the Western Visayas region of the Philippines. See the previous information in this eBook for more details for each item. Keep in mind that the population of Iloilo City itself is over 400,000 people and is no way near the 20 MILLION or so people that live in the Metro Manila area. The rural province that we moved from, Guimaras, has an estimated population of 130,000 spread across the whole island. All amounts will be in pesos.

We have three nieces and nephews that now live with us. The following budget figures is the most accurate estimate for my asawa and I before the kids moved in with us.

Our home association fees include Monday through Saturday garbage pick-up, security personnel for the subdivision, street lights, paved roads and sidewalk maintenance and lawn maintenance. They do just about everything for us here but scratch our nose.

RENT	P6,000
HOME ASSOCIATION FEES	P400
ELECTRIC	P3,200
CITY WATER	P400
INTERNET (SMART BRO)	P826
SATELLITE TV (CIGNAL)	P590
FOOD, MISC. HOUSEHOLD	P12,000
TRANSPORTATION	P1,000
MISC. (DINING OUT, MOVIES)	P3,500
SUN POSTPAID	P350

ESTIMATED MONTHLY TOTAL=P28,266 or approximately 700 USD

IT WAS TIME FOR A CHANGE!

Another reason for our move was that I wanted some change in my life and was *tired* of the same routine. Moving and living in the Philippines would be a *major* lifestyle change, and I felt such a radical move would really shake up my life. I was getting older and could not fathom living out my retirement years in our small town in Central Illinois just watching television from our DirecTV satellite dish and mowing our big lawn during the summer and shoveling snow in winter.

Our move to the Philippines certainly has altered my lifestyle! And for the *better.* We might not have as many material possessions that we had back in the United States, but my wife and I are content with our life in the Philippines. I wouldn't trade it for anything. The burden of making a daily commute to work and having a daily grind on the job has been lifted. It feels fantastic!

MY FILIPINA WIFE'S RELATIVES WERE ALL IN THE PHILIPPINES

The third reason why we decided to move to the Philippines was that I wanted to have the peace of mind that someone would take care of my wife after I had left this world. Although I am in good health, I am 60 years old at the time this E-book is being written, 13 older than my loving asawa.

My spouse has no relatives in the United States as is the case with some Filipinos living there. Without me around she would have had no one to take care of her. I did not want her to end up in a nursing home in her old age. I realize that she could probably take care of herself having spent years working overseas under extremely harsh conditions. But you don't know what life will bring. I wanted her back in her home country where I knew she would be watched over and cared for when I'm gone.

She has many good friends back in Illinois, but the bond of family is much stronger and reliable. My wife has countless nieces and nephews that will care for her. At the time of this writing, our 19-year-old twin nieces, April and Michelle, have moved in with us in June 2012. The twins call me "Dad," and they love their tita (aunt.) There is no doubt in my mind that these two hard working and devoted young ladies will take care of my beloved asawa.

April and Michelle

I WANTED TO RETIRE *NOW!*

Why make the move to the Philippines? Well, my Filipina wife and I had been discussing the possibility to move to the Philippines about a year or so before we actually moved. I knew we could live cheaper in the Philippines than we could in our small town in Central Illinois, Auburn, although compared to other parts of the United States our cost of living was not as high.

My job at AT&T had changed, and I was extremely displeased, bored, and frustrated with the new work we had which was in the billing department. I was thinking more and more of collecting my lump sum payment from the company as opposed to a monthly pension at a later date and taking an early retirement now. I had enough years of service (ended up with almost 30) and was old enough so I could retire with full benefits which included health care for my wife and myself.

Fortunately after I turned 55 the money in my company retirement account more than doubled, and the talk of selling our home and moving to the Philippines increased. My Mother had recently passed away after a year long battle with cancer, and my Dad had moved back to Las Vegas with a new companion he had found, so I felt I could leave the United States now and know someone would be taking care of my Dad.

My wife and I have no children, so we didn't have to worry about uprooting kids from their school and friends and moving them to a foreign country. Our union's contract was going to end in June 2009, and not wanting to jeopardize any changes that could be made to my lump sum payment with a new contract, I retired in April 2009.

I would have had 30 years of service at the end of July 2009, but as mentioned, I still retired with full benefits. I would have only gained about a $1000 in my lump sum payment if I would have stayed a few extra months, and it was not just worth it to me. I filed my retirement paperwork, swallowed hard, and started putting our planned move into high gear.

As you can imagine it was a highly stressful time for us since we wanted to put our house up for sale and avoid our almost $1000 a month mortgage payment let alone our monthly truck payment. After I received a check for my vacation pay, the only income we would have would be the small daycare home income my wife had which would soon be down to one child as we had notified the parents of our plans to move to the Philippines.

I had to roll my lump sum payment check over to a traditional IRA with Edward Jones which was set up as a T-72 account and would provide us with a fixed monthly income and defer taking a huge chunk of taxes out of my retirement account. However, I would not receive any money from that until July.

After doing some painting and preparing our house to sell, I contacted a retired co-worker that was now a real estate agent, and she sold our home within a month! We only had our house for four years, but we were still able to make a small profit on the sale and used that to help finance our move. We moved out of our home in early May and stayed with some good friends for a month, and then went to Las Vegas where my Dad's companion had a time-share which she generously allowed us to reside until we flew to the Philippines in mid-July 2009. It was a whirlwind of activity the past several months, but we were finally on our way!

BEFORE: OUR HOUSE IN AMERICA

AFTER: OUR HOUSE IN GUIMARAS, AFTER THE REMODELING

THE FUTURE: OUR NEW HOME IN OUR SUBDIVISION WILL BE A TWO-STORY STRUCTURE SIMILAR TO THIS

MY WIFE ALREADY OWNED HER OWN

HOUSE AND PROPERTY IN THE PHILIPPINES

The last major reason that I listed for moving to the Philippines is the fact that my wife owned a house and lot in a small town in Guimaras. My wife spent years working overseas as mentioned earlier to pay for the construction of the home. The house and lot are entirely paid for.

Since I am not able to collect Social Security yet, and we have a fixed monthly income, I did not want the added expense of renting a house. Why do that when we had one already sitting in the Philippines?

But as documented earlier, things did not work out after two years, but it has turned out for the better as we enjoy our life in our new rental home outside of Iloilo City. Plenty of privacy. Great subdivision. Close to shopping. No more tedious journeys on the pump boat.

In retrospect I would have moved to Iloilo City and rented a house a lot sooner than we did, but when we first arrived in Guimaras my wife wanted to keep supporting her Mother and our nieces and nephews.

That's my five major reasons for moving to the Philippines. There's many more I could add such as my celebrity status here, the fact I can openly pee in public streets without fear of getting arrested, and drink some of the best beer in the world, San Miguel Pale Pilsen etc.

TWO KEYS TO LIVING IN THE PHILIPPINES

Here's my two keys to living and surviving in the Philippines:

KEY # 1: USE COMMON SENSE

KEY # 2: DON'T THINK WITH THE WRONG HEAD!

KEY #1: USE COMMON SENSE

Common sense. Most of us have it. Some use it more than others. In the Philippines, if you want to survive, it is *absolutely essential* that you exercise some degree of **common sense**. You're not in Kansas anymore, my friend, and you will be exposed to a completely different culture and way of living that you are accustomed to.

What you don't know and who you piss off *can* result in extreme bodily injury or even *death*. No, I am not exaggerating one iota. In this E-book I'll explore the concept of "saving face" as it applies to Filipino and the SIR principle, Smooth Interpersonal Relationships.

I'll be relating some stories of when I personally and some other expats, that will go unnamed, did not exercise any common sense. Let them be cautionary tales that you could personally learn from. It's *vastly different* when you're on vacation in the Philippines as opposed to actually living here. Gritty, harsh reality sets in not long after you make your move. Some make it. Some don't. Which one you will be depends entirely on you. Exercise some common sense and take heed of some of the advice in this book, and it will increase your odds for survival in this archipelago.

Hey, I **want** you to make it. I've got more E-books on the way, OK?

KEY#2: DON'T THINK WITH THE WRONG HEAD!

Whether you're a single or married guy coming to the Philippines, you will likely find yourself the center of attraction no matter where you go. Doesn't matter how homely, fat and ugly you might think you are. **"Beauty is only skin deep, but ugly goes clean to the bone."** the humorist Dorothy Parker once wrote.

Brother, I don't frickin' care if your ugliness is the kind Dorothy Parker wrote about; you will discover that young, beautiful and drop-dead gorgeous Filipinas will be looking at you. I have expat friends that even tell me that some of the pretty pinays will stare right at your crotch (no need to stick some socks in your boxers guys, you'll be fine regardless.)

So it stands to reason that if a guy comes over from the States and hasn't had a date in 15 years or more, he's bound to go a little loco loco once he arrives in this paradise for single guys. I've known expats that have come over here that have lost tons of money in just a short matter of time to conniving, gold-digging Filipinas that think there's a huge ATM sign stamped on your forehead. But I'll have information on scammer warnings and more cautionary tales regarding this topic coming up.

So guys, don't think with your dick. It could lead to some serious trouble down the road. Please listen to me. I've talked to many guys that have lost everything because they did, indeed, listen to the wrong head. (Photo source: **Metal Injection**)

WHAT KIND OF LIFESTYLE DO YOU EXPECT TO HAVE IN THE PHILIPPINES?

Just as **location** plays a major part in what the cost of living can be in the Philippines, if you're planning a Western-type lifestyle with all of the conveniences you've become accustomed to over the years, then be prepared to pay for that once you make your move here.

If you expect to enjoy the same lifestyle you might be experiencing now, than **you might as well stay put unless you have a substantial monthly income that will support such a lifestyle.** That said, it's still cheaper to live in the Philippines, for the most part, than what it cost us in the States, and the US Dollar is **still** worth a lot more than a Philippine Peso. But don't expect the same amenities without paying for them.

Some people will tell you that you can **"live like in a king in the Philippines."** That might be true if you're raking in thousands of dollars income each month, but on just over 1100 USD, we're living comfortably and not extravagantly by any means.

I can't tell you if you have enough money to live in the Philippines. Everyone has different needs and expectations and their own comfort level. You'll have to make adjustments. Are you prepared?

Here's what one of my readers said in a recent comment in a reply to an expat that talked about living "native style" in the Philippines.

Hey Paul "native style" in Bacolod ain't that bad. lol. It's not exactly the sticks; but, anyway… these money discussion always come down to lifestyle. So many people seem to just want to live their American lifestyle in a "cheaper" US instead of actually living in the Philippines. Can't be done. These people are better off moving to a cheaper US state.

My wife and I divide our time between the US and the Philippines. When I'm living in the US, I don't eat a lot of processed foods. I keep things fresh and healthy so when I'm living in the

PHL, I'm not spending $$$ on imported American food. I don't eat McDo in the US so I'm not spending money at Jollibees when I'm in the PHL. I hate driving so I don't mess with a car in the PHL–I'm strictly a jeepney guy. No $$$ on gas, car, etc. If you live an expensive lifestyle in the US, it's going to be expensive no matter where you go. In fact, it will probably be more expensive outside the US because many of these "must-haves" are going to be imported goods. If you live a simple lifestyle in the US, then living that simple lifestyle just may be cheaper in the PHL.

Of course, my biggest coup was marrying a woman who already owned her own home free and clear AND no siblings so nobody asking for cash. lol Marrying well also saves $$$.

Larry

Larry is exactly on target with his statement: **"So many people seem to just want to live their American lifestyle in a 'cheaper' US instead of actually living in the Philippines."** Like he said, just move to a cheaper state.

Your lifestyle in the Philippines *can* be cheaper, but don't have unrealistic expectations.

Beach goers at Raymen Resort in Guimaras

ARRIVING IN THE PHILIPPINES: WELCOME TO THE REAL WORLD!

So you've entered the *long* lines at Immigration at the Ninoy Aquino International Airport, voted as one of the worst airports in the world. If it's your first visit to the Philippines you're understandably nervous. You don't want to piss off one of the Immigration officers and end up in some jail you have seen on *Locked Up Abroad*. And let me tell you, you *really, really* don't want to end up there.

I've had several Filipino relatives that have been in lock-up in Manila prisons. One was there for five years for a murder charge. He's currently on bail awaiting trial. Some guy held a knife to both his wife's and daughter's throat over a 20 peso debt his daughter owed the man. Alex, my wife's first cousin, was not home at the time. When he heard what the guy had done he killed him and took off. The authorities held his wife in jail until he came out of hiding and turned himself in.

Alex spent five years in the Manila jail before an former employer of his posted his bail. He came by our house in Guimaras one night not long after he was released. Alex was the foreman on the construction crew of the house my asawa had built for her mother before we got married. He didn't want any money. He had come to visit our place since he had heard we had returned to Guimaras to live. I gave him 500 pesos about 12 bucks. I wanted to keep on the man's good side since we would be living in the mango province now.

Another relative, one of my wife's brothers, was in jail for a week just recently. We had to help pay his P24,000, 571 US dollars, bail to get him out on his "frustrated murder" charge. My spouse had to sell one of her caribous in Guimaras to help raise the funds. My mother-in-law had to sell one of her cows.

Flores, my asawa's brother was pissed. He had caught some neighbors stealing water from his eldest sister's home in Caloocan City, near Metro Manila.

When he confronted the neighbors about the water theft, they attacked him with bolos, machetes. In retaliation he slashed the arms of the mother, or nanay, involved in the dispute.

Flores fled to Guimaras, the family home. He stayed there for a while and laid low but eventually returned to Manila and got a job as a messenger.

Until his arrest, he had eluded the authorities for almost eight years. He asked my wife to please get me on the phone after his release so he could personally thank me. I can assure you that he was *very* grateful. Like cousin Alex, he will have to await trial. Could take years before his case comes up in the courts. You think justice in America is slow? Welcome to the Philippines. You're now on "Filipino Time."

Understand this and understand it clearly. ***YOU HAVE NO RIGHTS IN THE PHILIPPINES.*** While you might be able to bribe your way out of trouble in one of the most corrupt nations in the world, are you willing to risk decades in jail for making a stupid mistake? So when you get out of that line with dozens of porters screaming at you and trying to grab your luggage and finally get out of that airport, be extremely cautious.

Use **all** of the common sense you have. Remember, this is one of my basic keys to living and surviving in the Philippines. But let me repeat that and emphasize it: **USE ALL OF THE COMMON SENSE YOU HAVE.** And brother, if you don't have any, you better keep your ass at home.

Once you have some cute Filipina decades younger than you smile in your direction, you'll possibly do some very stupid things that could get you into a lot of trouble. And I mean a *LOT* of trouble. I have some stories from expats that have met Filipinas and have been charmed by those pretty pinays. I'll be posting their accounts in this book. All names have been changed to protect the guys' identities. **NONE** of them are people that I have written about on my website, **PhilippinesPlus.**

But don't worry, it's not going to all "gloom and doom." You'll soon discover that you are a celebrity in the Philippines. You might even find yourself elevated to "rock star" status. And yes, I met a new expat friend from Great Britain the other day and that was some of the first words out of his mouth: **"I feel like a rock star here in the Philippines."**

You will find yourself being stared at by some of the most beautiful women in the world. Be prepared for all the attention. While it can be quite an ego booster, you still need to be aware of some popular scams currently in vogue and also discussed in the next chapter. But don't worry, you'll find out that is indeed, "more fun in the Philippines."

CULTURAL CHALLENGES OF LIVING IN THE PHILIPPINES

If you moved from the United States or another country not considered a Third World Nation, then be prepared for some *radical changes* in your lifestyle. If you have visited the Philippines before on vacation, you have just a very **small** taste of what your life will be once you decide to make the Philippines your permanent home. This is reality now and *not* a vacation. Here are some of the things that I have had to adjust to since moving to the Philippines almost three years ago. Some of the items I have since gotten used to and some I am still working on. Some I will probably *never* get used to.

Living with My Mother-in-Law and Relatives and the Lack of Privacy.

My wife already had bought and paid for the house and property we used to live on in the rural province of Guimaras years ago. Her mother and other relatives resided there, and it made sense at the time to move into this home which is in my wife's name since as a foreigner I cannot buy property in the Philippines, with some exceptions (to be covered later.)

My wife's mother is almost deaf and to compensate for her hearing loss practically shouts when she is speaking to anyone, and also had the annoying habit of peering into our bedroom/living room/computer room that we lived in. Because of her poor hearing she played her radio so loud that I often find it difficult to hear anything else so I just shut our bedroom door.

She had a remarkable built-in-radar that kicked in whenever I wanted to go to the cramped back kitchen area to do some cooking. I don't care what time of day I went there, my mother-in-law suddenly appeared and got in my way to wash just one cup or plate at a time.

My mother-in-law also had the annoying habit of loudly scraping her plate when eating. I have **never** in my life heard such a racket made from the simple act of eating, and I grew up with two younger brothers. After the plate scraping she would often burp very loudly without excusing herself, which I find very disgusting.

Having my 79-year-old mother-in-law living with us was something I probably would have *never* adjusted to so when we moved out of the house in Guimaras to our own place in Iloilo, I was extremely pleased. In fairness to her, if I were to list *my own* annoying habits it would take up a large portion of this eBook. I read on one website that a good rule-of-thumb is to live at least three hours away from any relatives, and I would have to agree that's a pretty good rule from my point of view.

Loaning Money to Relatives.

Do NOT Become Someone's Personal ATM

Want to survive in the Philippines? Well, in my personal opinion, which is the view of many other expats, living at least three hours from any relatives, as mentioned earlier, is key. Why? Living with relatives or having them live nearby by will invariably mean someone will probably always be asking you for money. This is something that you need to put a stop to *immediately*, or you may find yourself *constantly* approached by relatives asking for money.

While my wife and I waited for her immigration visa to be processed so she could join me in the United States she spent part of her time at our present home in Guimaras and faced *daily* visits from relatives asking for money. Word was out that she was married to a "rich American." I can assure you that such news travels very quickly.

I am well aware of how difficult life is in the Philippines, and we have helped out some relatives since living here when the situation called for it. However, I was not aware of the situation my wife faced at that time, and was not pleased that some of the monthly support money I sent was going for, in many cases, handouts.

The relatives might phrase it as a "loan" sometimes, but rest assured, that the "loan" will probably *never* be repaid. In fact, we almost did not move to Guimaras because of the concern with relatives asking for money, and what their reaction would be if we turned them down. It is a harsh life for many in the Philippines and *sometimes even relatives will retaliate if you refuse to give them money.*

My wife feared for our safety and was against moving to our present home. It proved to be the best financial choice for us at the time, so I convinced my spouse we should move to her home so as not to have any monthly house payments.

Here's a story I did about my wife and her loans to relatives.

My Filipino Wife is a Loan Shark!

Loans were being made at our home on Guimaras Island faster than two rabbits making babies in a sock! I had no idea my asawa had been providing pesos to various relatives in the past year. I accidentally discovered that my spouse was a loan shark when her cousin **Doning** stopped by the other morning. I spied him as he passed through our front gate.

I advised **The Sainted Patient Wife** that her relative was here. I recognized him as he was part of the crew that built our new **Comfort Room** (CR, or Restroom) almost two years ago. Doning always wears a distinctive headband and has a mole on the left side of his face with a long dark hair growing out from it. SPW went outside. He stood on our front porch, too shy to come in, and I went to the front door to greet him and saw him handing my spouse two 1,000 bills (about 26.64 in US Dollars each) Now that got my attention!

Seems Doming's son had been in the hospital this past June, and SPW had loaned him P1,000. He had borrowed money from my wife before and had always paid her back. I didn't mind her coming to the aid of a hardworking relative that needed a helping hand. After refusing the additional P1,000, I'm sure he could use the extra cash more than we did, I invited our relative inside and my asawa fixed him a cup of **Nescafe 3-in-4 Brown N' Creamy** coffee. His two daughters that worked in Lebanon as OFWs (Overseas Filipino Workers) had recently sent some money home, and thus he was able to pay off his debt.

I excused myself and left them to chat. An hour later after an exchange of some chiz miz (gossip) and pan de sal, my asawa's cousin departed for home, and my wife pulled a small, **duwende-sized** green notebook from her purse.

She flipped to a page which I could see was a list of names and proceeded to scratch off an entry for Doming's debt.

WHAT? YOU HAVE A LIST OF PEOPLE THAT OWE YOU MONEY?" I asked. **"I DIDN'T KNOW YOU WERE MAKING LOANS. WHO OWES YOU MONEY YET AND HOW MUCH?"** I was not very pleased to discover that The Sainted Patient Wife had been making secretive loans. We just had a recent incident in which one of her relative's would not respond to her texts concerning a loan her relative had promised to pay over a few weeks ago (that debt has now been settled by an outside concerned party.) My wife was irritated that her texts had gone unanswered. If the debt could not be repaid, she at least wanted the courtesy of an answer to her inquiry.

So when my wife advised me that four relatives owed her a total of P5,000 (118 US Dollars), I expressed my displeasure. She told me that the borrowing parties had *always* paid her in the past, and she did not want me to be bothered with it. She does not charge any interest for the loans, no matter how long it takes to repay them, but said **"5/6" loans** are common in the Philippines. A "5/6" loan is a 500 peso (11.82 USD) loan for thirty days and P100 (2.36 USD) interest is charged when the loan is repaid.

After reviewing the loans that were still unpaid, which my wife assured me would be cared for, I left the matter for future payouts in her hands. As long as we have money for food and can pay our utilities, I'll defer to her. It might mean an occasional reduction in my San Miguel consumption at times, but that's just the price I'll have to pay. I love my San Migs, but I love my wife more.

Many months later after this story was published, my asawa still has not seen the repayment of *any* of those "loans." At least in our new locations outside of Iloilo, we have not had any relatives coming over as we have not told many of them where we have moved to. They would have to get past layers of security guards anyway. Funny how we now have money left over every month now.

The Heat and Humidity. Weather in the Philippines.

GET AN AIR CON (AIR CONDITIONER) ASAP!

If you want to get a good night's sleep after moving to the Philippines, then put this purchase at the top of your list. *I cannot emphasize this enough.*

Our air con, a 3/4 horsepower Carrier cost around 325 USD, came with a remote, and cools our bedroom great. We only run it during the evening and put it on an seven-to-eight hour timer due to electricity costs. I only wish we would not have waited almost ten months before we had purchased it, but due to financial matters and construction costs on our home when we first moved, we delayed our purchase. In retrospect, I would have used some of our construction funds to install the air conditioner as soon as possible.

Here are some weather facts for our former province of Guimaras from the official **Guimaras website** and the Guimaras NMDRC. Weather conditions on Panay Island, Iloilo province, are very similar:

Dry Season – November to April
Wet Season – May to October
Average No. of Rainy Days/ Month: 16
Average No. of Rainy Days/Year: 141 days
Average Monthly Rainfall: 231 mm (9 inches a month)
Average Monthly Temperature : 27.3 C, 81.14 F
Average Maximum Temperature: 30.13 C, 86.23 F
Average Minimum Temperature: 24.58 C, 76.24 F
Average Monthly Relative Humidity: 87.08%

High temperatures in the summer months of April and May can easily reach over 37 C, 100 F, until the rainy season starts sometime in May or early June. July can see up to 16 inches of rain. Combined with the humidity, conditions can become brutal during those summer months.

My wife and I arrived in July of 2009 during the rainy season and slept under a mosquito net due to the very real threat of dengue fever, a mosquito-borne disease. That made sleeping even more difficult as the net would block some of the breeze from the fan that tried to cool us during the evening. I would often arise at 4:30 am since it was too hot for me to sleep anymore and go on an early morning walk in our town. After the air con was installed, I was sleeping until 5:30 or 6:00 am and discontinued my daily walks in Guimaras for awhile. I now walk on an almost daily basis for an hour in the evening with my wife along the paved subdivision roads of our home in Iloilo.

I *hate* hot and humid weather, and my favorite seasons back in Illinois were fall and winter. It has been hard for me to adjust to the weather and the fact is we basically have two seasons in the Philippines, rainy, hot, and humid and dry and very warm. As mentioned before, we do not use the air con until the evening, around eight pm, and I use a fan to cool myself during the daytime.

In December 2009, our first December in the Philippines, the temperatures did moderate, and there were even times in December when I did not even need a fan during the day. In February 2010, the temperatures started creeping up again, and by March 2010, the summer season started to kick in. It was extremely hot and dry our first summer, but in December 2010 and 2011 we experienced much cooler temperatures and more rainfall than 2009. There were many times I did not even run the fan during the daytime or the air con at night as the temperature these past two December dropped to 22 C (72 F.)

I was amazed by all the rainfall we had when we first arrived. There were periods of rain in August 2009 that lasted for ten days straight with just a few breaks of sunshine. And when it rains, it **POURS!** I have never seen such an onslaught of rain as I have witnessed in the Philippines. The rainy season is also the advent of the typhoon season, and we had to switch to a safer dock when we traveled to nearby Iloilo whenever a typhoon was present in the Philippines.

Our former home in Guimaras was spared the terrible damage that typhoons did in the Philippines in 2009; we just endured a few nights of high winds. Having lived in the Midwest back in America, the high winds I experienced during severe thunderstorms and nearby tornadoes, on occasion, were much more threatening than what I have thus far experienced in the Philippines. Flooding is not really an issue in our province of Guimaras, but has caused severe problems in nearby Iloilo where we now live, especially during the devastating Typhoon Frank of 2008, and of course in the heavily-populated Metro Manila area.

Be prepared to perspire profusely whenever you walk anywhere, and carry a handkerchief or small towel with you to wipe yourself down with. It takes but a few minutes for me to get drenched in sweat. While I wait for the jeepney to fill up with passengers, the heat makes me very uncomfortable. Carry water (tubig) with you. And even if you travel by taxi in the big cities a lot of the cabs have little or poor air con, so don't forget that towel to wipe yourself off with, you'll need it!

So for me personally, the weather and lack of seasons that I had back in the

Midwest, are at the top of my list for one of my biggest adjustments to living in the Philippines. It has been one of my biggest challenges to living in the Philippines. After almost three years here, I am still not completely adjusted. Some expats say that it take at least four years to acclimate. Your first year will be *brutal*.

My own Filipina wife who grew up in the heat and humidity of an actual jungle had some difficulty at first when we moved to the Philippines having spent nine years in a home with central air conditioning back in the States. She has since adjusted to the heat. However, I can honestly say I don't miss shoveling the snow out of my driveway back in Illinois or driving to work on ice-covered roads, so there are also some benefits to living in this type of climate.

Brownouts!

Power outages! Blackouts! Or brownouts as they are called in the Philippines, are a common problem throughout the Philippines, and the source of much irritation to me. I estimated we have had over 150 brownouts the first year we resided in our town of San Miguel in Guimaras province, lasting from 15 minutes to three hours and sometimes occurring twice daily and on some occasions, three times a day. I started a log to track the brownouts, and we averaged about five brown outs each month in 2011 in Guimaras. Some of the outages lasted as little as two minutes all the way up to one in December 2010 that was 11 hours and 35 minutes long.

A maze of wires at our front gate in Guimaras

We have had 61 brownouts (as of late August 2012) since moving to our subdivision in Iloilo in the middle of October 2011 with two of them lasting almost 13 hours each. Despite a coal plant that has recently gone online, it seems that power outages will continue to be a recurring problem in our new location.

Purchasing a gas generator is an alternative, and several years ago, while still living in the States, my wife wanted us to send extra money so a generator could be purchased for her father because he needed it for his farm. I believe the cost was around 200 USD, but the generator eventually ended back up at the home in Guimaras where it was tested occasionally, but is not used for back-up because some wiring changes had to be done in our home to enable that.

So for now, we have decided to live with the brownouts, and wait until we move to our new home in the Philippines which we are going to have built in a few years and have a generator installed there. We have purchased rechargeable flashlights to cope with the outages and rechargeable fans are also available.

Sadly, it seems to me, that most Filipinos just accept the way things are, and say that's just the way it is. The infrastructure in the Philippines is sorely lacking and greed, corruption, and politics often block any improvements that could be made. As an American, it is difficult for me to understand the attitude of doing nothing, but after numerous calls to our local power company where I just get frustrated and angry, I have decided to try and live with the situation, and just complain to my poor wife when a brownout does occur.

If the outage occurs during the daytime, I work on organizing my paperwork, take a shower, or go outside and take some pictures for my website. You'll find that you will adapt once you live here for awhile, and this from a guy that had such a rigid routine back in America and hated change. Just give yourself some time.

The Language Barrier.

English is taught in schools in the Philippines as one of the two official languages, the other being Filipino (formerly called Tagalog.) Wikipedia states that *"English is used in education, religious affairs, print and broadcast media, and business, though the number of people who use it as a second language far outnumber those who speak it as a first language."*

In the rural province of Guimaras that we used to live in and the nearby big city of Iloilo, I have found that many of the Filipinos that I encounter have very limited English skills. Of course, I have even more limited language skills and know just a few phrases or words of the local language of the area, **Illongo**, or **Hiligaynon**, the third most spoken native language of the Philippines. I would recommend that you try to learn some common phrases and words while living here.

The locals love it when you use some words from their language, and since I am a guest here, I cannot expect everyone to know my native language. I am often told by the locals that they do not understand my English accent because I speak " English slang" which Wikipedia states: *"May refer to strong foreign accents and pronunciation "Your English is very slang". Often implying that someone is hard to understand or that an American accent is used by the speaker.* I have had more than one Filipino politely tell me that.

And don't forget, **Taglish.** You'll find a lot of Taglish, a mixture of Tagalog and English, on television programs in the Philippines. I don't notice that much of it spoken as such in our region, but you will encounter it once you're in the Philippines.

"THE CHIEF" AND OTHER CHARACTERS

You'll meet some interesting characters in the Philippines. Some of the most interesting ones are the locals. *Most* Filipinos that I have encountered in my past three years living here like to meet foreigners. They are usually very friendly and helpful. And sometimes you receive offers of help that you never imagined back in the States. When you meet guys like "The Chief," it's best to exercise some of that "common sense" I was talking about earlier.

Several months ago I met a somewhat large Filipino man at a birthday celebration (not the one in the photo above standing next to me.) He was introduced as **"The Chief."** He works in law enforcement and had a unique way of dealing with shabu (meth) dealers. He killed them before they could even get locked up. Talk about "The Punisher" and Charles Bronson's character, Paul Kersey, in the Death Wish movies!

And you know what? "The Chief" was absolutely serious. He was a friendly but no-bullshit-kind of guy. He put his arm around me and told me that if I *ever* had any problems to let him know. He would take care of the problem. I believed him. Note to self: "Never piss off 'The Chief!'"

Haven't seen my new amigo since then. But rest assured, I kept that info he gave me in the back of my head. Though I would never consider asking "The Chief" for the help that he offered, he is one example of vigilante justice that is often practiced in the Philippines. If a local neighborhood has a problem with a shabu dealer, thief or rapist, they will often take matters into their own hands. That's just the way it is. It's justice, with "no holds barred." And let me tell you, "The Chief" is one tough son-of-a-bitch that you *do not* want to mess with.

Be careful who you might piss off. When we moved to the Philippines in July 2009, I managed to make a security guard angry at the Iloilo International Airport. We had just left NAIA in Manila and I was in no mood to deal with what I call the "taxi vultures" at the Iloilo airport. Loud, obnoxious and shouting out to you and trying to con you into using their taxi service. These folks annoy me greatly.

At the time I did not know that a FX van service operated right across the street so I talked to the taxi drivers parked nearby, ignoring the irritating vultures. As I was speaking to one and was able to get a reasonable P350, 8.30 USD, ride to the Ortiz Dock where we would catch a pump boat to Guimaras, one taxi hawker continued to yell at me.

I asked the guy what his problem was. **"Don't you understand my English?"** I angrily asked. I turned around to an airport security guard and said to him: **"I bet *YOU* understand my English, don't you?"** He didn't. He thought I was angry with *him*. He said something to my wife in the local Ilongga language. She angrily replied. We got into the taxi.

"What did that guard say?" I asked my asawa. **"He said you better be careful or he will have you killed,"** was her response. Welcome to the Philippines. Problem was. He was right. Haven't seen him since. I had caused the guard to "lose face," a concept explained in the following chapter.

SAVING FACE IN THE PHILIPPINES

Like other Asians, Filipinos believe strongly in saving face if they feel they are slighted. This is why, in response to an invitation, when a Filipino says yes, it might mean **"yes"**, but could mean **"maybe"**, or even **"I don't know."** It is often difficult for Filipinos to bring themselves to say no, and it is a good idea to confirm a dinner invitation several times to ensure that they did not say "yes" because they could not find a proper way to say no.

Also tied to saving face are *amor propio*, which means self respect; and *hiya*, which means shame. A Filipino would be thought of as lacking amor propio if, for example, they accepted criticism weakly or did not offer honored guests the proper hospitality.

Hiya is felt by those whose actions are seen as socially unacceptable, and one of the ultimate insults in Philippine society is to be labeled *walang-hiya*, which roughly translates to being shameless. Everyone is expected to have hiya, and to win the respect of others by conforming to community norms.

Those who change allegiances for personal convenience are seen as double-faced, and labeled *balimbing* (after the many-sided fruit). Also, in order to save face, Filipinos are not allowed to express anger or resentment, so their hostility can take the form of withdrawal of cheerfulness from someone who has displeased them. This silent treatment is known as *tampo*. After a "cooling off" period, it is important to respond to this person with a friendly overture or relations will deteriorate.

(Source: **Carousel Pinoy Entertainment**)

HERE COMES PABLO WITH HIS HAND OUT...
AGAIN.

When my asawa and I lived in the rural province of Guimaras we were sometimes approached by a jeepney dispatcher at the Jordan Wharf, "**Pablo.**" I wasn't too happy when Pablo's father, "**Sam,**" another jeepney dispatcher at the dock, rode along with our multicab driver to our home in Guimaras when we first moved to the rural province. I had no doubt that he was checking out the home of the "rich kano."

Son of Sam, Pablo, did the same thing as his Dad one day. Hopped on our multicab to ride along, no doubt to check out our location. A couple of weeks later, I was not too surprised to see the dispatcher at the front gate to what I jokingly called "The Compound," our home, asking for money for a basketball team he was on.

My asawa was out front talking to him and came in to tell me what he wanted. I decided to give him a 100 peso note, 2.38 US Dollars. I didn't want any trouble from him in the future and felt the 100 pesos was a good "investment."

So I'm sure you're not surprised that I was approached by Pablo again with a request for money. This time it was when I was making a solo trip to Iloilo City on the Iloilo Strait via pump boat. Pablo conveniently hopped on the same boat as I did.

At that time I was only using taxi cabs and not jeepneys to get around in Iloilo. Pablo said he was headed over to Doctor's Hospital to see his grandmother who was very ill. I invited him to ride along in the cab as I was also headed there for a dentist's visit and could drop him off to see his lola.

Before exiting the taxi as we reached the entrance of the hospital, he asked me if I could "loan" him 200 pesos to buy medicine for his grandma. I said "OK" and handed him the money. My wife and other relatives were very angry to learn about this "loan" when I returned home later that day. I did not know the different excuses one uses as described in the article at the beginning of this chapter.

From that point on, my wife or brother-in-law, who lived on our property also, went to our gate when someone approached it. They made it very clear that if Pablo returned, that *they* would speak to him. They told me that they would never directly tell him **"no,"** but would not give him any money and would make up an excuse so the dispatcher could **"save face."**

Pablo made a couple of more trips to our house, always asking for money, of course, and with a new excuse for why he needed it. His lola that was sick died, his wife was sick, etc. Each time my wife or brother-in-law told him that I was taking a nap and was not available.

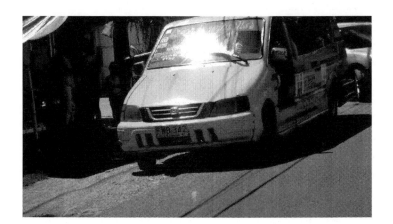

At one time my wife wanted our relative, a local policeman, to talk to the jeepney dispatcher. I firmly opposed that suggestion. It was best, in my opinion, not to stir things up. Especially when we heard from a jeepney driver one day that "Sam," Pablo's father, was in the local jail for murder.

"Sam," who was reported to be on shabu, meth, had killed his cousin over a dispute regarding a jeepney passenger. "Sam" felt his cousin, a fellow dispatcher, had robbed him of a fare and had taken a passenger that should have gone on one of his jeepneys. So he killed his relative over a 13 peso fare, 30¢. Each dispatcher receives a cut from the drivers based on how many passengers are on a particular vehicle they are in charge of supervising.

Not long before we left to live in Iloilo, Pablo made his last visit to our home in Guimaras. I saw him through our front window facing the gate, but he did not see me before I got out of sight. My wife was already outside. Let me assure you that my asawa *does* have a temper when provoked. Pablo wanted some money to buy cigarettes and snacks for his tatay, father, in jail. My wife told him that I was not at home but that I *would not* be giving him any money for his father. He left.

Next time I encountered Pablo at the Jordan Wharf, he gave me a very cool reception. He did not greet me as I got off the jeepney and headed for the pump boat wharf. On my return trip back home, he *did* direct me to one of his jeepney with a **"over here, David."** Haven't seen him since.

The Concept of SIR (Smooth Interpersonal Relationships)

Here's some great advice from one of the faithful readers from my website, a law student at a university in Manila, "**Kaltehitze,**" when he read about the situation with our jeepney dispatcher:

"But please, do not confront it the way you do back in the US where confrontation and being frank is a normal way of resolving a potential conflict head on.

Please be aware that the Philippines, despite the trappings of American culture and Spanish religiosity on the surface is still an Asian country. As such, **SIR (Smooth Interpersonal Relationships)** matters very much. SIR means that personal relationships are highly valued and what follows it is honor. Personal Honor that is. When an Asian is being confronted directly, he will feel humiliated and a loss of 'face' or personal honor. This in turn can lead to bigger problems and can escalate especially when the 'offended' person perceives that he has been unjustly aggrieved, this in turn can lead the offended person to take it to the next level, that is, physical contact.

To know more about the Filipino values, society, social mores and culture, just read up any book about sociology or culture written by a Filipino.

At any rate, I recommend…no, I *STRONGLY* recommend that you do not confront. What you do is, be evasive. Be like the Japanese in confronting a problem (read books or articles on how the Japanese say no. The Japanese don't say no directly to you, instead, they make many explanations, dropping some hints here and there about what they're really trying to say).

As for your situation, you could give out lots of excuses like you're still waiting for your check from the states, wear the crappiest clothing you could find if you're just staying in the compound and establish a reputation as a poor, struggling American so that needy people won't ask money from you, and don't be too generous.

The thing is, in the Philippines, the really poor people still have this colonial mindset, cascaded through the stories of parents and grandparents, that white equals wealth therefore it won't hurt for a white to share a little and if you don't share (which you have every right to do so), then you're greedy. You're this exploitative Spanish (or American) aristocrat who just wouldn't share with the community.

Ask some members of the academe also if you know one (there are 7 universities and 10 colleges in Iloilo City) about the veracity of the concept of SIR and the ways on how to deal with potential problems."

Peeing in Public in the Philippines

Another cultural difference I soon encountered after my arrival in the Philippines were Filipino men that would urinate in the public streets right on the main roads of our rural province. They would stop their motorcycle or tricycle, and with their backs to the road, not even seeking out a tree or bush to hide behind, pee in broad daylight.

Back in the Midwest, such behavior could get you arrested for indecent exposure. The above photo of a "Public Male Urinal" in Iloilo where we now live, is something that Guimarasa does not have. I have only seen one person use that facility. The first couple of times you see someone urinating in public, you might be startled. After that, it's no big deal. However, I've occasionally seen women (usually older lola's) squat down and pee. That is something I will never get accustomed to. Here's an early story from my first blog, *"The Rooster Crows at 4 am!"*:

"To Pee Or Not To Pee!"

"Thankfully I don't have to be politically correct in my blog, because it probably is not "PC"to write about peeing. I'm talking about peeing in public in the Philippines. As I have said before, I just try to observe daily life in the Philippines from my viewpoint. I write about. That's it.

Peeing in public in the Philippines really came to my attention about six weeks or so ago. My twin nieces and I were taking a walk to the nearest Internet cafe in Guimaras since my 50 ft broad ban tower had not been set up yet. We take a short cut behind one of the buildings leading up to the Internet cafe, and there is a guy peeing in public on the side of the building. I was a bit taken aback with this since it was broad daylight.

Now don't get me wrong. I have seen peeing in public back in America before (remember Billy Carter?) Most of the time it involved late night drinking and peeing in a dark alley. I remember one time on the way to Montana with my friend Rocky, when I pulled off the road in the middle of the night, and took a pee. Have you ever been on a Montana interstate in the *wee* hours of the morning? If so, you know there is not much traffic, and you could be hours from the next town or rest stop.

But I thought it a bit much to have this going on in front of people, especially my nieces. But they really didn't say anything about it, and it didn't seem to upset them, so I thought OK, just go on to the Internet cafe. Well, about two weeks later Sainted Patient Wife Melinda and I are eating pizza and chicken and spaghetti at a local place in Guimaras right on the main road called the "The Crossing." I see a motorcycle rider get off his bike across the street from us, and with his back to us (thankfully), pees as he stands just about a couple of feet off the road . We're talking about traffic, people going by, it's noontime!

I say something to the wife. She says it's no big deal. All the guys do that here. We go home and I ask my sister-in-law (since she is a teacher but I guess that doesn't make her a pee expert) if it is against the law to pee in public. In the country (which Guimaras qualifies as since it is a rural province) it is OK, but in a big city like Iloilo where we go shopping, it is against the law. So later my 3-year-old nephew Jorreal goes outside from his nipa hut (no bathroom there) and pees on the side of our house (I guess just to follow in the footsteps of his elders.) What the heck! He's only three. And we're in the Philippines. Always an adventure. Never dull."

In full disclosure I will confess that I do pee occasionally in the evening outside of our home in Iloilo. Since we only have running water three times a week, I do this in an effort to conserve our water supply. But I keep my back to the street, following the custom of the locals.

Toilet Paper and the Lack of it

While I'm on the subject of urinating, let me also mention that when you travel in the Philippines it is best to bring your own toilet paper. The Comfort Room's, CR's here, do not have any toilet paper, so it's a good idea to carry some if you are accustomed to using it.

You *can* go native if you choose and use what most Filipinos use, a tabo, or water dipper that is kept in the CR along with a pail of water. I can remember my first visit to the Philippines where I used the Comfort Room of our present home (we did not build a new private bathroom until we moved here) and had to ask my wife for some toilet paper. There was no toilet with a toilet seat to sit on, just a bowl which I just hovered my butt over. Quite an experience! It was not a flush toilet, so you just use the water in the bucket to flush the toilet with, and it can be refilled by a handy spigot in the CR.

But if you don't have any toilet paper handy and want to go native then just soap your hand, wash your butt, rinse off with the water dipper, and you're done. I've done that before but still cling to my Western culture and use the toilet paper while at home, and hope I don't forget it when we go shopping.

Our new rental home in our subdivision had sewer problems just a few days after we arrived. We couldn't flush our toilet without it backing up into our shower. Not a pleasant situation. Our landlord had his plumber put in a new sewer pipe for us and took care of the problem, but I cannot flush any toilet paper. I have to wrap it up and throw it away in the CR trash can. We recently had some problems when I flushed our toilet using the handle instead of using a bucket of water.

We had some sewage backup again but after using a local drain cleaner and not putting any more toilet paper in the bowl itself, haven't had any problems since. You learn to adjust. My asawa strictly lectured me on throwing the toilet paper in the trash can and not the bowl, so I am adhering strictly to her policy.

The Rude Filipino! Butting in Line!

Another practice I found in the Philippines that I did not expect to experience, is the practice of some Filipinos to butt into lines. Being from the States and having experienced people trying to jump in line ahead of you at times, I was completely surprised and irritated when I first encountered it since my overall impression of the Filipino people is that they are warm, smiling, and friendly. In my past almost three years of living in the Philippines I have had this happen to me more than my previous 57 years of living in America.

"Filipino Time," which is the rule of thumb and is a state of mind where every one seems laid back and is in no hurry, somehow *doesn't* apply when standing in line for a pump boat ticket or at a pharmacy counter (which is where I have encountered this problem the most.) I have also been jumped ahead of line at SM Department Store checkout counters and at grocery stores in Manila and pan de sal bake shops in Guimaras.

I *always* make a comment to the person stepping ahead in line much to the chagrin of my Filipina wife. In my opinion, rude is rude no matter where you live, and I *will* speak up. Sometimes I just get stares from the offender so I proceed to make another remark. Some of the people do not understand my English, but I did have one occasion where the lady went back in line and apologized.

If you happen to step in front of my wife at the pump boat line, however, you will see a six foot tall, 200-pound kano step in *front* of you, and you *will* wait your turn. That's just the way I am. My wife fears for my safety at times when this happens as she thinks someone will stab me with a knife. I have not been stabbed yet, and it is probably wiser if I did not say anything, but I do not know if I ever will be able to just "turn the other cheek" when it comes to those situations.

Here's an example of what I'm talking about taken from my website.

I Am The Invisible Man in the Philippines!

Yeah, who would have thought a six foot tall, 200-pound, loud, overbearing white guy in the Philippines would be invisible? Getting a pump boat ticket at Ortiz dock in Iloilo City, and as I was standing at the counter, a lady in her 50's, accompanied by a female companion, pushed a 50 peso note in front of my 13 pesos, the cost of the ticket. I pushed her bill back, and said: "**Excuse me, but am I *invisible*, and you do not see me standing in front of you?**" She laughed and said "**Yes!**" "**Really?**" I replied. "**But I am so much bigger than you, and you still don't see me?**"
By this time I had gotten my ticket for the ride home on the *Ric Rac* as the line jumper waited to purchase her ticket back to Guimaras. "**Is it because you are older that you think you can push ahead of me?**" I asked.She had no reply, so I walked away and boarded my boat. As soon as I took my seat, the engines started as I was the last one to board, mine was the *last* ticket sold. As the *Ric Rac* crew pushed the boat off the dock, I saw the rude lady and her companion walking to the next boat. But she would have to wait. The pump boat doesn't leave the dock until they have a full vessel.

Lady Boys (She Males or Bayut) in the Philippines.

I was quite amazed as I went shopping with my Filipina wife to the various malls in the Philippines to see such a large amount of "lady boys", men who dressed and acted like women. Cebu is said to have the largest concentration of lady boys, but I have seen many as I travel in Iloilo City. After living in the Midwest for 57 years, with one year living in Las Vegas, I had never seen so many guys dressed like women in my whole life. Not even in Vegas.

Many have certain female characteristics while not attempting to hide their original maleness. For example, a lady boy may sport a typically male haircut, but speak in a feminine way. Gays are not ostracized in the Philippines which I found surprising due to the largely conservative Catholic population.

My wife has a lady boy named **"Bambi"** that cuts and styles her hair in a large salon in Iloilo and does a fantastic job and is very personable. I have had a few "bayuts" also wait on me at different shops and always found them to be very pleasant and polite. Just another cultural difference to expect in the Philippines.

There is one particularly friendly lady boy at SM City in Iloilo that works at a shop where I buy a newspaper. I always chat with him for a minute or two, but to be honest, even after almost three years of living in the Philippines, I am still am getting adjusted to this part of Filipino culture which I find peculiar, especially for a nation that is about 84% Catholic. Different strokes for different folks, I suppose.

Drugs in the Philippines

You cannot find aisles and aisles of over-the-counter pain relievers in the Philippines. You have to buy it at the pharmacy counter. I've tried to adjust to the inconvenience of that (to me), and usually handle it by letting my Filipina wife stand in line.

Of course if you can purchase a generic brand of medication it will be cheaper, but please note that some shops in the Philippines sell medication that has been "cut" to lessen the dosage but still sell it for the same price. A chain of drug stores across the Philippines, **Generics Pharmacy**, is a reputable outlet for generic drugs, however.

It is better to deal with the major pharmacies in the Philippines such as **Mercury Drug** or **Watson Drugstores**, and never buy any medication that someone might try sell to you off the street such as Viagra. But I am sure the readers of this eBook are smart enough to realize that. So my advice would be to purchase as much prescription medicine you might need, and other medications and vitamins, before moving to the Philippines. The following is an article from my website, PhilippinesPlus.com:

Fake Drugs in the Philippines

Over 10% of drugs sold in the Philippines are fake. That's according to a report in the **Inquirer.net**, Nov. 16, 2010 edition. The article states that Asia is the largest producer of counterfeit medicines, and different organizations in the Philippines are joining forces this week to launch the first "National Consciousness Week against Fake Medicines."

Aside from counterfeit drugs being sold in the Philippines another problem I have encountered in the local provinces, such as rural Guimaras where my Filipina wife and I live, is the sale of potentially harmful drugs at the local pharmacies. In the fall of 2010 my wife injured her knee, and her sister-in-law purchased a steroid, which could not have been bought without a prescription in the nearby larger city of Iloilo City. The medicine caused my wife's knee and entire leg to become extremely bruised.

We took a pump boat to St. Paul's Hospital in Iloilo City to have her knee checked out, and the specialist (who was trained in a university in Boston and had a private practice in New York City) said that if my wife would have continued taking the medication it could have been potentially life-threatening. To say that I was upset with my sister-in-law would be an understatement, but fortunately the doctor's treatment and prescribed medication healed my wife's knee.

Dr. Vicente V. Pido's fee, the head of Orthopedic and Hand Surgery for St. Paul's, was only 600 pesos (about 13 US dollars at the time.) He and another physician that initially examined my wife warned that it was very common in the provinces to sell medications without a prescription. Not only are counterfeit drugs a problem in the Philippines, but also medications taken without a prescription.

The Inquirer article says to look for the Rx symbol and expiration dates. Look at the labels and be wary when the price is significantly or unusually low. Good advice to follow. We try to purchase the bulk of our medications from legitimate established drug stores in the Philippines, and I am very cautious of even buying a simple thing like an aspirin at one of our local provincial pharmacies in light of the episode with the steroids. Just exercise caution and some good common sense, and you should be fine.

Another piece of advice: don't stand near your wife when she purchases any medicine. I made that mistake once at a Mercury Drug Store in Iloilo and my wife ended up paying 600 pesos (13.88 USD) more for her mother's high blood pressure that she had paid in previous months. Did not matter how much my wife complained (I didn't know what was going on at the time, and you can be sure I would have LOUDLY protested.) This is a classic case of the **"skin tax."** Also sometimes referred to as the **"foreigner tax."** After that I just stood on the other side of the store out of sight of the pharmacy counter and chatted with the security guard posted at the front door.

Armed Guards in the Philippines. You WILL Be Searched.

You *WILL* face armed guards, either carrying a pistol, shotgun or assault rifle, that pat you down and search you when shopping at the malls and many retail outlets in the Philippines. If you're carrying a backpack or purse, it will be opened up and looked at. Don't complain. Don't make any remarks. Just greet the guard with a **"Good Morning"** (you can even use "Good Morning" in the afternoon since many workers at the SM Malls greet me with "Good Morning" even in the pm.) I always raise my hands high up in the air to let the guards quickly frisk me. Guess I've watched too many cops shows back in the States.

When I first experienced armed security guards during my initial visit to the Glorietta Mall in Makati City, I was surprised, but of course complied. I had never experienced this before in America aside from being frisked at an OzzFest concert in Missouri many years ago.

My first visit to the Philippines was in January 2000, before the 9/11 tragedy in New York City. That same Glorietta Mall was bombed in May of 2000 and injured 12 people. An explosion in October 2007, rocked the mall and killed eight people and injured 126. Authorities blame the explosion on a leaking LPG tank, and the Philippine government still clings to the *"official"* gas explosion theory even as the site smelled of gunpowder and some reports revealed traces of C4 explosives being found.

Of course I was also carefully searched upon my first arrival to the airport in Manila, but did not expect it at a shopping mall. The Philippines has experienced many terrorist bombings in the past, and this continues to be a threat to this day, so I do not mind the extra security, in fact, I welcome it. I usually pass through in a few seconds while my wife and anyone carrying any purses or backpacks with them have those quickly searched. I have never seen anyone have to empty their purse or backpack in front of the guards which one can expect to find at most businesses in the Philippines, not just the large malls.

In Iloilo City where we do our shopping, many mall guards such as at the The Atrium were not even searching us at all. That is until the "Wild West" shooting which killed one person at the SM Delgado store and critcially wounded another, a place we have shopped at many times. Here's the story on that:

Wild West Shootout at the SM Delgado in Iloilo City

One dead. One critically wounded. Words were exchanged in the CR (Comfort Room/Restroom) of **SM Delagado in Iloilo City** this past Friday around 6:40 pm. A place my asawa and I have shopped at numerous times since moving to the Philippines in Guimaras province over two years ago. I can guarantee you that the mall was crowded that Friday, and it was fortunate no innocent bystanders were hurt.

Mayor Jed Patrick Mabilog, in true damage control mode, stated that the incident was an isolated case and expressed confidence that the mall will institute tighter security measures to avoid a repeat of any similar events, that according to a report in the **Panay News** August 1, 2011 online edition.

The article states that **Chief Supt. Cipriano Querol Jr.**, regional police director, ordered a thorough investigation of the incident.

He wanted to find out how Cahuya and Gumire were able to enter the mall despite the security checks in all of its entrances.

"If the security guards thoroughly checked (the persons) entering the mall, they should have discovered that the two had guns," Querol said.

Chief, let me clue you in on something you are **certainly fully aware of**. During the *countless* times I have gone through security guard checkpoints at SM Delagado or SM City in Iloilo, I have noticed many occasions where backpacks or purses were not thoroughly checked. Shoot, (I mean, "shucks,") I could probably have stashed an old Volkswagen in a plastic bag and gotten past the guards with it.

I *will* say, however, that the vast majority of guards are extremely polite and respectful, but after the shootout, I would think they might be pressed to be more thorough in their inspections. However, if the security personnel only make 265 pesos (about six US Dollars) a **day**, same as the SM Department Store employees, I cannot blame them for being too motivated. But still, a job is a job. No one even gets checked at the entrance to **The Atrium Mall** in Iloio and rarely do I see anyone checked at the local **Mary Mart Mall**, so at least SM security is attempting some kind of search.

Forty-seven-year-old **Marcos Cahuya**, a retired member of the **Armed Forces of the Philippines**, was pronounced dead by attending physicians of the St. Therese Hospital where he was rushed. His adversary was 52-year-old **Alfredo Gumeri** of Aurora Subdivision in Iloilo City. He was taken to Iloilo St. Paul's Hospital for treatment.

The two had long-standing personal grudges, an initial investigation showed.

They chanced on each other inside the mall and a verbal tussle ensued prior to the shootout.

Shoppers, sales attendants and even the **mall security guards** (with the male guards being armed, to my knowledge, with some carrying shotguns, but remember the six-dollar-a-day salary now) **scampered** for safety when they heard successive gunshots. Nobody else was injured in the shootout and the ensuing pandemonium.

Cahuya was armed with a .45 pistol while Gumire had a .40 pistol. Outside of the mall there is a sign depicting a gun with the the universal red slash through it, indicating no weapons are allowed. It is common in Iloilo City and the Philippines to see signs with **"Check your weapons at the door"** emblazoned across them. Wild Wild West indeed.

A utility personnel of the mall, Elmer Barnuevo, witnessed the shooting incident. He said Gumire and Cahuya crossed paths on the hallway of the mall comfort room. They had a heated argument. Cahuya later rushed out of the comfort room, with Gumire running after him and shooting him.

The Panay News reports that Gumire reportedly went back to the comfort room and then casually passed by the felled Cahuya thinking he was already dead. Unknown to Gumire, the critically wounded Cahuya was still alive. Cahuya shot him, but his foe survived. Wild West West Shootout in Iloilo City. Things **can** get a little crazy here.

I have always found the guards to be very professional and polite and have never had an issue with any of them as it is wise to *always* be civil to someone that is carrying a pistol or assault rifle. I am not usually searched at any other places but the large malls and am accustomed to it now.

With such terrorist groups as **Abu Sayyaf** (a Muslim group with ties to al-Qaeda and based in the southern Philippines), the **NPA (New People's Army**, the armed wing of the Philippines Communist party), and **MNLF (Moro National Liberation Front)** from which Abu Sayyaf split from in the early 1990's), present in the Philippines, I understand the need for the heightened security. The threats these terrorists groups pose are very real and are not to be taken for granted, but I personally have not experienced any safety issues since living here and will bring up the issue of personal safety later in this eBook

Food in the Philippines.

Another major cultural difference I have is with the food available in the Philippines. Adjusting to the food in the Philippines is something to deal with once you arrive here. For those of you married to Filipinas such as I am, you have probably already eaten plenty of Filipino food, but things are quite different once you actually arrive in the Philippines and go to the local wet markets. I probably ate at fast food restaurants about once a week in America and prepared most of my own meals, some frozen, or those that weren't very healthy. While there are many Western style fast food restaurants in nearby Iloilo City and through out the Philippines: **McDonald's, Pizza Hut, KFC,** and **Shakey's Pizza**, there were none on Guimaras.

My Filipina wife is a great cook and has prepared many fantastic Filipino dishes, but native ingredients were sometimes very difficult to find in our area when we lived in America, and once she started working, and opened a small home daycare center later, I prepared my own food as she did not have the time or energy.

We were able to find an Asian market in the city I worked in where she could buy 25 or 50 pound bags of the rice she enjoyed while working as an **OCW (Overseas Contract Worker**, now called **OFW, Overseas Filipino Worker)** in Taiwan. We purchased a rice cooker, a necessity in the Philippines and for our home in America, as rice is a *mainstay* in the Filipino diet and many times served at both breakfast, lunch, and dinner.

When we moved to the Philippines, my wife and I used to eat a delicious bread called pan de sal, famous throughout the Philippines, for breakfast and at snack time, *merienda time*, usually ten in the morning and four in the afternoon. But that was when we lived in Guimaras and our bakery was only a five-minute walk from us. At our new location in Iloilo, the nearest pan de sal outlet is a 25-minute walk from us, and is not nearly as tasty as the bread we enjoyed in Guimaras.

Other times my asawa will eat some buttered raisin bread she buys at the SM Supermarket in Iloilo City along with her Nescafe 3-in-1 coffee. I will usually have some instant Quaker Oats oatmeal (I've tried the SM Bonus brand and an Australian brand, but pay a few extra pesos for Quaker which I like the best.) I also have a cup of Earl Grey tea with my oatmeal, and have pancakes on Sunday morning which my wife prepares and will have eggs once or twice a week for a break from the oatmeal.

Thankfully, I have been eating healthier in the Philippines as I now eat fresh fish, either tilapia, or milkfish (bangus) three times a week, and have lost about 15 pounds since moving here. My wife prefers small tuna or squid.

For those coming here without Filipina spouses or girlfriends, then you might have a period of adjustment, or you could just be adventurous and try a lot of the traditional foods when you arrive. Western-style foods are available in the supermarkets in the Philippines but usually at western-style, higher prices. Be prepared for that.

Local Government in the Philippines and Establishing Residency

Barangays, or barrios, are the smallest administrative division in the Philippines and is the native Filipino term for a village, district or ward. You will find barangays all throughout the Philippines. The local barangay is the pulse of the neighborhood. *Always stay on good terms with your local barangay officials.* You may need a favor later.

I met our local barangay chief, captain, after just a couple of weeks after moving to our small town in Guimaras. A very friendly man and pleased to greet a foreigner visitor, a "kano", or American, such as myself. You will discover that the majority of Filipinos are very friendly and happy to meet a foreigner, even though many will be shy.

Filipinos are a warm people and quick with a smile. I found myself somewhat of a "celebrity" in Guimaras. I still get my fair share of attention in Iloilo so if you don't like attention and being stared at, then you will have some difficulty adjusting to that.

My Filipina wife had to register as a resident of her barangay after having lived in the United States with me for the past nine years because we had some construction to be done at our home, and she had to be registered as a resident in order for her to be authorized to sign the construction permits that the local barangay officials also had to sign off on. My wife is the legal owner of our home and property in the Philippines.

While at the city hall, my wife also obtained a general permit from the barangay captain which authorized the construction at our home. The total cost of the residency requirements and general construction permit was approximately five dollars in US currency.

I, personally, have never registered as a resident though when I signed up for my Smart Bro account for my Internet service, I was advised by the **Smart Bro** official that I would have to register later in order to have my Smart Bro service established in my name. Well, I started my service in Guimaras in

August 2009 and transferred my Internet in October 2011 when we moved to Iloilo. I still have Smart Bro service in my name without going back to any barangay hall to register as a local resident.

I *would* advise, however, having a utility service such as an Internet provider in your name. I have needed such documentation later to prove my residency in the Philippines in order to have my cell phone contract in the States ended at an earlier date without any termination fees. You might also need such a utility bill here in your name if you plan to make any credit purchases or apply for a bank account.

I did make an inquiry about getting our electric bill in my name but that involved too much of a process and has not been proven to be necessary. The utility bill in Guimaras was in my mother-in-law's name. The utility bills at our new location in Iloilo is in the home owner's name. I did not need any proof of local residency when I applied for my **ACR-I** card in Manila this past June 2010 or when I obtained my Permanent Visa in past May 2011.

"The Crossing" in San Miguel, Jordan in Guimaras

"Filipino Time."

"Filipino Time" is another major cultural difference that takes some getting used to. I'm still adjusting to it after almost years in the Philippines (and after being married to a Filipina for over 12 years), but at times it can be quite maddening and irritating. For the uninitiated, **"Filipino Time"** is a laid back state-of-mind practiced by nearly all Filipinos where being on time for functions, appointments or deadlines mean very little and are not observed. In short, **"Filipino Time"** can mean always being late and things get done when they get done.

In fact, my wife and I were late for our civil wedding ceremony with the City

Clerk that issued our license to marry. My sister-in-law who made arrangements with the City Clerk prior to our getting married and had to be at the Clerk's office with us, was still sweeping the floors of her house (where we staying that day) an hour before the time we were to get married. It takes an half hour to get to the office.

We were 30 minutes late, and I was not very pleased with my first exposure to **"Filipino Time."** As an American that worked almost 30 years for a company that would penalize you if you were one minute late, and as someone who prided himself on always being punctual and arriving early for every function, **"Filipino Time"** was difficult for me to deal with at times, but I do find myself adjusting to it better, though, the longer I live here. Just takes some, well, time.

Here's a story I did about a recent Philippine government program to attempt to put an end to Filipino Time.

The End of "Filipino Time?"

A recent story in the **Philippine Daily Inquirer** disturbed me. While GMA idles away her time under hospital arrest watching *"Wil Time Bigtime"* and Supreme Court Justice Corona facing an upcoming impeachment trial, Philippine Science Secretary Mario Montejo is calling on the nation to synchronize watches and clocks with Philippine Standard Time (PST) so everybody can greet 2012 at the same time. Worse yet, is news of this nefarious **"Juan Time"** project which is an initiative that aims to redefine the notoriously late **"Filipino Time"** by encouraging Filipinos to synchronize with PST and encourage timeliness. I find this *extremely* unsettling.

"Let us synchronize our time pieces with the PST so that we will all celebrate at the same time the coming in of the New Year. We will be one nation using one standard time," Montejo said in a statement.

The weather bureau, the country's official timekeeper, displays the official time on its Web site **www.weather.gov.ph**. They use a precise time system that consists of a rubidium atomic clock and a Global Positioning System. I don't understand the need for this. What's wrong with having six or seven clocks in a household, business or government office with six or seven different times?

My OCD, Obsessive Compulsive Disorder, once controlled me so much I **HAD** to have the same time on my watch, cell phone, microwave, electric stove, alarm clock. clock radio, etc., back at our home in the States. I would absolutely *cringe* if any time piece was a minute off from any of the others. I worked for a company, AT&T, that disciplined a co-worker for *being 20 seconds late* to his desk at start time. And the Department of Science and Technology (DOST) is worried about clocks being synchronized in the Philippines? I just don't get it.

The science department partnered with the local office of Discovery Channel (don't *they* have anything better to do?) for the Juan "initiative." DOST also tapped its fellow government agencies to synchronize clocks in offices to carry the national standard time.

The Inquirer article goes on to report that the Department of Education adopted the campaign earlier this year and ordered all offices and schools to synchronize clocks with PST.

"The national launch of Juan Time paved the way for Filipinos to understand the value of time. This socio-cultural initiative, where science is central, has made the public appreciate the existence of the PST..." said Montejo.

I urge the government to **embrace** Filipino Time and junk this "Juan Time" crap. And why pick on anyone named "Juan" in the first place? So what if you show up one or two hours late for a party? Or work, for that matter. And if you call the police to come out to your house and they show up the next day, what does that all matter? I'm just now adjusting to "Filipino Time," and the government wants to junk it? It's ingrained in the culture. What's next, Mr. Secretary? A ban on balut?

Sticking out as an Expat! Celebrity Status in the Philippines.

I'm a six foot tall, 200-pound Caucasian American that used to live in a town of over 20,000 mostly Filipinos. I got noticed *a lot* whenever I walked around, and heard *"Americano"* every where I go. Sometimes I got the occasional *"Hi Joe!"*

As mentioned earlier, I feel like a celebrity at times and have gotten used to the attention. The longer I'm here, the more I have adjusted, but be prepared to have people stare at you wherever you go. It's not that the Filipinos are being rude, they are just curious. I have passed groups of little kids whose jaws drop in amazement as I walk by.

So if you don't like attention, then you should stay where you are or keep holed up in your home if you do move. Actually, you guys might enjoy the extra looks you will get when you go shopping at your local SM Mall from some of the Filipinas that work there and from Filipinas that shop at the malls. You will find the sales people very friendly for the most part, and happy to converse with you.

Of course since most expats *do* stick out in the Philippines, that means you have to be aware of your surroundings as you might find yourself the target of pickpockets and other thieves. In nearby Iloilo City, which has a population of over 400,000, I always try to avoid the crowded downtown streets as much as possible and always keep my wallet in my front pocket (which I also did when going to Las Vegas.)

I have had one Canadian expat that lives in Guimaras that told me he was the victim of a pickpocket in Iloilo, but after almost three years of residing here, I have not had any problems. And I travel via jeepney almost exclusively now when in Iloilo without any difficulty at all. My wife always clutches her purse when she goes to Iloilo, also, and it is wise to be on your guard. Do I obsess about it? Absolutely not!

However, if you travel in the Manila area, I *would* advise extra caution. When

I arrived in the Philippines in January 2000, my future spouse and I went to the Glorietta Mall in Makati City to buy her wedding ring. As we were shopping in the mall a Filipino gentlemen approached me and said *"Hello, sir! Do you remember me? I am your security guard at your hotel. Could you give me 600 pesos for my daughter's birthday today so I can buy her ice cream?"*

I was taken aback, and since I had only been in the Philippines a couple of days, and I was staying at a hotel, I gave the man the money as I did not want to appear cheap in front of my soon-to-be wife and didn't want any trouble with any security guards at our hotel. As soon as the man left, my future wife said she was ashamed of the behavior of some of her countrymen, and apologized. I told her there was no need for an apology, and advised her that I had doubts about the man's story, but went ahead and gave him the money to avoid any trouble. Yes, I was scammed, the man wasn't a security guard at our hotel, but I learned from it.

Beggars in the Philippines.

I have had *numerous* encounters with street beggars and others (non-relatives, as opposed to relatives which I previous covered) asking for money. I'll just give you my observations on begging as it relates to my former province, Guimaras, and nearby Iloilo City. Of course larger cities like Manila will have more problems with beggars, but I'll just cover what I know from personal experience.

My wife's residence in San Miguel, located in Jordan municipality on rural Guimaras province, is a small town whose main shopping areas are divided into two sites, the **"Old Site"** and you guessed it, **"The New Site."** I used to take a daily early morning walk between the Old and New Site, and encountered a smiling Filipino middle-aged gentlemen who said to me *"Hey Joe! Give me some money!"* I turned my pocket inside out to show him it was empty and said *"Wala!"* ("none".) I then continued my walk. I met the gentleman several times after that and would purposely avoid him whenever possible. He never asked for money after that initial meeting but always said *"Good morning, Joe!"*

I did have a lola (grandma) ask me for money when accompanied by my wife at the Old Site Market, but did not give her any and was also asked by a lolo (grandpa), but did not give him any money, either. There once also was a young boy playing some homemade drums at our jeepney dispatch site in Guimaras and asking for some pesos, but I advised him that he could play as much as he likes, but I would *not* be giving him any money.

I also encountered a Filipino gentlemen on my way home from a walk early one morning in Guimaras that was standing with a group of people at our local funeral home that *ran after me* and demanded money. I told him to get away from me in no uncertain terms, as I was not in the mood that day to be bothered. But that's been the extent of any begging I have encountered in San Miguel.

Iloilo City is another story. Of course being a large city, you would expect to encounter more incidents of begging. We used to be by approached by a lot of beggars when we went shopping at **SM Delgado** or **The Atrium**. Many street people there asking us for money. There was an older blind gentlemen that I would give a few pesos to and to the occasional young kid who would open a taxi door for us. Some actually grabbed me by the arm, which always provoked a negative response from me.

However, a big problem in Iloilo have been the syndicates or gangs who force children into begging and take all the money they get. If they don't collect enough for the day, the poor kids are beaten. Some parents actually *sell* the kids to the gangs. *Absolutely horrific and evil!*

The Iloilo City government passed an ordinance which prohibited begging, and I *had* seen a dramatic decrease in the beggars for a few months. However, the begging has increased again in the SM Delgado or Atrium area and is back to its normal levels. The law also makes it illegal to give money to any beggars.

At SM City, where we do the bulk of our shopping and is far from the downtown area, we have only had one instance of someone asking us for money. It really is more of a minor annoyance than a problem, and with the level of poverty you are surrounded by, you can understand the extremes that some people have to go through to survive. However, again, my first responsibility is to my wife and to myself as we live are supported by my fixed income.

Divorce and Annulments in the Philippines

My wonderful Filipina wife and I have been married over 12 years. Thank God, she has the patience of a saint. She has to put up with my constant complaints and bad attitude and has done so most of the time without getting angry at me, but over time we have had a huge argument when she can't take it anymore and explodes. Can't blame her. But we get through it, and love each other just as much.

Sad to say, my first marriage to my American wife only lasted nine months before she kicked me out of the house and threw my belongings in the front yard (but at least she packed them in garbage bags.) I wasn't physically abusive, but the main reason for the split was that her young daughters did not want to "share" their Mom with a step-dad (she had been divorced for over six years before we were married) and threatened to live with their Dad if I continued to reside there. At least after the divorce she admitted she said was 50% responsible, too, and several years later I met my current wife.

That said, the Philippines is the only county in the world (not including Vatican City) without a divorce law (Malta, another predominantly Catholic nation, was the only other nation on the planet that did not allow divorce, but enacted a law in October 2011 allowing it.) The Philippines only allows an annulment under certain conditions (infidelity is not one of them) and at a cost of 150,000 pesos to 300,000 pesos or more.

Annulment in the Philippines has been called "Catholic divorce for the rich and famous." President Aquino's own sister, Kris Aquino, was granted an annulment in February 2012. She was married to basketball star James Yap in July 2005. The couple campaigned for her brother and separated after Aquino assumed office in 2010.

About 95% of all annulment requests are denied. A divorce outside of the Philippines where the couple is married in the Philippines, is not recognized in the Philippines so an annulment would have to be obtained.

However, my wife has a cousin whose wife left him for another man, and he has since "remarried" (though it is not a legal marriage.) It is my understanding that this practice is quite common in the Philippines because of the stringent laws prohibiting divorce but since the overwhelming majority of Filipinos are of the Catholic faith, the fact that there is no divorce law is not a huge surprise.

My own personal feeling on the subject is that in cases of infidelity or spousal abuse, then divorce should be allowed, however, I do not believe in a "Las Vegas," or "quickie" style of divorce and remarriage.

Culture shock in the Philippines? You'll experience all of the above topics I have covered plus more. Just be prepared to change, try to be patient, and you'll adapt. I did. And if *I* can do it, I have no doubt that you can also.

WANT TO SPEND SIX YEARS IN A PHILIPPINE JAIL? COMMIT ADULTERY.

Here's an article I wrote that tells about the dangers of dating someone in the Philippines that is married. You can wind up in jail *for a long time* if your "special someone" is married.

Would you care to spend up to six years in a Philippines jail? I believe the majority of my readers would probably answer with a resounding *"NO"* to that question. However, a new bill proposed by a House of Representatives committee in the Philippines has been approved that would impose stiff penalties on married citizens engaging in sexual intercourse with an individual other than his or her legal spouse. That's according to a recent April 22, 2012 report in the **Manila Bulletin.**

Despite the proposed new legislature, adultery is *already* considered a crime in the Philippines. Here's what the Revised Penal Code Book Two, Title Eleven **Article 333** states:

- "Who are guilty of adultery. — Adultery is committed by any **married woman** who shall have sexual intercourse with a man not her husband and by the man who has carnal knowledge of her knowing her to be married, even if the marriage be subsequently declared void.
- Adultery shall be punished by prison correccional in its medium and maximum periods.
- If the person guilty of adultery committed this offense while being abandoned without justification by the offended spouse, the penalty next lower in degree than that provided in the next preceding paragraph shall be imposed. "

- But the new proposed law by the House Committee on Women and Gender Equality, **House Bill 5734**, *also* eliminates gender bias in laws penalizing the crimes of adultery and concubinage.
- In an article I did back in November 2010, I was amazed to learn that under Filipino law, murder is essentially allowed for **spouses caught in adultery!** but the new law, as mentioned above, is going to eliminate the current gender bias.
- HB 5734, a consolidation of five bills filed by various House member, defines sexual infidelity as an act committed by any legally married person who shall have sexual intercourse with another person other than his or her legal spouse.
- It does not exempt a person whose marriage has been subsequently declared void.
- **However, the crime cannot be prosecuted by anybody except upon the complaint of the *offended spouse.***
- The bill eliminates the disparity between the penalties imposed by existing laws on the crimes of concubinage and adultery.
- Again, under the above-mentioned current Article 333 of the Revised Penal Code, adultery is committed by a *married woman* who engages in sexual intercourse with a man not her husband. Offenders are punishable by a *maximum jail term of six years.*

- On the other hand, Article 333 of RPC only metes out on the offender a penalty of "destierro" or banishment from the community where the couple lives for a certain period of time.
- **HB 5734** treats the two crimes as the *same acts* that constitute sexual infidelity.
- Also, lawmakers proposed that an offended party can no longer file charges against the alleged offender if the former is also guilty of sexual infidelity or had abandoned the guilty spouse without just cause for more than one year.

So for you expats that come over to meet a *married* Filipina and think you don't have a thing to worry about, think again. It is a very distinct possibility that you could wind up in a Philippines jail. Don't think it can happen to you? Yeah, I'm sure that's what those foreigners already languishing in jail for committing adultery thought, also. Better make sure you know what "head" *you're* thinking with.

I've received several emails over the past year or so from guys that were coming over to the Philippines and were well aware that the girl that they had been chatting with online was married. They have never stepped foot in the Philippines and have no idea the danger they are placing themselves in. If the husband finds out that his wife has a boyfriend, and it makes no difference how long they have been separated, the husband *CAN* press charges and have both parties arrested.

Here's a story I recently read:

"For three months a 62-year-old Filipino man had been suspecting his wife was having an affair with another man. He finally found proof that she was.

The report, from said "Wilfredo" saw his wife's car parked outside a motel in this city, leading him to suspect that she was with another man there.

"Wilfredo" tried but failed contacting his 50-year-old wife through her cellphone. With the help of a friend, he was able to barge into the motel room where he saw his wife was with a man, allegedly a former government official of Negros Occidental.

With the help of the Women and Children Protection Unit of the Bacolod City Police, the woman and her lover are now in custody of authorities who said that she will be charged with adultery." (Source PhilSTAR.com.)

Culture shock in the Philippines? You'll experience all of the above topics I have covered plus more. Just be prepared to change, try to be patient, and you'll adapt. I did. And if *I* can do it, I have no doubt that you can also.

Visitor at "The Farm" in Guimaras

OBTAINING A VISA IN THE PHILIPPINES

This detailed section of my E-book will focus *entirely* on obtaining a **visa for living in the Philippines** since it one of the most *sought after* topics of information desired by those planning a move to the Philippines or for those currently residing in this archipelago of 7, 107 islands.

I have included a *detailed* section on obtaining a Permanent 13(a) Visa which I am not publishing in its entirety on my website, PhilippinesPlus.com, since it would be too lengthy of an article to print; I also wanted to include something special for those that purchased this book.

ENTERING THE PHILIPPINES

First, I will explain what I did concerning visas to the Philippines *before* moving here. I researched extensively and put many hours and hours of work on the Internet checking various established websites maintained by expats

that had been in the Philippines for years trying to find some definite answer on what to do about a visa once I get to the Philippines. I also extensively researched the Philippines Bureau of Immigration Website.

Some of the information I found was confusing and contradictory. And why? Well, as an official at the **Bureau of Immigration's** main office at **Magallanes Drive, Intramuros, Manila** told me during a visit for my **ACR-I Visa** on June 2010 (more on that later) when you arrive at the airport *"it just depends upon what immigration officer you talk to."* Very true.

Some immigration officials at the Ninoy Aquino International Airport (NAIA) will *strictly* enforce the immigration law, may or may not ask for you to show them a return ticket for onward travel to your next destination, and some may be quite pleasant and helpful like the official that checked us in when we arrived in the Philippines in July 2009 to take advantage of the Balibayan Visa, or Privilege (more on that later also.)

For those that have already made trips to the Philippines, you know it can be a bit intimidating and confusing after you get off that 13-19 hour flight and face the long immigration lines at the **Ninoy Aquino International Airport** in Manila. Most of you reading this probably are already aware of the following information from the **Bureau of Immigration website** of the Philippines:

Guidelines on Entry Visas of Temporary Visitors to the Philippines
The 9a Tourist Visa

"Nationals from the following countries (see list **here**) are allowed to enter the Philippines without visas for a stay not exceeding twenty-one (21) days, provided they hold valid tickets for their return journey to port of origin or next port of destination. Department regulations require that passports are valid for a period of not less than six (6) months beyond the contemplated period of stay. However, Immigration Officers at ports of entry may exercise their discretion to admit holders of passports valid for at least sixty (60) days beyond the intended period of stay."

This is the **"9a" Tourist Visa.** Become *very familiar* with this visa if you are a single guy. Unless you've got big bucks to qualify for a Quota, SRRV or SVEG Visas (to be discussed later), the **9a** (the "a" gets tacked on when you extend your original 21 days entry, it is just a "9" when you first arrive) and you will become good friends. Be prepared to shell out 5-6 thousand pesos every two months for the privilege of using this particular option. My American expat friend living in Iloilo City estimates his annual cost for his temporary visa to be around 600 US Dollars a year.

But what if you want to stay longer? Here's what the Immigration website states:

"How can aliens admitted under E.O. 408 (non-visa required nationals admitted for 21 days) extend their stay in the Philippines beyond 21 days?

"Aliens admitted under E.O. 408 (non-visa required nationals admitted for 21 days) may extend their stay in the Philippines beyond 21 days by applying for a visa waiver at his nearest Immigration Office before the expiration of the 21-day period. This will entitle him to stay in the country for more than 59 days, he should secure extension of stay and register with the Bureau of Immigration, and pay the necessary Immigration fees." (See following screen shot from the B.I. **website** for the latest look at the fees as of February 2012.)

TOURIST VISA EXTENSION AFTER 59 DAYS

Non-Visa Required Nationals

PARTICULARS	MINOR		14-16 YEARS		ADULT (16 years old and above)	
	1 month	2 months	1 month	2 months	1 month	2 months
› Every month of extension	P 500.00	P 1,000.00	P 500.00	P 1,000.00	P 500.00	P 1,000.00
› Application Fee	P 300.00	P 600.00	P 300.00	P 600.00	P 300.00	P 600.00
› Alien Certificate of Registration Fee	P 500.00	P 500.00	P 1,000.00	P 1,000.00	P 1,000.00	P 1,000.00
› Head Tax (over 16 years old)					P 250.00	P 250.00
› Certificate Fee	P 500.00	P 500.00	P 500.00	P 500.00	P 500.00	P 500.00
› Express Fee	P 1,000.00	P 1,500.00	P 1,000.00	P 1,500.00	P 1,000.00	P 1,500.00
› Immigration Clerance Certificate Fee/Certificate of Exemption Fee	P 200.00	P 200.00	P 700.00	P 700.00	P 700.00	P 700.00
› Legal Research Fee (LRF) for each immigration fee except Head Tax and Fines	P 50.00	P 50.00	P 50.00	P 50.00	P 50.00	P 50.00
Total	P 3,050.00	P 3,550.00	P 4,050.00	P 4,550.00	P 4,300.00	P 4,800.00
I-Card for Tourist	$ 50.00	$ 50.00	$ 50.00	$ 50.00	$ 50.00	$ 50.00
Express Fee (for I-Card)	P 500.00	P 500.00	P 500.00	P 500.00	P 500.00	P 500.00

The 9 (a) Tourist Visa is the most simplified and easiest visa to obtain in the Philippines. The Immigration Department has a fixation about adding lower-case numbers to their visa classifications. So you married guys don't feel left out, I will be discussing at great length later on the **13a Permanent Visa** as opposed to the 13 d, e, g, etc.

Note the following posted right after the fees schedule:

Fine for Overstaying (Additional P 500.00) per month Motion for Reconsideration for Overstaying (Additional P 500.00) Legal Research Fee (LRF) of P 10.00 Re-issuance of ACR for (2nd entry of every entry after 59 days) P 250.00

So it would be in your best interest to make sure you are not late in getting your visa extended. You *can* be booted out of the Philippines at the discretion of the Immigration office.

What is the maximum extension of stay that can be granted?

"Foreigners holding temporary visitors visa pursuant to Philippine Immigration Act of 1940 and aliens admitted under E.O. 408 may extend their stay in the Philippines every 2 months for a total stay of 16 months. Extension of stay after16 months, up to 24 months need the approval of the Chief of the Immigration Regulation Division. Extension of stay after 24 months need the approval of the Commissioner."

Now some expats don't like to wait in long lines. If you have a severe lack of patience you can always hire an *authorized agent* to represent you at the Bureau of Immigration to do all your dirty work for you. I never have. I'm too cheap. But for 500 pesos or so, you have that option. I would suggest checking with another expat that has used the agent before and would recommend them.

THE BALIKBAYAN VISA (PRIVILEGE)

I entered the Philippines with my American passport accompanied by my Filipina wife who held a Philippines passport and who has a Permanent Resident "Green Card" from the United States, and requested a "Balikbayan" visa. Now just a month before we arrived in the Philippines I was confused by the information I found on the Internet from various sites. Maybe it was just me.

And then there is the matter of the infamous **"throw away"** ticket (which is not needed if you hold an **ACR-I Card,** to be discussed later) to another location out of the Philippines which was mentioned in the majority of websites I looked at, and which I did not need (but had previously purchased) before I arrived in Manila. Officially, you must have a ticket for onward travel to enter the Philippines. This applies both to those who apply for visas before arriving in the Philippines and those who hope to receive a 21-day visa on arrival. In practice, immigration inspectors at the airport *don't always ask* to see an onward ticket.

I also thought I had to fill out some paperwork for the **Balikbayan** visa, or privilege. However, thanks to a helpful official at the Philippines Consular Office in Chicago, I was advised to ask for the **Balikbayan** visa when arriving in Manila, make sure I have a NSO certified copy of our marriage contract with us (I did), and tell the immigration officer I would just be staying for three or four months.

When we arrived in Manila on July 15, 2009, and faced extremely long lines, we were fortunate to find a lane that just opened up and the friendly female Immigration officer I had mentioned earlier just looked at my passport and my wife's, and did not even request a look at our marriage certificate. She did *not* ask for a ticket from me for another destination in the future. She did *not* ask me how long I was staying (and I did not volunteer that information.) She wrote a small **"BB"** by my passport stamp for Balikbayan visa and that was it.

Again, from the official Philippines Immigration website, here is information on the "Balikbayan" visa or "Balikbayan Privilege":

THE BALIKBAYAN PRIVILEGE (R.A.6768 as amended)

By legal definition, a Balikbayan is:

1. A Filipino citizen who has continuously been out of the Philippines for a period of at least 1 year;
2. A Filipino overseas worker; or
3. A former Filipino citizen and his or her family, who had been naturalized in a foreign country and comes or returns to the Philippines.

- The "Balikbayan Privilege" may be availed of by foreign family members of all 3 classifications provided that they travel together everytime they enter the country (MEMORANDUM dated July 1, 2008 issued by Atty. Edgardo L. Mendoza, Chief, IRD).

- "FAMILY" shall mean the spouse and the children of the Balikbayan who are not Balikbayan in their own right traveling with the latter to the Philippines.
- Correspondingly, all Balikbayans 14 years and below and 60 years of age shall be allowed to extend their temporary visitor visa under Section 9a of the Philippine Immigration Act of 1940 as amended, for a maximum period of 6 months for every extension PROVIDED that all appropriate fees are paid. Thus, Balikbayans are allowed a total maximum stay of 2 years inclusive of all extensions.

A very painless entry to the Philippines for me but again keep in mind what the Immigration official that I saw in June 2010 said: *"it just depends upon what immigration officer you talk to."* I believe that statement explains some of the contradictory information found on the Internet on obtaining visas to the Philippines.

PLEASE note that a Balikbayan is someone that has been *OUT* of the Philippines *for at least one year*. Some people have asked me if their fiancee, who has **NEVER** left the Philippines, can "avail" of the Balikbayan Privilege once they are married. They wanted to fly out to Hong Kong for a few days and return together. Nope, have to be gone at least ONE YEAR to use the privilege.

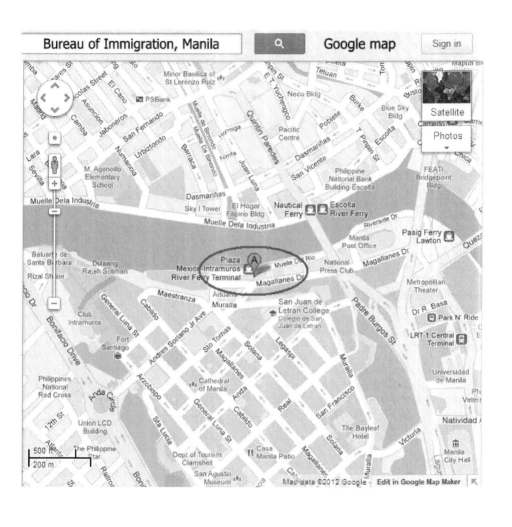

Can You Obtain Your Visa Before Moving to the Philippines?

But can you obtain your visa before moving to the Philippines? Of course you cannot obtain a Balikbayan visa before arriving, but an **ACR-I Card (Alien Certificate of Registration)** can be secured before moving to the Philippines if your spouse is Filipino. This can usually be done at the nearest Philippines Consulate General Office to you. My wife and I went to the Chicago office to apply for her new passport to the Philippines, and my intention was to file the 13a immigrant visa application there along with a Letter of Petition from my wife, but when I found all the information about the Balikbayan privilege I decided to opt for that since it seemed simpler to do at the time.

In retrospect, and after that initial visit to the Bureau of Immigration in Manila in June 2010 to obtain my ACR-I card to stay in the Philippines for another year, I could have applied for my visa at the Chicago Consulate Office and saved myself some future expenses and trouble.

I also acquired the 13a Temporary Visitor's Probationary Residence Visa during my June 2010 visit to Immigration, which my wife petitioned me for, and I applied for and was granted a Permanent Visa in May 2011 when I returned to the Immigration office after filing the necessary paperwork. However, I *could* have cared for that earlier in the Consulate Office and would *recommend* anyone with a Filipino spouse to consider doing that.

However, I *have* read of a *few* cases where those that were granted a Permanent Visa before arriving in the Philippines were *not given one* once they reported to the Bureau of Immigration and had to start the whole process over again. Read what I have to write about the three-week process in obtaining my 13(a) Permanent Visa in Manila and make your own informed decision.

My personal advice and opinion would be to tell you that the easiest way to enter the Philippines, as long as your are married to a Filipina and enter the country with your spouse, is to ask for the **"Balibayan Privilege."**

I think it's the cheapest (it's free), and affords you the least hassle. After you arrive in the Philippines and have decided to stay, I would then recommend obtaining the 13a Temporary Visa and then after a year's probation, secure the Permanent Visa.

Every expat has their own opinion on this and some swear by the Balikbayan Privilege and leave the country every year. Since my wife and I live far from Manila, it is more costly in our situation to fly there every year and get an international flight out. I *personally do not* want to be concerned with that every year.

With my Permanent Resident Visa I can stay in the Philippines as long as I like without leaving the country. I only have to renew my ACR card every five years (and have since found I can do that at the Iloilo City or Cebu Immigration Office and do not have to travel to Manila.) I also have to make a required annual report (see the next section), to the local office in Iloilo City and pay 310 pesos (7.15 USD) for my yearly registration as a foreigner.

FOREIGNERS ANNUAL REPORT TO THE BUREAU OF IMMIGRATION

From the Philippine Bureau of Immigration Website:

BI reminds foreigners to make ANNUAL REPORT
The Bureau of Immigration (BI) reminded that all resident foreign

nationals in the country that they have only until this March 1, 2010 to report in person to the bureau their presence in the country, lest they face deportation for being improperly documented aliens.

This was something I did not know about until I was in the Philippines and accidentally stumbled upon it as I was doing research for my ACR-I application. I went to my Immigration office in nearby Iloilo before the March 2010 deadline and was advised by the officials there that since I had a Balikbayan visa I would not need to register. However, that was the opinion of *that* local office.

In 2011, I had to make a return trip to the Bureau of Immigration Office in Iloilo to make my Annual Report since I now had my **Alien Certificate of Registration** card and **Temporary 13(a) Visa** and no longer held a **Balikbayan Visa.** I had researched the Philippine Bureau of Immigration Website to see what documents, other than my passport, I might need to bring. What the Bureau of Immigration website *doesn't* tell you is that you will need **two 2"x2" photo ID's** the *first time* you register as an alien.

I made the 15-minute-pump boat ride to Iloilo City to report in person. The office is only a short distance from the Ortiz Dock where the pump boat from Guimaras drops us off so I had looked up the address and printed out a Google map.

Immigration only looked like it was about 3-4 blocks from Ortiz so I told my wife I was going to walk it. My Filipina spouse did not come with me. After I arrived at the office I met an American who had some previous difficulty with the Iloilo B.I. Office and made it a point to bring his wife with him this time. Now when applying for a **13a Temporary or Permanent Visa** it is absolutely *imperative* that you bring your Filipina spouse. She is the one sponsoring you for the 13a, after all.

Didn't make sense to hire a taxi or tricycle to go the short distance to the Iloilo office. Before I left our home in Guimras, my asawa expressed concern. *"You're an American."* she said. I was already aware of that fact, but she thought I would be a target for possible robbery since I kind of stood out from the locals. I told her I would be fine. I was going in broad daylight and never have had any problems in Iloilo since we moved to the Philippines in July 2009. I had already advised my wife that she and her little niece could go on ahead to SM City, and I would catch up with them later.

I made it through the side streets of Iloilo without any problems and a minimum of stares though I was the only kano in sight. I managed to find the Immigration Office without even having to stop to ask for directions. Walked into the facility and knew I was going to be in for a wait as the room was filled with a large group of people of all nationalities.

However, an immigration officer quickly came over to me. I told him what I wanted and filled out a couple of duplicate forms which asked some general information. Handed the forms back to the gentlemen that had helped me before, and that's when he advised me I would need the two 2"x2" photo id's. I politely remarked that the Immigration website did not make note of that, but he said there was a photo booth outside, and they would process my paperwork while I was getting my id's.

I stepped outside and looked around and could not see any photo booth. I walked down the street a short distance and spoke to a Filipina lounging on the sidewalk next to a tricycle driver evidently waiting for their next fare. The helpful lady told me to go down the sidewalk and cross the street where I would find a photo shop. After dodging some jeepney traffic, I crossed the street and still could not locate a photo business.

I walked into a little shopping area that held a restaurant and asked a security guard where I could get my picture taken. He pointed to a small photo shop only about ten feet away. I had my ID photos snapped, and they were in my hands in about 15 minutes. Dodged some more jeepneys, thanked the lady still languishing by the tricycle, and she wished me a **"Happy New Year"** (it was now mid-January.) I responded in kind and could tell she was quite pleased to have helped me and to talk to a kano. Another example of that celebrity treatment that I often encounter in the Philippines.

Walked back into Immigration and handed my photo ID's to another clerk and was led into an large air-conditioned office where a middle-aged Filipina dressed in a smart blue outfit, the Director, advised me that I would need to go to Manila in June to renew my ACR (which I knew), and politely told me I could go outside to the immigration officers and that everything was in order.

The Immigration Officer handed me my official receipt which the Immigration Officer in Manila had **stressed** to me to make sure I receive and bring back with me when I renew my ACR and obtain my Permanent 13(a) Visa. The whole process at Immigration took about an hour, but that included my travel time to get my photo id's. The office had good air-con, and all of the employees were helpful and respectful. Aside from having to get my picture id, it was a pleasant experience.

When I made my report to the office in Iloilo City this year, in 2012, the director I had spoken to the previous year was replaced and now taking my payment for the registration fee. I was not led into the new director's office this time, and the whole process only took about 15 minutes.

THE ALIEN CERTIFICATE OF REGISTRATION, ACR-I CARD, PROCESS

Visa information, again, is one of the most sought after areas of information on moving to the Philippines. It can be frustrating, confusing, and complicated. I have already covered the Balikbayan visa which I obtained when first arriving in the Philippines, and touched on some other basic visa information. I also mentioned I obtained an **ACR-I, Alien Certificate of Registration** in June 2010, which enabled me to legally stay in the Philippines for another year. The following information on the ACR-I card is from the Bureau of Immigration of the Philippines website:

To the ACR I-Card Holders:

- They are provided faster processing time at the ports of entry and exit with a maximum of 10 seconds for the verification process.
- They are assured that they are holding a genuinely issued ACR.
- They receive faster and more efficient service at the BI offices for immigration requirements.
- They are provided incomparable convenience as they are holding

only one immigration document. No more paper-based ACR and ICR/NBCR/CRTV/CRTT/CRTS/CRPE, ECC, SRC and RP.

- Online payment of immigration fees.
- Quick verification of information.
- Eliminates illegal and unwarranted detention of alien residents. The implementation of the ACR I-Card Project will prevent and eliminate instances where aliens are indiscriminately accosted, harassed and detained on mere suspicion of possessing fake or fraudulent immigration documents.
- It decreases the cost of transacting business with the Bureau of Immigration as the ACR I-Card Project will eliminate fixers, illegal middlemen and syndicates issuing falsified documents.

To The Bureau of Immigration:

- Automates process of alien registration.
- Eliminates fraud in all aspects of alien registration as well as in the immigration entry/exit points in the country.
- Reduces the resources needed for manual passport checks and encoding of pertinent data while drastically improving immigration process time.
- Achieves higher revenues for the Bureau and the national government through increase in number of aliens who will register and improved efficiency in collection of fees.
- Enhances security of national borders against entry or exit of terrorists and transnational criminals; eliminates human smuggling activities.
- Increases efficiency of services to the resident aliens.
- Improves internal governance by eliminating fixers and illegal personnel issuing falsified documents.

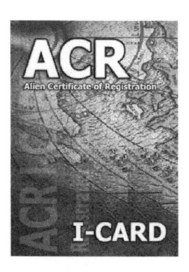

COVERAGE OF THE ACR I-CARD

All registered aliens, including their dependents, who have been duly issued paper-based ACRs are required to replace their ACRs with the hi-tech microchip-based ACR I-Card.

All aliens who have been duly issued immigrant or non-immigrant visa and all other aliens who are required to register under the Alien Registration Act are required to register and apply for the ACR I-Card. They are the following:

1. Native-Born

2. Permanent residents under:
   - a. Section 13 and its sub-sections
   - b. Republic Act Nos. 7919 and 8274 (Alien Social Integration Act of 1995)
   - c. Executive Order No. 324 (series of 1988)
   - d. Note Verbale No. 903730 dated Sept. 17, 1990 between Philippines and India

3. Temporary residents under:

- a. BI Law Instruction No. 33 (Series of 1988)
- b. BI Law Instruction No.13 (Series of 1988)
- c. BI Law Instruction No. 48 (Series of 1988)
- d. BI Memo Order No. ADD-01-038 (series of 2001)
- e. BI Memo Order No. ADD-02-015 (series of 2002)

4. Temporary visitor under Section 9(a), PIA –one who is coming for business or pleasure or for reasons of health if his stay exceeds six (6) months

5. Treaty trader under Section 9(d), PIA

6. Temporary student under Section 9(f), PIA

7. Pre-arranged employee under Section 9(g), PIA

8. Such other aliens as may be required by law to registerFor those who are required to register but exempted from immigration fees, they may opt to avail of the ACR I-Card subject to payment of the card fee.

FIRST VISIT TO BUREAU OF IMMIGRATION IN MANILA

THE ACR-I CARD AND TEMPORARY 13(A) VISA

In June 2010 I obtained an **Alien Certificate Registration** card along with a "**Temporary Visitor's Visa to Probationary Residence under Section 13 a**" (the official title of the document) Or, more simply put, a **13 (a) visa.** As mentioned before with my new 13 (a) Permanent Visa, it is *still necessary* to renew your ACR card every five years but not annually as is the case without a Permanent Visa.

During my first visit to the local B.I. Office in Iloilo, I was told by an official that I would need *eight* 2"x2" id photos for my ACR-I Card. (I only ended up needing four. There are numerous photo id shops located in most malls, and I believe my cost for the eight photos was under four USD.) I also needed a **NSO, National Statistics Office,** certified copy of my marriage certificate in the Philippines along with my Filipina's wife NSO copy of her birth certificate. Copies of some pages from my passport were also required. I had all the required documents before going to the Immigration office on Magallanes Drive, Intramuros, Manila. The Immigration office also has copying machines available near the front entrance for a charge of two pesos per copy (about five cents.)

My initial visit to the Immigration office in June 2010 was a *nightmare.* Some expats have had a far better experience, while some share my views.

It's chaos when you first arrive inside the office, so many people, so much confusion. It just pays to try and keep a level head, as it can get frustrating. Fortunately I spotted a section which dealt with ACR-I cards where a gentlemen behind the window told me I would have to apply for the 13A Immigration Visa *first* before applying for an ACR card.

He told me the office to go to, but I had difficulty in understanding his English (as he probably had difficulty in understanding mine.) I called my Filipina spouse over and had her write down the name of the office we had to go to. I thought we were going to another office within the Immigration complex, but after consulting with a local outside the main office, we found we were going to a place just outside the complex which turned out to be an attorney's office. No doubt the Immigration official who referred me to this attorney was receiving some kind of compensation from the lawyer for directing me to his office.

My wife and I entered the darkly lit attorney's office, whose location we found with the help of one of the Filipinos standing outside the main immigration building eager to help (and who I tipped P20.) A standing fan was giving us little comfort from the heat and humidity in this summer month of May. We were greeted by the attorney's wife who had us fill out some forms and after briefly speaking to her husband, dressed in an undershirt, we had the forms notarized and completed which were necessary to apply for my ACR-I card and 13A Temporary Visa. The lawyer advised us that for a fee of P26,000 he could expedite my ACR card application, but we declined and paid the very reasonable fee of P400 (almost nine USD) for his services.

After going back to the main Immigration office we applied for my ACR-I card and 13A visa, and after two more visits (a court hearing, actually a visit before a BI attorney , is also required), I was able to obtain my ACR-I card and Probationary 13A visa which became a permanent visa in my visit to the Bureau of Immigration this year, 2011. Here's a list of fees directly from my Bureau of Immigration Official Receipt, all amounts listed are in Philippine Peso:

Form Fee	100
Implementation Fee	1000
ACR	1000
Change Status Fee	600
CRTV	1400
Head Tax	250
Passport Visa Fee	200
Legal Research Fee	50
Express Lane Fee	500

Total for fees was P5,100.00

As most expat websites will advise you, *just pay* the express lane fee. There's nothing "express" about the whole process, but it's fruitless to argue about this charge.

After the initial trip to the Immigration Office, the Immigration officials took my wife's official NSO (National Statistic Office) copies of her Birth Certificate and our Marriage Contract. That is standard practice now. I guess it's a way for the government to generate more income because you have to go back to the **NSO** for more official copies. **Xeroxed copies *ARE NOT accepted*.** Those documents were needed for the processing of my 13(a) temporary visa.

Want an easy way to get the necessary NSO documents (which also can be done online but payment cannot be made online at this time)? It can be a long and hot wait at your local National Statistics Office for your Filipina spouse or fiancee to stand all day in long, non-air con offices at local NSO offices. My wife spent many frustrating days years at the NSO facilities in Manila when she had to obtain the paperwork for her Spousal Immigration

Visa to the United States.

Your local **SM Business Center Office** located in many SM Malls throughout the Philippines can process your request for the cost of only **160 pesos ($3.69 US Dollars)** each and a wait of only **five business days.** You can obtain the necessary documents delivered right to the SM Business Center Office. The NSO office charges 140 pesos each for each document, so for only P20 for each document, it is much more convenient to have the SM Business Center Office handle this for you. Had no problems at the office, just filled out a short request form, gave it to the friendly SM associates, and we picked up the paperwork a week later.

PERMANENT VISA PROCESS

As mentioned earlier, I obtained my **13(a) Permanent Visa** to reside in the Philippines on May 2011 after a three week stay in Manila to complete the process. What's the advantage of having a Permanent Visa over some of the other visas available in the Philippines? Well, the *number one advantage* for me is that I no longer have to leave the country every year which is the case for someone that uses the Balikbayan Privilege. I don't have to invest a substantial sum of money which is required for the SRRV for example. Don't have to file any visa extensions every month or two.

The Permanent Visa gives me peace of mind and simplifies my life. Only have to renew my ACR-I Card every five years and not annually, and just have to visit the local Immigration Office every year to register as a foreigner at the cost of P310 (7.16 USD.)

If you're already married to a Filipina, which is the first basic requirement for obtaining a Permanent Visa, since your Filipina spouse is your sponsor, or petitioner, of your visa request, *I would absolutely encourage anyone who is residing in the Philippines and married to a Filipina to apply for one.*

OK, so you've received your Temporary Visa, and your year probationary period is coming up. My probationary 13(a) was going to expire on June 17, 2011, but my wife and I didn't go the Bureau of Immigration Office in Intramuros in Manila until May 10, 2011. I sort of panicked when I saw that other expats had recommended going to get the Permanent Visa three months before it expired.

I recall that the Immigration Officer I had spoken to in May 2010 during our initial visit recommended coming 30 days before the expiry (as it's called here.) Well, I already purchased our tickets for Manila and made reservations at the Binando Suites in the Binando, or Chinatown section of Manila, about a five-minute pedicab ride from our hotel, so I decided to stick with our original plan and go the B.I. Office early on Tuesday, May 10.

Arrived around 7:30 Tuesday morning and went to the **VIMS (Visa Issuance**

Made Simple) counter located behind the main front entrance after surrendering my Illinois Driver's License to the guards as I signed in at the front entrance. I handed the gentleman at the counter my paperwork that I *thought* I needed and placed in the proper order. Here's what I submitted to him:

- A **General Application Form, BI Form MCL-07-01** which can be downloaded from the Immigration website. I had this notarized by an authorized Notary Public in Guimaras, an Attorney. I also attached a small package of six 2"x 2" photos of my self. The application form has a blank area in the right hand corner in which to attach your photo, but when I handed this form to the Immigration Officer that handled my paperwork the year before, he told me to leave my picture unattached.

- **A letter from my wife requesting the conversion of my visa status to Permanent Status.** I used a sample document from the Bureau of Immigration Website and also had it notarized. If you don't want to track down a Notary Public or pay for one, there is a free Notary Public Service offered at the **Public Information and Assistance** counter which has a **Public Attorney Desk** alongside it. The helpful ladies at the Public Attorney's Desk will notarize any documents you have for free, but **will not** *compose* any documents for you.

- NSO certified copy of my **wife's Birth Certificate** proving she was born in the Philippines.

- NSO certified copy of **our Marriage Certificate** which showed we were legally married in the Philippines.

- Three Xerox copies each of the NSO Birth Certificate and NSO Marriage Certificate along with three copies of pages from my United States Passport, **the bio page with my photo and the page with my passport stamps admitting me to the Philippines.**

I had all the above documents clipped to a document check list which I had also downloaded from the Bureau of Immigration website. Imagine my surprise when the Immigration Official at the Visa Issuance Made Simple counter handed everything back to me but my **General Application Form, BI Form MCL-07-01** and informed me that the document cover sheet I had downloaded was for Indians. I assumed he did not mean Native Americans from the United States.

He didn't need any of my NSO documents or the petition letter (the original petition letter the lawyer drew up for my original application back in May 2010 was sufficient.) Seems that the documentation needed for the Permanent Visa is covered when you apply for the Temporary or Probationary 13(a) Visa. If I correctly recall I did need a copy, front and back, of my ACR-I Card and copies of my Passport pages.

After visiting the VIMS counter I was instructed to go to Window #15 where I would receive a document and receipt which will inform me when my wife and I would have our hearing before an Immigration lawyer at Immigration Office.

I was directed to make a copy of the document, which gave us a hearing date for Friday, May 13th. After that I had to pay at the Cashier's Window next to Window #15 and then return to Window #15. Went back to Window #15 and showed them my paid receipt and was instructed to return on the 13th of May. I was getting dizzy.

The instructions on the document stated the following:
"In connection with your application you are hereby directed to personally appear together with your applicant and bring all the original documents in support of the application. The hearing will be held at Room 401 of this Bureau on 13 May 2011 at 10:00 o'clock in the morning otherwise your application will be summarily dismissed for lack of interest. No postponement shall be allowed."

You can bet I wasn't going to be late for that appointment and start the process all over again. **Here's the breakdown of fees for this visit** (All amounts will were in Pesos, I will list the approximate US Dollar charge after the Peso amount):

APPLICATION FEE	P 1,000 (23.11 USD)
LEGAL RESEARCH FEE	P 20 (46 cents)
CERTIFICATE FEE	P 500 (11.54 USD)
TOTAL COST	P 1,520 (35.11 USD)
EXPRESS LANE FEE (CERTIFICATION)	P 500 (11.54 USD)
EXPRESS LANE FEE (FILING)	P 500 (11.54 USD)
TOTAL COST EXPRESS	P 1,000 (23.08 USD)
GRAND TOTAL	P 2,520 pesos (58.19 USD)

The whole process for the day only took 30 minutes. However, as noted   in an earlier section, I would *strongly recommend* arriving early.   Here are the hours for the Main Office in Intramuros in Manila straight from the Bureau of Immigration Website:

Transactions are entertained during Mondays thru Fridays, 7:00am to 5:30pm.

Well, I don't know how entertaining the whole process is, but I was pleased with the results of Visit #1.

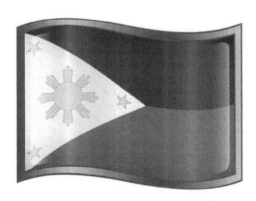

THE HEARING

"In connection with your application you are hereby directed to personally appear together with your applicant and bring all the original documents in support of the application. The hearing will be held at Room 401 of this Bureau on 13 May 2011 at 10:00 o'clock in the morning otherwise your application will be summarily dismissed for lack of interest. No postponement shall be allowed."

I repeat this section from the B.I. document I received on my first visit in my quest to obtain a Section 13(a) Permanent Visa to stay in the Philippines because a couple of items caught my eye and concerned me. The phrase *"bring all the original documents in support of the application"* had me scratching my head a little, as I had already turned over all my documents to the folks at the **VIMS (Visa Issuance Made Simple)** Counter on our first visit to Immigration.

I noted that they had put all my paperwork into a folder, and figured if I needed anything else when we went for the hearing a few days later someone would let me know (turns out we didn't need any more supporting documentation. Just make sure you bring your passport and ACR-I Card.)

The phrase **"No postponement shall be allowed"** of course meant I better show up on time. Since my wife and I were staying at my sister-in-law's home in Caloocan City, about two hours away if there are not any major traffic jams, I made sure we got an early start Friday morning, the day of our appearance before the immigration lawyer.

Woke up at 5am and left the house at 6am. Made it to the Bureau of Immigration Office in Intramuros around 8:15 am, and I reported to Room 401 to make sure someone knew we had arrived even though our appointment was not scheduled until 10:00 am. Told the clerk working the window at Room 401 that we were here for our scheduled hearing, and she took note of my name. A tall, friendly Filipino with glasses and dressed in a white T-shirt and jeans (must have been Casual Friday) showed me the attorney's office on the fourth floor where our interview would be conducted.

My wife and sister-in-law, who I had mentioned was our guide to reach our destination, sat in chairs provided outside Room 401, and I roamed the hallway and spotted our friendly Filipino friend with the glasses taking a smoke break on a balcony down the hallway. Discovered his name was **"Noel"** ("like the Christmas carol", he said), and I asked him how long it would take after the interview before we would hear if our application was approved or not. Two weeks he advised. Told me to go to Window #1 and to bring my passport and ACR-I Card. When I see my application status on the Immigration website be sure to get the reference number.

I passed some more time with Noel, and in our conversation he asked me if my wife and I have any children, a question my spouse and I are constantly asked by most people that we encounter in the Philippines. I reply with my standard *"no, we don't, my wife already went through the change-of-life, menopause, when we got married even though my wife was only 35 at the time."* Noel, then jokingly asked if we could adopt him, and I said sure. We had a good laugh about that, and I left him to finish his cigarette uninterrupted as I joined my wife and sister-in-law.

I was glad to get that information from Noel, as petitioners are not individually notified anymore if their visa has been approved, **the results are posted online at the Bureau of Immigration website**. I had been checking the website at the LIST OF BOC ACTED APPLICATIONS link and noticed it was updated every week.

After sitting for about thirty minutes I noticed Noel walking down the hallway near us, and I called him over. *"Noel, I want you to meet your future nanay"*("mother," as I pointed to my wife) and advised my asawa we were going to adopt Noel. The man sitting next to me laughed as did my spouse, and Noel jumped back and exclaimed: *"I was only joking, sir!"* *"I know"*, I replied, *"I was only teasing you."*

It doesn't hurt to ask a friendly employee like Noel for help. His information turned out to be exactly correct.

My wife and I went to the immigration lawyer's office on the fourth floor for our interview about 9:30, about 30 minutes before our scheduled 10:00 am appointment. The lawyer's aide advised us that our interview would be delayed for awhile, but that he would contact us when the attorney would be available.

He had us fill out a brief form which we had to get notarized and copied, but took advantage of the free notary service mentioned earlier, that is located right behind the **VIMS (Visa Issuance Made Simple)** Counter on the first floor near the entrance. Just look for the Public Information and Assistance Desk where you will find the Public Attorney Desk behind VIMS. Don't waste your money on those people outside the entrance holding up the "Notary Public" signs.

Around 11 am we were summoned by the lawyer's assistant and called into the outer office. We heard the authoritative voice of what sounded like an older Filipino, but when we were escorted inside his office discovered him to be a young man as my wife exclaimed to him **"Oh, I thought you were much older when I heard your voice, and you are quite young."** He didn't reply but asked my asawa how long we had been married.

- **"We got married in 2000,"** my wife replied (great, I thought, she only gave him the year, couldn't she been more specific, I thought, and tell him January 28, 2000 or at least January 2000?)
- **"Do you have any children?"** (I answered with the aforementioned "change-of-life-reply" but added that we must have about a 1000 nieces and nephews in the Philippines. He nodded his head in agreement.)
- **"You were divorced before?"** he asked me. (He evidently had records of such information as that was something I did not recall being asked in any of the information I had to previously submit.)
- **"Oo, po,"** (Yes, sir) I replied. **"My wife kicked me out of the house after nine months."**
- **"Nine months?** he asked. **"What happened?"**

I explained to him that my wife's younger children, my step-children, had spent the past six years before our marriage without anyone but their mother, and threatened to leave and live with their father (who had married a woman he had an affair with when he was married to my ex-wife.)

- **"Too easy to get a divorce in America."** I told him. **"My wife and I have disagreements some time, but I think that is normal in any relationship."**
- **"Yes, everyone does,"** he replied (evidently a married man himself.) He then stood up and announced: **"Well, what else can I do? You've already been married 10 years."** We shook his hand and thanked him.

WAITING FOR APPROVAL OF MY PERMANENT VISA

I checked the Bureau of Immigration website daily at my sister-in-law's home as my brother-in-law has a computer with a good Internet connection from PLDT. Even though the attorney at the immigration office had left us with *"Well, what else can I do? You've already been married 10 years."* I still would not feel completely relieved until I saw our names on the Immigration website as "approved" by the Board of Commissioners. The Board of Commissioners has to review every application given to them by the lawyers that conduct interviews such as the one we had gone through.

I searched past applications on the website under **"LIST OF BOC ACTED APPLICATIONS"**, **Petition for Visa Conversion (Change Status)**, which was what we had applied for, a *conversion* of my Temporary or Probationary 13(a) status to Permanent Status. Some of the visa types listed on of BOC acted applications were MISSIONARY CHANGE, TOP 1000 CORPORATION, TRV CONVERSION, TRV EXTENSION, 13(A) PROBATIONARY (which had a listed validity of one year), and of course, 13(A) PERMANENT, which has the validity date left blank, because it has no expiration. It is unlike a Permanent Resident Visa ("Green Card") my wife possessed while living in the States which *does* expire after 14 years.

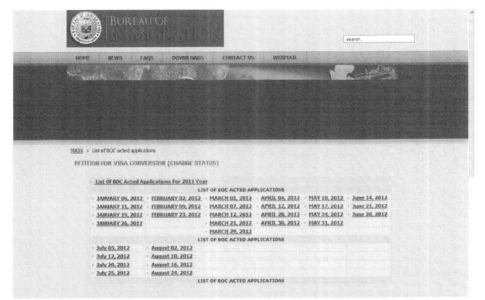

Here's a recent screen shot from the Philippine Bureau of Immigration to help illustrate what I'm talking about:Look for the next screen shown above (from the Philippines Bureau of Immigration website), for example, and click a date to find this section online. Look for the closest date which would apply to your application. You will open up the following screen which will have several pages of approved visas for the various categories, including Temporary and Permanent Visas.

I did not see any 13(a) Permanent Visa applications that were denied in the few previous weeks I searched on the Immigration website but did see one

19	MAIN KERST STEPHEN WALLACE	ITALIAN	KERST SOPHIA	JULY 16 2012	13(A) PERMANENT	PERMANENT	ATTY DERAY
20	MAIN MICHAEL PROVOST BERGERON	AMERICAN	ROBIN GOMEZ CABATAC	AUG 1 2012	13(A) PROBATIONARY	1 YEAR	ATTY RODULFO III
21	MAIN OKAMOTO AKIO	JAPANESE	OKAMOTO CONSTACIA M	JULY 18 2012	13(A) PROBATIONARY	1 YEAR	ATTY DERAY
22	MAIN JONATHAN TYACKE	BRITISH	NANCY ROBLE TYACKE	JULY 27 2012	13(A) PERMANENT	PERMANENT	ATTY MAMINTA
23	MAIN ROBBIE PAUL HETTERICK	AMERICAN	GLENN HETTERICK	JULY 27 2012	13(A) PROBATIONARY	1 YEAR	ATTY ARELLANO
24	MAIN TOKUZO IWAI	JAPANESE	LORDWILL IWAI	JULY 24 2012	13(A) PROBATIONARY	1 YEAR	ATTY MAMINTA
25	MAIN CASPER WOUTER KAPTEIN	DUTCH	AILEEN ESPINAR KAPTEIN	JULY 26 2012	13(A) PERMANENT	PERMANENT	ATTY SULIT
26	MAIN BENJAMIN GEOFFREY THOMPSON	BRITISH	EUREKA RAMIREZ THOMPSON	JULY 31 2012	13(A) PERMANENT	PERMANENT	ATTY TUBBAN
27	MAIN CHUN SANG LAM	CHINESE	MARISSA LAM	JULY 31 2012	13(A) PROBATIONARY	1 YEAR	ATTY MAMINTA
28	MAIN MARCELO DA SILVEIRA LABRE	BRAZILIAN	LETICIA LABRE	AUG 6 2012	13(A) PROBATIONARY	1 YEAR	ATTY SANTOS
29	MAIN STEVEN VERN YOCUM	AMERICAN	NORA YOCUM	AUG 1 2012	13(A) PERMANENT	PERMANENT	ATTY SANTOS
30	MAIN WILFRIED SCHOTT	GERMAN	MAY BELLE GUILLERGAN SCHOTT	AUG 2 2012	13(A) PROBATIONARY	1 YEAR	ATTY TUBBAN

Canadian who had applied for a 13(a) visa (the website did not denote if it was a temporary or permanent visa type, and he had *no* petitioner listed) with the words *"ORDER TO LEAVE"* posted by his name.

I kept checking the website to see if our petition had been approved, and when I did not see anything updated on the website on the Friday following our Friday 13th hearing date, I was getting anxious even though Noel, the helpful Bureau of Immigration employee, had advised me that it takes two weeks for applications to be approved. I searched the Bureau of Immigration Website to try and find a number to call to see if someone could give me the status of my visa or at least tell me when the website's information would be updated.

After trying several numbers and having no one answer the phone, it just kept ringing and ringing, I was able to reach someone on the following number: 527-5660, who, after asking my name and my petitioner's name (my wife), informed me that my application had just been received today. She advised me to call back next Thursday afternoon after the Board of Commissioners would have have reviewed my case. The person I spoke to was very polite and helpful, and after hanging up the phone (my brother-and-sister-in-law have a land line in addition to a cell phone), I told my wife that we will be in Manila for another week. Looks like Noel's information was right on the mark.

Called back the next Thursday and was told our application was approved. The helpful employee also advised me of my reference number (which would correspond to our listing in the **"BOC ACTED APPLICATIONS"** on the Immigration website), and to make sure I brought my passport and ACR-I Card. I was told that if we arrived in the office early, my Implementation could be processed before noon, in 2-4 hours. I was ecstatic, and told my wife that we would be going to back to Immigration early tomorrow since our application was approved. I was eager to get back home. Manila, with all the traffic and millions of people, was too much for me. Life is definitely more laid back in the province.

IMPLEMENTATION OF THE PERMANENT VISA

Again, I would *highly recommend* going to the Bureau of Immigration office in Intramuros *early.* The crowds, and I *do* mean crowds, thicken considerably after 9 am (the office opens at 7 am) as does the corresponding noise level. Since I had been advised the day before to arrive early so the Implementation of my Permanent Visa could be processed before noon, we arrived at the office around 6:45 am, or 15 minutes before opening. What I didn't know was that the cashier's windows did not open until later, but I'll address that shortly.

It is *extremely difficult* to hear the Immigration employees even early in the day with less people at the office, and I had to put my ear up to the small circular opening to be able to listen to the employee's instructions. The best way to describe the conditions at Immigration is controlled chaos. Talk about heightened stress levels! I don't how the employees deal with it, but they are generally courteous and helpful.

Made ten different stops that day.

1. Even though I was at **Window No. 1** ten minutes before their 7 am opening, the pleasant lady behind the window asked me what I wanted and started to process my request. I was also asked if I want **Single Express Service** (which cost 500 pesos, and transactions would be completed in 10 hours or less) or **Double Express Service** (1,000 pesos, and transactions completed in 2-4 hours.) I opted for the Double Express service. I was advised to go to Window No. 9, the Cashier's Window, to pay my Implementation Fee and Express Lane fees. **Pay for Double Express!** The Immigration website states that only certain functions are performed on certain days. Double Express will take care of that.

2. I had no idea that the **cashier** at **Window No. 9** did not start work until 7:30 (or 8:00 am, depending on whom you asked), so I politely stood

sentry by the window at 7:10 am as my wife and sister-in-law, Emily, our guide to Immigration, sat down. At 7:15 a middle-aged lady came up to her computer station by the window, logged in, and *sternly* advised me she was not open yet but would take my payment **only** in exact change. She was not pleased, as I wouldn't haven't been either, to start work early off the clock, but I was just following the instructions of the nice lady at Window No. 1. Plus, I was paying for the **Double Express Lane Service** and was determined to get my money's worth.

3. Back to **Window No. 1**. Gave the lady my receipt for my Implementation Fees and Double Express Lane Fee. I handed her my passport, as requested, and was given a receipt or stub, for it and on that stub it told me to return to Window No. 1 at 10:30 am. It was now 7:30 am. My wife, sister-in-law, and I decided to go down the street and get some breakfast at a nearby Jollibee's to pass the time.

4. Went back to **Window No. 1** again at 10:25 am. My implementation was already done, and my passport was taken from a stack of passports already processed and was about in the seventh or eighth position from the top. In light of that, I would advise you to check on your passport *before* the scheduled time they give you to return. Checked my passport to see my Permanent Visa stamp and paid five pesos at the window for a copy of the passport page with the new stamp. The implementation process was now completed. I was then instructed to go to Window No. 37 to start the processing of my revised ACR-I Card which would reflect my new Permanent Visa status.

5. Go to **Window No. 37**. I am given a form to fill out which I have to get copied along with the front and back of my present ACR-I Card. When I have that completed, I am to go to **Window No. 35**.

6. At Window No. 35 a friendly man behind the window takes my form I was given to fill out from Window No. 37, along with the copy of my ACR and tells me he will call out my name when he is ready for me. A few minutes only pass as the friendly official comes away from the window, stands by me, announces the name of "John Wayne," and we all laugh as a young Chinese man stands up. Guess his parents were fans of "The Duke." He then calls *my* name and instructs me to go to Window No. 38 and receive a document I will give to *another* cashier to pay for my new ACR-I Card. After I pay for the card, I am to return to Window No. 35.

7. Go to **Window No. 38** and receive the necessary paperwork. It is so loud that the lady behind the window has to hold up four fingers on one hand and one finger up (not the middle one) on the other hand to direct me to Window 41.

8. Arrive at **Window No. 41** and the older gentlemen at the Cashier's

window is somewhat grumpy. Can't blame him, the noise level is terrible. Pay him for the new ACR-I Card and receive my receipt.

9. Return to **Window No. 35**, and I'm told to wait for my name to be called again. Doesn't take long before the friendly official, who is in total control of the chaos surrounding him, calls my name again, addresses me as his "buddy" and sends me to the the second floor where the ACR Division is located.

10. I have some difficulty finding the window, but after dropping into a couple of the wrong offices, arrive at a **window for the ACR Division.** I'm asked to wait for my name to be called again, but after a few minutes I'm escorted inside the office and given a slip of paper which instructs me that my new ACR Card can be picked up the following Monday, May 30th. The paper had instructions to stop at Window No. 43 first to obtain the serial number of my card and then proceed to Window No. 4 to pick it up. Since this was only the Friday before, I was pleased that I wouldn't have to wait long for the new card.

Picking up the new card and only making a stop at two windows for my fourth and final trip to the Bureau of Immigration was going to be a breeze---or so I thought. The final trip was anything but that.

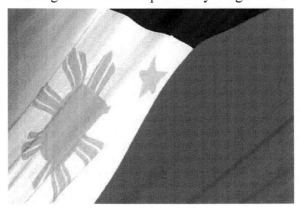

FINAL VISIT TO IMMIGRATION.

PICKING UP MY NEW ALIEN CERTIFICATE OF REGISTRATION CARD.

Went to pick up my new ACR-I Card on Monday, May 27, 2011, the last step in the processing of obtaining my 13(a) Permanent Visa to the Philippines. Little did I know at the time that this visit would be my most trying and stressful out of all previous trips to Immigration.

The slip of paper given to me by the ACR Division on Friday instructed me to first go to Window No. 43 where the serial number of my ACR card was to be written and then proceed to Window No. 4 to pick up the actual card.

We did not plan to arrive too early that Monday figuring that the card would probably not be ready for pick up. Arrived at 9:15 and was informed by the personnel at Window No. 43 to go to Window No. 4 at 11 am to pick up my card.

A serial number and the time to pick up the card was written on the slip of paper given to me by the ACR Division. Wasn't overly concerned about waiting 90 minutes, after all, the process was almost completed, and we had already purchased our return tickets to fly back home the next day, Tuesday, putting our stay at Manila at just a little over three weeks. I had faith that my ACR would be issued the day we were instructed to receive it, though as the day unfolded that confidence *did* get shaken.

Standing in front of me at Window No. 43 was a retired American Navy man and his Filipina wife. I had met and spoken to them the past Friday. He needed an ACR Card in order to adopt a child. We both were instructed to go to Window No. 4 at 11.

I decided to head over to Window 4, which displays an **"I-Card Receiving"** sign on its counter, on the off chance that the card was already available. Saw the retired Naval man and his wife already sitting in front of the window area, and he told me that the clerk at Number 4 had advised him that his card would be ready in 15 minutes after just being told it would be available at 11 by the employees at Window No. 43.

Of course I ask the young Filipina clerk at Window No. 4 if *my* card would be ready in 15 minutes as she had just advised the other American. She said she did not know when it would be ready, and if I had any questions I should go back to Window No. 43. Let the games begin!

Instead of going back to Window 43 I decide to return to the ACR Division on Floor 2 where my slip of paper for my ACR pick up was issued on Friday. I explained to the lady at the window that my card was supposed to be ready at 11 am, but an American that was in line with me at the same time and also instructed to go to Window No. 4 at 11, was now told *his* card would be ready in 15 minutes.

After several minutes of checking, the Immigration employee at the ACR Division wrote down the batch number that my card would be released in. I asked if it would be released today since I have a flight booked home for tomorrow. She asked if I had given anyone a copy of my ticket itinerary Friday. I told her I hadn't done so, didn't purchase my ticket until the day after, Saturday, and was counting on getting my ACR Card today as I was told. She told me to go back to Window No. 43.

The bespectacled young lady at Window No. 43 looked at the batch number, and told me to come back at 11. I asked her if she wanted me to come here, to Window No. 43 or Window No. 4. She told me to come back here, to No. 43. However, a co-worker standing next to her told me to return to Window No. 4 at 11. After a minute of watching the two wrangle over which window to return to, the male clerk advised me to go to Window 4 at 11.

I decided to return to Window 4 right away, over 30 minutes had passed by now, and I saw the Naval man still seated. He said they have *now* told him to come back at 11. The young Filipina at Window 4 then told me that my card was not ready yet, so I sat down next to my wife and sister-in-law and fumed.

At ten minutes before 11, the time the employees at Window No. 43 had told me my card would be ready, I went returned to Window No. 4. I was advised by the same employee I had been dealing with all morning that my card was *not* ready, and she had *no* idea when it *would* be ready. She was getting very irritated as was I at this point. **"You mean I could be waiting here all day? You have no idea when it will be ready?"** I asked. **"Sir, you need to go back to Window No. 43 and ask them,"** she loudly replied to me.

Off to Window 43 again. The clerks I had spoken previously to at Window 43 were in the back of the office as I explained my situation in polite but frustrated tones to another employee. The young man that had dealt with me earlier stepped up to the window and said the following: **"I apologize for the delay, sir. We had to bring an employee to the hospital and that put us behind. Wait for just a few minutes, please."**

It was now 11 am. Other frustrated people expecting their card at 11 at Window No. 4 also started appearing at the window per the request of the employee at No. 4. I stayed at Window 43 for 35 minutes until I was finally told my card was now ready for pick up at Window No. 4. **"Are you sure?"** I asked, **"that employee at Window 4 is getting very irritated at me."** He smiled and assured me that it was there.

Went back to Window No. 4 *again.* Now there was a line of eight people in front of me, including the retired American Naval guy, and I told him what they had said to me at Window 43. About 15 minutes after standing in line, I finally got my new ACR-I Card, and the Permanent Visa process was completed!

It was now around noon. I was just glad the whole thing was over. I should never have to return to the Immigration Office in Manila from this point as my ACR-I Card, as mentioned before, only has to be renewed ever five years instead of annually, and I will be able to that at my local Bureau of Immigration Office in nearby Iloilo.

My wife and I hitched a ride from my brother-in-law the next day to the **Ninoy Aquino International Airport**, and my wife and I were back in Guimaras that evening and very thankful to be home. Felt a big weight had been lifted off my shoulders now that I had my Permanent Visa and was happy that it was now cared for.

I would recommend to anyone that does file for the 13(a) Permanent Visa to plan on staying at least three weeks in the Manila area. We were fortunate to have relatives to stay with and did not have any hotel expenses aside from the first night we arrived in Manila.

The closer you can get to the main office the better since at least four hours of travel time were involved for us with each visit. Taking a cab each of those days would have been fairly expensive. I was happy to have my sister-in-law as our guide as we were able to travel much cheaper on the local jeepney's, FX vans, LRT's and pedicabs. Plus, it was an adventure traveling there and much more interesting then just taking a taxi or having a driver deliver us.

Here are the costs for the Implementation Fees and ACR-I Card:

Implementation Fee	P 1,000.00 (23.11 USD)
Form	P 100.00 (2.30 USD)
ACR(Alien Certificate of Registration)	P 1,000 (23.11 USD)
Change of Status	P 600.00 (13.79 USD)
Head Tax	P 250.00 (5.74 USD)
Passport Visa	P 200.00 (4.60 USD)
Legal Research Fee	P 50.00 (1.15 USD)
Express Lane Fee	P 500.00 (11.54 USD)
Grand Total	P 3, 700 (85.34 USD)

TOTAL COST, INCLUDING CERTIFICATION, FOR THE WHOLE PERMANENT VISA PROCESS: P 6, 220 (145.19 USD)

Not bad considering it costs about P6,000 to obtain a visa extension every two months and cheaper than flying out of the country every year.

IMMIGRATION FAQ'S

The next section consists of some **Frequently Asked Questions (FAQ's)** directly copied from the Bureau of Immigration website concerning the 13 (a) permanent visa process.

"I am an alien whose country has an immigration reciprocity agreement with the Philippines. I am also married to a Filipina. Am I qualified to apply for a permanent residence visa?

Yes, under the Philippine Immigration Act of 1940, Section 13 (a) you are eligible for permanent residency in the Philippines. This visa is issued to an alien on the basis of his valid marriage to a Philippine citizen.

To qualify for this visa, the applicant must prove that:
- He contracted a valid marriage with a Philippine citizen.
- The marriage is recognized as valid under existing Philippine laws.
- There is no record of any derogatory information against him in any local or foreign law enforcement agency.
- He is not afflicted with any dangerous, contagious or loathsome disease.
- He has sufficient financial capacity to support a family and will not become a public burden. (***PERSONAL NOTE: I was *NOT* asked for financial records or bank records of any kind during any of my visits to Immigration. I did, however, have copies of such information with me just in case.)
- He was allowed entry into the Philippines and was authorized by Immigration authorities to stay.

NOTE: This visa is only available to citizens of a country which grants permanent residence and immigration privileges to Philippine citizens.

How can I apply for 13 (a) visa?

Ask for an application form (Form number RBR 98-01) from the Public Assistance Unit of Commissioner Window One (1) or from the Makati Extension Office and accomplish the form properly. If you will be accompanied by your unmarried minor children they must fill up a separate form.

All documents to support your application must be properly certified as true copy. Sworn statements or affidavits should be notarized.

Foreign documents must be duly authenticated by the Philippine Embassy or Consulate at the place where they are issued.

You may submit the duly accomplished application form with the supporting documents to window (1) located at the ground floor of the main building of the Bureau of Immigration or to the Makati Extension Office."

Special Retiree Resident Visa, SRRV.

Another visa available is the **Special Retiree Resident Visa, SRRV.** Again, directly from the Bureau of Immigration website is this detailed information on the **SRRV.**

Who May Apply for a SRRV?

A retiree who applies for a Special Resident Retiree Visa (SRRV) has the option to enroll to the program based from his retirement status.
Retirement Option and their Required Time Deposit
   With Pension - 50 years old and above - the required time deposit is US$10,000.00 plus a monthly pension of US$800.00 for a single applicant and US$1,000 for couple.
Without Pension
   - 35 to 49 years old - US$50,000.00 time deposit
   - 50 years old and above - US$20,000.00 time deposit
   - Former Filipino Citizens (at least 35 years old, regardless of the number of dependents - US$1,500.00)
   - Ambassadors of Foreign Countries who served and retired in the Philippines, current and former staff members of international organizations including ADB (at least 50 years old) - US$1,500.00
A resident retiree can bring with him, without additional deposit, his spouse and child who is unmarried and below 21 years old or if the spouse is not joining, two(2) children (provided they are unmarried and under 21 years of age.) Additional children with the same qualifications may also be allowed to join the principal retiree provided there is an additional deposit of US$15,000.00 per child. The said time deposit however, is subject the same and conditions with that of the principal deposit. This does not apply to former Filipino Citizens.

What is the validity of SRRV?

The holder of the SRRV may reside in the Philippines without securing extensions of his stay from the Bureau of Immigration.

Are SRRV holders exempted from Travel Tax?

PRA members who are holders of valid SRRV are exempted from paying travel tax provided they have not stayed in the Philippines for more than one year from the date of last entry into the country.

Can SRRV holder own real property in the Philippines?

No. If he or she is legally married to a Philippine citizen, he or she may construct a residential unit on a parcel of land owned and/or registered in the name of Philippine spouse. Natural-born former Filipinos whose SRRV has been issued may own/acquire a maximum area of 5,000 square meters of urban land and three (3) hectares of agricultural land.

Is the dollar deposit convertible to other currency?

The dollar deposit may be converted into peso after 30 days upon issuance of the Special Resident Retiree's Visa (SRRV).

Where do I get the approval of the SRRV?

The approval of your application will come from the Bureau of Immigration. The pre-evaluation of the application is made by the Philippine Retirement Authority where applications are filed.

How long is the processing time?

Processing time takes seven to ten working days upon receipt of complete requirements.

Can my spouse and unmarried minor children be granted an indefinite privilege to reside in the Philippines?

Yes. Your spouse and a legitimate or legally adopted unmarried child under twenty-one (21) may be given an indefinite status if they are accompanying or joining you soon after your admission into the country as such.

Is there an additional deposit for unmarried children if they are following or accompanying me?

Yes. There is an additional deposit of US $15,000.00 or any equivalent acceptable foreign currency for each additional legitimate or legally adopted unmarried child under twenty-one (21) years of age.

*More information on Special Retiree Resident Visa on the Philippine **Retirement Authority website.**

SPECIAL VISA FOR EMPLOYMENT GENERATION (SVEG)

There is yet another immigration visa available called the **Special Visa for Employment Generation (SVEG).** Here's what the BI website has to say about it: **"The SVEG is a special visa issued to a qualified non-immigrant foreigner who shall actually employ at least ten (10) Filipinos in a lawful and sustainable enterprise, trade or industry. Qualified foreigners who are granted the SVEG shall be considered special non-immigrants with multiply entry privileges and conditional extended stay, without need of prior departure from the Philippines."**

More detailed information about the **SVEG** can be found at the Bureau of Immigration website

Again, it can be at times confusing and somewhat overwhelming when applying for a visa in the Philippines. Come prepared with the proper documents you need for your visa, and be prepared to spend some time waiting at the immigration office you go to. I found the employees at both the Iloilo City and main Immigration office in Manila to be courteous and respectful.

Be sure you dress in proper attire when going to any immigration office as this is stressed on their website. I wore a polo shirt and blue jeans with shoes, not sandals. That said, I saw many people dressed in shorts and T-shirts inside the Immigration office, but why take a chance? I always wear jeans, a polo shirt and casual shoes.

Not Married to a Filipina? There is the Quota Visa Option.

What if you are not married to a Filipina and would like to obtain a permanent visa to stay in the Philippines? What other options other than the ones previously mentioned are available? Well, thanks to an informative and helpful reader of my website, **Billy**, my readers and myself were given some detailed information about the **Quota Visa**. Here's what Billy had to say on the topic:

"Of course the lawyers are going to tell you that its all wrong and bad and they advise you against it because they could not get it. My first year here I waited for 12 months for the processing of my 9G working visa. Conveniently it was finished right about time for renewal. When they asked me about renewing, I told them it is too late, I had a permanent residency Quota Visa already.

She was quite angry with the loss of revenue at first, but after a while she asked how much it I paid and then she said. OK, that is a fair price, and she went on to say that they aren't able to get them for their clients. The fact is, they want to ding you every year or two for 2/3 the price of a quota visa instead of once in a lifetime.

The process is very simple, quick and legal.

The Quota visa is very limited and usually by about April or May the slots for countries with a lot of Expats here, like the USA are taken up. And the price seems increase when there are only a few slots left… like a bidding war. There are about 50 a year per country. If you know someone in immigration, that is the simplest way, because if you go into Intramuros and try to get it done, you are lucky to even get past the first few steps. Here is what you need:

1. To know a lawyer in immigration.

2. Have the funds. The costs are typically up to PHP180K-PHP220K (4,155-5,078 USD) depending on country.

3. Have a bank account with $30,000USD in it... you can either borrow the money from your friend during the process, or this can be facilitated. It is no different than when you tried to get your girlfriend a visa back to your country. You had to fill her bank account full of money so the embassy would believe she could afford the journey. Conversely, if you have a company that shows you are an owner of more than 10%, you will not need the money in the bank account.

4. Go to Intramuros to have your photo taken for your ACR I-card.

5. Pay a yearly renewal fee of less than 400 pesos at Immigration. If this is not paid, they will ding you when you replace the I-card.

6. Replace the I-Card after 5 years. The residency is lifetime but the card needs to be renewed every 5 years due to our physical changes.

7. When your passport expires, have the stamp transferred from your old to your new passport(about 500 pesos) or you will have to tote around both passports for a while as the stamp is the actual Visa.

And that is it."

Billy goes onto to respond to some previous comments:

"What you have been told about the visa is partly right. The previous commissioner was not corrupt, but he was not strict enough with the requirements. For example, the $30,000 USD in the bank was never an issue. But now, it might be with the new commissioner. I believe in the future, it will be the same, but technically someone will have to provide a piece of paper that says you have money or own a company.

As for the lawyer trying to frighten you, believe me, you are far more likely to go to prison for something completely different that getting a permanent residency visa. I have helped about 10 people get their visas now and not a single one of them have had an issue. Personally I leave the country on business and personal trips about 12-15 times a year and have never had a problem. It is a complete and legal visa. The same as a spousal visa, without the ball and chain."

If you are sure you are going to reside in the Philippines, the Quota Visa, is an option, although initially a costly one, but considering that if you don't use a Balikbayan Visa you'll have to renew your visa on a continual basis for a cost of around P6,000 (138 USD)every two months and file your extension at your local Immigration Office. Just another option to consider. What's another option that some foreigners living in the Philippines use, but I do not recommend? Staying in the Philippines illegally.

STAYING IN THE PHILIPPINES ILLEGALLY.

First of all, don't do it. I'm married to a wonderful Filipina and would not want to do anything to jeopardize my stay in the Philippines, thus I went to the trouble of obtaining my Permanent Visa. *Here's a tip: Keep your visa and ACR-I Card current. Register annually as a foreigner at your local Bureau of Immigration Office.*

Here's a story I ran on my website, *PhilippinesPlus.com* concerning the issue of Americans living illegally in the Philippines.

Americans Living in the Philippines Illegally

How many Americans are living in the Philippines illegally? After posting a recent article about illegal Filipino aliens living in the United States, I thought it would be only fair to explore the issue of Americans residing in the Philippines with current or expired visas. If you're a foreigner staying in this archipelago of 7,107 islands, and your visa has expired *or* you have stayed past your original 21 day grace period, *you are an illegal alien.*

What's the penalty for visa expiration? According to the Philippine Bureau of Immigration website: **"if expired, additional fees for the following: Fine for overstaying per month P500, Motion for Reconsideration P510."** So if you want to leave the Philippines, you could be paying a substantial fine depending on how long you have been here. In the past it was possible to pay the fine right at the Manila Ninoy Aquino International Airport, but violators are now being directed to the main Bureau of Immigration Office in Intramuros, Manila.

I have no idea on how many American expats are living in the Philippines illegally. However, the Philippine Bureau of Immigration website reported that 142 illegal aliens were deported from the Philippines in 2008, and nine of those were Americans. And a March 25, 2011 report from the Immigration website noted that two U.S. fugitives were recently sent back to the United States. **Destor Cabasada Gatchalian** and **Alan Brian Carillo**, were deported aboard a Philippine Airlines flight to San Francisco, California. Gatchalian, 39, is a wanted child rapist, while Carillo, 29, was charged with multiple counts of mail fraud. It was determined that the deportees were both undocumented aliens at the time of their arrest as their passports were already revoked by the US State Department. They are now banned from re-entering the Philippines as a result of their inclusion in the immigration blacklist.

I only have met one American, **"Mickey,"** not his real name, that I encountered at the SM Hypermarket in Iloilo, who told me his visa had expired quite a long time ago. Since "Mickey" evidently has no plans to return to the United States soon, and is engaged to a Filipina while still married to one and trying to get an annulment from her, I guess he isn't too concerned about staying in the Philippines illegally.

Though the law requires a person to always carry their passport, I **never** carry mine with me unless I'm going on a flight to Manila or Cebu or, of course, going to the Immigration Office. I do, however, carry my **Alien Certificate of Registration** card with me, though I just obtained that on June 2010. Before that if I ever needed to show any ID, I just offered my Illinois Driver's license.

No one, absolutely **no one**, has ever stopped me and asked for my passport. I doubt that anyone will ever stop "Mickey," either, as long as he keeps a low profile and stays out of trouble. So if you entered the Philippines and decided to stay without having any visa, my guess is that you probably could do that without ever being detected. But why in the world would you want to do that?

More than 65,000 foreign nationals **did** travel to the Bureau of Immigration (BI) for their annual report this year (I was one of those 65,000), according to statistics from the immigration bureau's alien registration division. That's 5,123 more than registered last year. That figure does not include those who take advantage of the Balikbayan Privilege (those foreigners who have a Filipina spouses are the only ones who can use this type of visa and do not have to register for the annual report, as mentioned earlier.) Those who **do not** comply with the annual report may be subjected to criminal sanctions and deportation for violating the Alien Registration Act of 1950 as amended.

After I posted this article I received comments from some American expats who knew of similar people like "Mickey" who were staying in the Philippines illegally with expired visas. One reader told me of someone he knew that had been living in the Philippines for over 28 years without a visa! Like I said before, why risk it. Follow the visa laws and make your life easier. Why take any chances?

PERSONAL SAFETY IN THE
PHILIPPINES

Maybe you've heard of the hostage "rescue" attempt in Manila on August 23, 2010, that resulted in the deaths of eight Hong Kong tourists on a tour bus. Or perhaps you have heard of the shameful "Mindanao Massacre" in November 2009 that resulted in the deaths of 57 innocent people, many of them journalists, slaughtered in a political dispute by a rival political clan. Or you've probably heard reports of terrorist groups such as Abu Sayyaf, a

Muslim terrorist group, which is aligned with Al-Qaeda and operates in parts of the southern Philippines and has beheaded many of those they have kidnapped. Despite the killing of their leader Osa bin Laden, the group is still active in the Philippines.

The United States Department of State recently issued the following warning concerning travel in the Philippines on January 5, 2012:

The Department of State warns U.S. citizens of the risks of terrorist activity in the Philippines. While most of the recent incidents of terror have occurred on the island of Mindanao and in the Sulu Archipelago, U.S. citizens are reminded that terrorist attacks could be indiscriminate and could occur in any area of the country, including Manila. Public gathering places may be targeted, including (but not limited to) airports, shopping malls, conference centers and other public venues. This Travel Warning replaces the Travel Warning dated June 14, 2011, and reflects continuing threats due to terrorist and insurgent activities.

U.S. citizens should exercise extreme caution if traveling to Mindanao or the Sulu Archipelago. Regional terrorist groups have carried out bombings resulting in injuries and death. Sporadic clashes have occurred between criminal groups and the Philippine Armed Forces throughout Mindanao, particularly in rural areas. U.S. government employees must receive authorization from the Embassy to travel to Mindanao or the Sulu Archipelago.

Kidnap-for-ransom gangs continue to be active throughout the Philippines and have targeted foreigners, including U.S. citizens. U.S. citizens should exercise caution when traveling in the vicinity of demonstrations, since they can turn confrontational and possibly escalate to violence.

A state of emergency is in effect for the Maguindanao and Sultan Kudarat provinces, as well as for Cotabato City in Mindanao. Travelers should expect heightened police activity and a significant military presence in these areas as well as restrictions that Philippine government officials may impose on travel in those areas.

The Department of State remains concerned about the continuing threat of terrorist actions and violence against U.S. citizens and interests throughout the world. The **Worldwide Caution** reminds U.S. citizens that terrorism can occur anywhere.

Well, the Philippines *can* be a dangerous place to live such as there are dangerous places to live back in America where I am from. I personally do not feel any danger while living here, and have not had any concerns for personal safety for my wife or myself aside from an event in Guimaras when my wife and I heard someone at 4 am turning the doorknob of our front door.

Fortunately our door was locked that evening as sometimes our niece and nephew that lived with us would sometimes forget to lock the door. We turned our outside porch lights on and saw no one, but took the precautions of adding a deadbolt to our solid wood mahogany door, and installing a motion-sensing floodlight above our front porch. We have not had any further incidents.

As mentioned before, we live in a subdivision outside of Iloilo City which has multiple layers of guards. Security personnel are posted at the main front gate. A guard with a loaded shotgun is near our entrance which has an additional two to three sentries on duty. Security patrols on foot and bicycles routinely patrol our area.

Now when I have to travel to the Metro Manila area, I am more aware of my surroundings since it is vastly more populated area than Iloilo. But I had my guard up when I traveled to Chicago and walked around the downtown area. Again, *common sense* is your greatest friend. Just be aware of your surroundings, don't be stupid and flash around any money.

Now that may seem obvious, but there *are* people that do that. They'll take out a huge wad of pesos and pay their fast food bill with it or even count their money out in the open at their restaurant table. Count what you need to pay your bill with *under* the table. Also, I mentioned earlier in this eBook about the man at the mall who asked if I remembered him, he claimed to be a security guard at the hotel I was staying. It's the "Hi! Remember me from so-and-so hotel" scam. Yeah, I got hustled on that one, and it is a fairly common one in the Philippines. Don't be stupid and fall for it like I did.

If you do have a wallet keep it in your left front pocket, *NEVER* in the hip pocket. If your wallet seems too bulky and obvious, it probably is safer just to carry your cash in that left front pocket.

However, as mentioned earlier, I haven't had any problems with pickpockets since residing here. I have been told that jeepney waiting stations are favorite places for pickpockets to operate, at least in Iloilo City where we travel to oftentimes, so keep that in mind, also. OK, and here's another obvious one. Don't get drunk in public. That's about one of the stupidest things you can do as a traveler in any country. You're inviting trouble. Just drink your San Miguels at home. Or make sure you have plenty of trusted relatives and friends with you if you do find you have had too much to drink.

But really you shouldn't have any safety issues. Just exercise caution and again, just use some **plain old common sense**. You'll be fine.

CAN YOU SURVIVE IN THE PHILIPPINES WITHOUT A FIXED PENSION?

I've lived in the Philippines for over three years and have been blogging about living in the Philippines shortly after moving here with my beautiful Filipina asawa (spouse.)

I've always focused on retirees, foreigners, that were planning to make their move to this archipelago of 7,107 islands, and would have a fixed pension. I've even written articles discouraging anyone from making the move unless they had that fixed income or a guaranteed job (not promise) upon their arrival.

I saw a need to try and help those guys that might be years from retirement and wanted to move to the Philippines ASAP. Maybe they have a girlfriend waiting for them here already or a fiancee, or even a wife they had to leave behind. So in order to do that, I had to think "outside the box." The following sections of my new E-book, **"The Philippines Expat Advisor,"** will hopefully force you, the reader, to do the same. Don't think it's going to be easy to move here without some sort of fixed monthly income. It's not.

But if you put a *LOT* of effort into it, follow my advice, and are *ABSOLUTELY* 100% convinced you want to make that move with out the security blanket of a regular paycheck like you might be used to now, this book will help. I can't guarantee that you *will* make it but I'm giving you a fighting chance with this information.

There are guys living here on $3,000 a month or more and still not making it. But they're living beyond their means. And I know Peace Corps volunteers making it on $250 US Dollars a month.

I'll show you what businesses and jobs might be available and how to set up a business in the Philippines, plus much more.

START YOUR OWN BUSINESS IN THE PHILIPPINES

Time to switch gears. So you want to **make your move** to the Philippines but don't have any guaranteed source of income? There a multitude of businesses you could get involved with, but as a foreigner you cannot own a small business outright.

Foreigners or non-Filipinos can not own any percentage of a "small" retail business in the Philippines (e.g. Internet Cafe) as indicated in Section 5 of Republic Act 8762.

As of this writing, the only way you can have full foreign participation is if you have a paid-up capital of $2.5 million dollars (US) or more, provided that investments for establishing a store is not less than $830,000 (US).

So how *can* you own a business in the Philippines?

You can own an business "indirectly" if you're married to a Filipino because it will be a conjugal property. In case your natural-born Filipino wife/husband has gained foreign citizenship through naturalization, he/she can apply for Filipino citizenship to gain dual nationality thus re-acquiring his/her Filipino citizenship and may open a business under his/her name. My own wife never became a citizen of the United States and held a "green card," "Permanent Resident" status. She never gave up her Filipino citizenship.

You may not work in the business to gain any salary unless you have a work permit.

But as a couple you can always receive financial support from your spouse as long as you don't piss her off, right? **Make sure that you don't have your name on the business and no records whatsoever that you are being paid by the business.**

For you single guys out there wanting to start a business with your Filipina

girlfriend, you better be *absolutely sure* you can trust her. Many a foreigner has lost his life savings financing a business for his "true love" who figuratively *and* literally stabbed him in the back later.

Starting a Business in Iloilo City – Philippines

Alright, kids, this next section is by no means exciting and kind of frickin' boring, if you want to know the truth.

But if you're *serious* about moving to the Philippines and want to make your move *NOW* and not years down the line before you can collect a pension, I've included the following information in this E-book. I've used Iloilo City as the example for this particular section since this is where my asawa and I reside.

Below is a detailed summary of the bureaucratic and legal hurdles an entrepreneur must overcome in order to incorporate and register a new firm, along with their associated time and set-up costs. It examines the procedures, time and cost involved in launching a commercial or industrial firm with up to 50 employees and start-up capital of 10 times the economy's per-capita gross national income.

The information appearing on this page was collected as part of the _**Doing Business**_ subnational project in Philippines.

No.	Procedure	Time to Complete	Associated Costs
1	**Verify and reserve the company name with the Securities and Exchange Commission (SEC)** The company can verify the availability of the company name online. Verification is free but reservation of the name, once approved by the SEC, costs PHP 40 for the first 30 days. The company name can be reserved for a maximum of 120 days for a fee of PHP 120, which is renewable upon expiration of the period.	2 days	PHP 40
2	**Deposit paid-up capital in the Authorized Agent Bank (AAB) and obtain bank certificate of deposit** The company is required by law to deposit paid-up capital amounting to at least 6.25% of the authorized capital stock of the corporation. This paid-up capital must not be less than PHP 5,000. Some banks charge a fee for issuance of the certificate of deposit.	1 day	No cost
3	**Notarize articles of incorporation and treasurer's affidavit at the notary** According to Sections 14 and 15 of the Corporation Code, articles of incorporation should be notarized before filing with the SEC.	1 day	PHP 500
4	**Register the company with the SEC** The company can register online through SEC i-Register but must pay on site at the SEC. The following documents are required for SEC registration: a. Company name verification slip; b. Articles of incorporation (notarized) and by-laws; c. Treasurer's affidavit (notarized); d. Statement of assets and liabilities; e. Bank certificate of deposit of the paid-in capital; f. Authority to verify the bank account; g. Registration data sheet with particulars on directors, officers, stockholders, and so forth;	3 days	PHP 2,695 (PHP 1,667.99 filing fee equivalent to 1/5 of 1% of the authorized capital stock or the subscription price of the subscribed capital stock, whichever is higher but not less than PHP 1,000 + PHP 16.68 legal research fee (LRF) equivalent to 1% of filing fee but not less than PHP 10 + PHP 500 By-laws + PHP 150 for registration of stock and transfer book (STB) required for new corporations + PHP 320 STB + PHP 10 registration for SEC bulletin + PHP 30 handling fee)

No.	Procedure	Time to Complete	Associated Costs
	h. Written undertaking to comply with SEC reporting requirements (notarized); and i. Written undertaking to change corporate name (notarized). The SEC Extension Office charges a handling fee of PHP 30 to cover the cost of transmitting the documents to the SEC Head Office in Metro Manila.		
5	**After issuance of the SEC certificate of incorporation, pay the annual community tax and obtain the community tax certificate (CTC) from the City Treasurer's Office (CTO)**	1 day	PHP 500
6	**Obtain barangay clearance** This clearance is obtained from the barangay where the business is located and is required to obtain the business permit from the city or municipality. Barangay fees vary for each barangay since they have the discretion to impose their own fees and charges for as long as these fees are reasonable and within the limits set by the Local Government Code and city ordinances. Barangay fees may depend on: a. the location and the area (size in square meters) of the place of business; or b. the company's paid-up capital and the area it occupies; or c. whether they issue clearance plates or certificates.	1 day	PHP 100
7	**Submit business permit application form and requirements to, and obtain tax order of payment from City Treasurer's Office (CTO)** The application form is downloadable at the city's website. Notarization is not required. The CTO issues a tax order of payment after conducting an inspection and assessing the appropriate fees. Requirements: 1. Barangay clearance 2. SEC registration 3. CTC 4. Certificate of no real property	1 day	No cost
* 8	**Receive inspection from the CTO**	1 day	No cost
* 9	**Obtain certificate of no real property from the City Assessor's Office (CAO)** The applicant must apply for a certificate of no real property in view of the fact that it does not own any real estate and is only leasing commercial space.	1 day	PHP 115 (PHP 100 for certification + PHP 15 documentary stamp tax)
10	**Obtain temporary fire safety approval from the Bureau of Fire Protection (BFP)** In applying for a business permit, the applicant is allowed to secure a Fire Safety Inspection Certificate (FSIC) within 60 days from issuance of the business permit. In the meantime, the applicant is required to secure temporary approval from the BFP.	1 day	No cost (fees included in procedure 12)
* 11	**Obtain locational clearance from the City Planning**	3 days	No cost (fees included in procedure 12)

No.	Procedure	Time to Complete	Associated Costs
	and Development Office (CPDO)		
12	Obtain Mayor's Permit from the Business Permits and Licensing Division The applicant must submit the following requirements: a. Locational clearance b. Temporary fire safety approval	7 days	PHP 5,458 (PHP 278 business tax (1/30 of 1% of paid up capital) + PHP 1,000 mayor's permit fee + PHP 200 sanitary inspection fee + PHP 2,400 garbage fee + PHP 340 fire inspection fee + PHP 500 business plate + PHP 200 PTR fee + PHP 100 zoning fee + PHP 440 FSIC (10% of all regulatory fees))
13	Buy special books of account at bookstore Special books of accounts are required for registering with the BIR. The books of accounts are sold at bookstores nationwide. One set of journals consisting of four books (cash receipts account, disbursements account, ledger, general journal) costs about PHP 400. If the company has a computerized accounting system (CAS), it may opt to register its CAS under the procedures laid out in BIR Revenue Memorandum Order Nos. 21-2000 and 29-2002. The BIR Computerized System Evaluation Team is required to inspect and evaluate the company's CAS within 30 days from receipt of the application form (BIR Form No. 1900) and complete documentary requirements.	1 day	PHP 400
14	Apply for Certificate of Registration (COR) and Taxpayer Identification Number (TIN) at the Bureau of Internal Revenue (BIR) The company must register each type of internal revenue tax for which it is obligated by filing BIR Form No. 0605 and paying the annual registration fee of PHP 500. Upon registration, the BIR will issue to the company the certificate of registration—BIR Form No. 2303. To obtain the TIN, the company has to file: a. Barangay clearance; b. Mayor's permit; and c. Copy of its SEC registration. For company registrations filed with the SEC Head Office in Metro Manila, the BIR confirms the pre-registered TIN issued by the SEC. New taxpayers are required to attend a seminar.	7 days	PHP 115 (PHP 100 certification + PHP 15 documentary stamp tax)
15	Pay the registration fee and documentary stamp taxes (DST) at the AAB The company must pay DST on the original issuance of shares of stock. The rate is PHP 1 on each PHP 200 or a fractional part thereof, of the par value of such shares of stock. This payment with the BIR should be made on the 5th of the month following registration with the SEC. The COR will be released only after all the DSTs are paid. The company must also pay DST on its lease contract at the rate of PHP 3 for the first PHP 2,000 or fractional part thereof, and an additional PHP 1 for every PHP	1 day	PHP 4,670 (PHP 500 registration fee + PHP 4,169.97 DST on original issuance of shares of stock. DST on the lease contract is not included in the computation of the cost)

No.	Procedure	Time to Complete	Associated Costs
	1,000 or fractional part thereof in excess of the first PHP 2,000 for each year of the lease as stated in the contract.		
16	**Obtain the authority to print receipts and invoices from the BIR** The authority to print receipts and invoices must be secured before the sales receipts and invoices may be printed. The company can ask any authorized printing company to print its official forms, or it can print its own forms (i.e., it uses its computers to print loose-leaf invoice forms) after obtaining a permit from BIR for this purpose. To obtain the authority to print receipts and invoices from the BIR, the company must submit the following documents to the Revenue District Office (RDO): a. Duly completed application for authority to print receipts and invoices (BIR Form No. 1906); b. Job order; c. Final and clear sample of receipts and invoices (machine-printed); d. Application for registration (BIR Form No. 1903); and e. Proof of payment of annual registration fee (BIR Form No. 0605).	1 day	No cost
17	**Print receipts and invoices at the print shops** The cost is based on the following specifications of the official receipt: 1/2 bond paper (8 ½ x 5 ½ cm) in duplicate, black print, carbonless for 10 booklets.	14 days	PHP 4,000 (between PHP 3,000 – PHP 5,000)
18	**Have books of accounts and Printer's Certificate of Delivery (PCD) stamped by the BIR** After the printing of receipts and invoices, the printer issues a Printer's Certificate of Delivery of Receipts and Invoices (PCD) to the company, which must submit this to the appropriate BIR RDO (i.e., the RDO which has jurisdiction over the company's principal place of business) for registration and stamping within thirty (30) days from issuance. The company must also submit the following documents: a. All required books of accounts; b. VAT registration certificate; c. SEC registration; d. BIR Form W-5; e. Certified photocopy of the ATP; and f. Notarized taxpayer-user's sworn statement enumerating the responsibilities and commitments of the taxpayer-user. The company must also submit a copy of the PCD to the BIR RDO having jurisdiction over the printer's principal place of business.	1 day	No cost
19	**Register with the Social Security System (SSS)** To register with the SSS, the company must submit the following documents: a. Employer registration form (Form R-1); b. Employment report (Form R-1A); c. List of employees, specifying their birth dates, positions, monthly salary and date of employment; and	7 days	No cost

No.	Procedure	Time to Complete	Associated Costs
	d. Articles of incorporation, by-laws and SEC registration. Upon submission of the required documents, the SSS employer and employee numbers will be released. The employees may attend an SSS training seminar after registration. SSS prefers that all members go through such training so that each member is aware of their rights and obligations.		
20	**Register with the Philippine Health Insurance Company (PhilHealth)** To register with PhilHealth, the company must submit the following documents: a. Employer data record (Form ER1); b. Report of employee-members (Form ER2); c. SEC registration; d. BIR registration; and e. Copy of business permit. Upon submission of the required documents, the company shall get the receiving copy of all the forms as proof of membership until PhilHealth releases the employer and employee numbers within three months.	1 day	No cost

•   Takes place simultaneously with another procedure.

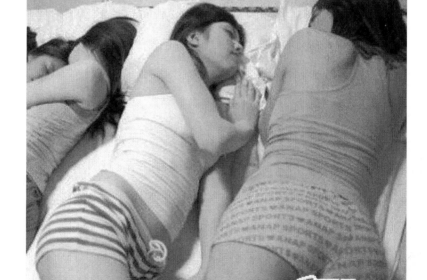

Stay with me guys, wake up from that nap.

Are you overwhelmed yet? It *can* be trying making your way through the maze of permits and mounds of paperwork. But some of my expat friends that have opened businesses in the Philippines were able to get some assistance from locals, such as barangay officials, that helped expedite the process. Don't let that long list of requirements scare you off. There is *ALWAYS* someone in the Philippines that can help you out and speed up the process. That I can guarantee you.

WHAT IS THE BEST BUSINESS TO GO INTO?

Eating with friends at a local talabahan, oyster bar, in Guimaras

In many entrepreneurship forums, the most frequently asked question by aspiring entrepreneurs is: **"What is the best business to go into?"**

The standard answer they often receive is: **"It depends,"** which is then explained in detail in terms of the many internal and external variables on which "it" depends.

Often, this answer disappoints the listeners. Does it disappoint you too?

But an answer that may be considered acceptable now may turn out unacceptable sometime after. If it is announced, for example, that the business to go into is the sago pearl business, then everybody would join the mad rush to set up a sago business and before you know it, the market has become overcrowded. That actually happened to the sago pearl business – as it did with the shawarma business. Before that, the hot pandesal business. So many people engaged in these businesses until competition became cut-throat. With thousands of shops competing for a share of the market, all but a few folded up.

You should be better advised to look within and outside to identify what is the best business for you to go into.

Looking Within

In a way, the best business for you actually depends on you – who you are, what you know, what you have.

Begin by looking for products, processes, or services about which you already know something. It is now a fact that many ideas for small businesses were the direct result of experience in a previous job. Carpenters would be confident going into construction, furniture making or sash-making. Seamstresses would have a best chance going into garment making or stuffed toy manufacturing, or setting up a modista or tailoring shop. Cooks would be good in starting a carinderia, a tapsilog stall, or a small restaurant.

By starting with what you know and what you have, you would not miss your goal.

Similarly, a hobby could become the basis for a full-time successful enterprise. Do you have one which you can expand into a business? Is it gardening? Bonsai plants and desktop garden-fountains are very much in demand. A commercial garden on an idle lot which you can rent for a small fee would also be a good possibility. There was this housewife who loved collecting ornaments and home accessories. Her friends liked her taste and convinced her to sell them some of her items. Before she knew it, she had begun a small home-based business which eventually prospered.

Technical training is also closely linked with entrepreneurship. You will do well to begin a business based on some vocation or trade skills you have learned, such as auto repair, metalworking, computer assembly, desktop publishing, or bookkeeping.

Looking Outside

After looking within, then you can look around you.

By looking at the total business environment, you identify business opportunities. In other words, you observe developments and trends in the economy, demography and society as a whole – including political, ecological, and technological events. What is happening in the broad picture will greatly affect your decision on what products to produce or services to offer.

(Source: Your Guide to Starting a Small Enterprise -dti.gov.ph)

My brother-in-law in Guimaras makes 2,000 pesos a month with his salted egg business

LIST OF POSSIBLE BUSINESS OPPORTUNITIES IN THE PHILIPPINES

1. FOOD CART

Whether it's a pork barbecue, chicken, hotdog, or even "isaw" (grilled chicken intestines), there is a market of Filipino BBQ lovers waiting for you.

The Booming of the Food Cart Business

Small capital, easy set-up and a good chance of success are just some of the reason why the Food Cart Business is thriving in the Philippines. If you will look at the market trend today, Food cart business is the choice of most aspiring entrepreneurs.

A mobile food cart is a business where you can start on low capital ranging from P30,000 to a maximum of P300,000. But it could be a little lower though, depending on how you will put it up — by franchise or on your own. Some companies offer food cart franchise for as low as P10,000 per package that includes, the cart, product, uniform for the crew and training.

Over the last few years, food service carts have sprouted all over the metro — from MRT and LRT station, malls, sidewalks,church, schools, markets etc.- name it and for sure, you'll find a food cart there. Today, there are about

800 different food cart formats available in the market–pizza, waffle,fishball, siomai, rice toppings, baked goodies, rice in a box, hotdog and a lot more.

Industry estimates that more than P1 billion in sales is turned over every year from the food cart businesses. With this amount, no doubt that Food Cart is the hot business in the market!

Some cart owners features were asked why they chose a cart setup over a full store. Their answer varied, but they have a consensus that:

- Carts are easier to manage and operate;
- They require less capital and rental cost:
- Carts are easy to transfer if the location is not good
- They need less maintenance and few workers; and
- Carts are ideal for businesses offering limited products or services.

Other reasons are:

- Carts are easy to launch;
- It is easier to get a space or location for a cart because it requires just small area; and
- It is easy to expand a cart business because it entails less capital

Cart businesses have another advantage: because they are normally located along the walkways of malls and commercial centers, they can capture a wider market.

Indeed, a cart business is something aspiring entrepreneurs would want to start with. Jorge Wieneke, who founded Potato Corner in 1992, however, gives entrepreneurs and would-be entrepreneurs five points to ponder before riding on the bandwagon, so to speak:

- Make sure the cart or kiosk has a focused concept. "If it's flavored fries food cart, then sell fries," he says.
- Don't just use any kind of material, but make sure the cart is good aesthetically.
- Plan a layout for the cart's equipment; it will help make the work flow within the cart more efficient.
- Enter the cart industry with a unique business concept.

- Have a strategy: "Enter the major malls first, then the other smaller malls before you go to the commercial centers, schools and terminals."

But, wait before you jump on the bandwagon, you need to consider a lot things. First is your cart–which is the basic component of the business.The cart must have a colorful and bold big signage to catch the attention of the customers. Your cart is a self-contained kitchen, so you need to keep it clean all the times. The sturdier the cart the better, since it is mobile, it will be easier to go from one location to another.

If you have a nice cart, then the next thing to consider is Location. Location,plays a big part in the success of your food cart or in any business for that matter. You have to think of a good location where people frequents and can see what you are selling. But not all places cramming with people is a good venue just like MRT and LRT station.

Lastly, you have to match your good location with the right product at a good price. People will keep coming back on you food cart biz, if you sell good quality products at a very reasonable price. When you are just starting your business don't be too greedy with the profit and be prepare for setbacks. Be creative and update your products every two months so that your customers will not get tired of what you sell. Always think that there are a lot of competition in the market.

*Sources: **Foodcartlink.com,** Mishell M. Malabaguio, entrepreneur.com.ph, Mark So, businessmaker-academy.com*

2. CARINDERIA BUSINESS

Carinderia is a local eatery selling and serving affordable food for the masses. It's also known as a "turo-turo" wherein customers literally point what they want to eat. If your house is located in a busy area or surrounded by a lot of office buildings and schools, then putting up a carinderia business is a wise choice. You can start your business right in your own home with a small capital investment!

Things to Consider in Putting up a Carinderia Business:

Capital:

You need about P15,000 to open a small carinderia or food kiosk. The money will go to two weeks' worth of inventory of food and ingredients, equipment and utensils, space rentals, and barangay permit fees. You may need a lower amount if you will do business in your own backyard or front yard (deduct P1,500 to P2,000 from the original estimate if this is the case) and if you will use your own existing kitchen utensils (deduct their brand-new cost).

Assuming an income of P600 daily six days a week, you can expect to recover your investment by the second month.

Materials:

You will need a space to accommodate your kitchen equipment and one to two small tables for your customers; a stove with an LPG tank (or charcoal supply if you prefer to use a charcoal stove); and cookware, plates, spoons and forks, and other utensils.

Workforce:

You need not hire staff to get started in this business. However, when you feel it's time to expand or offer a wider variety of dishes, you will likely need one or two staff to serve customers, wash dishes, and clean up the place.

Process:

To do this business, you must have determination and a real interest in cooking. According to Rene Jose Macatangay, a carinderia owner-operator for 11 years now, he would wake up as early as 2:00 or 3:00 a.m. to get the freshest produce when he does his marketing for food ingredients. Promptly at 4:00 a.m., he would be back at his food kiosk to do the cooking.

Location:

Finding a good location for your food kiosk is extremely important. A place very near or easily accessible to your target customers, say taxi or tricycle drivers, would be ideal. It's also advisable to check with your barangay council if a permit is needed for a small carinderia.

Menu:

Decide how many meals you will serve for the day and prepare a menu plan for at least a week. Some carinderia owners stick to a fixed menu plan particularly if they have already established best-selling dishes. In the case of Macatangay, however, he only serves merienda (snacks) and lunch. He opens at 10:00 a.m. and closes by 4:00 or 5:00 p.m. He regularly serves goto and lugaw (both rice porridge snacks) and tokwa (soybean cake). Although he changes his lunch menu every day, he has standard fare for particular days, like ginisang munggo (stewed mung beans) every Friday.

Price:

Make your pricing reasonable and within the reach of your target market. Macatangay says he keeps his prices low to maintain the loyalty of his regular customers.

Marketing:

Word-of-mouth advertising is your best promotional tool for this type of business. Satisfied customers will talk about your carinderia and recommend it to their friends who happen to be in the vicinity. And for Macatangay, it is a source of great satisfaction to see his loyal customers come back every day for his food fare.

With tasty, clean and affordable food with variety; and good marketing and location, you're carinderia business will surely be successful.
(Source: entrepreneur.com.ph)

3. FRANCHISE OPPORTUNITIES

In conjunction with the food cart business are the multitude of franchising opportunities in the Philippines. Remember, have the business in your spouse or trusted girlfriend's name before venturing into any endeavors. The food business is big in the Philippines.

But in this category you must possess roughly at least Php 500,000 to start a business. Why? Because you will sell name brand products, like Goldilocks or Jollibee that are known throughout the country. That is why it is very expensive.

But if you opened a small time eatery you could possibly do so on Php 10,000 or less, about 240 US Dollars, depending on the location. But you must do all the buying and cooking and waking up in the early hours of the day at 4 am to start your day or hire someone to do that. It is hard work. But who said a personal business is **not** hard work?

In the Philippines, food is "Number One," because Filipinos love to eat. Food is the best business in the Philippines and before you venture with any of it consult an expert opinion on what to do and what not to do.

4. MONEY CHANGING BUSINESS

There are many places that have a strong demand for a money changing business. The growth of tourism and the large OFW population of the Philippines has guaranteed a huge market to be tapped by money changers. This is one opportunity you may not want to miss. It is a simple business if you know how to start and operate it. Below is a shortened and simplified step by step procedure to give you a basic idea on this business:

1. Find an ideal location.

The key to success in this business is to secure a location in a place where there are many potential customers who feel safe when changing money. Previously this was limited to areas where there are many foreigners like the tourist belt. Now, some of the best locations are public markets, commercial areas, malls, and other places where a lot of people find it convenient and secure to change money. A location where you see money changers overflowing with customers are prime spots for putting up this business.

2. Registering a money changing business.

A money changer business can be a sole proprietor, corporation, or partnership. Sole proprietors need to go to the department of trade and industry, while corporations and partnerships must go the Securities and

Exchange Commission. You then must get a barangay clearance before proceeding to get a mayor's permit and then registering with the Bureau of Internal Revenue and having your receipts printed.

3. Requirements of the Central Bank.

You also need to register with the Central Bank. One of the key requirements of the Central Bank is attendance at the Anti-Money Laundering Law Seminar.

4. Capital needed.

While there is no legally mandated minimum amount, it is recommended that you have around five hundred thousand pesos to start this business excluding a minimal amount for renovation, furnishings, and equipment. A bigger capitalization will enable you to have more transactions.

5. Learn buying and selling prices of different currencies.

You make your profit from the difference in value between your buying and selling of currencies and so you must know the way of rapidly updating buying and selling prices.

6. Learn counterfeit money detection.

The most critical operational skill you and your staff must acquire is to learn how to detect fake currencies. To do this, you must have the tools of the trade: the lens, ultra violet money detector, and white light.

7. Attracting and retaining customers.

On the surface it seems that your product or service is hard to differentiate. However, there are many aspects that could be made more appealing to increase the chances of customers preferring your shop. Physically, make external facade look neat with your signage prominent and clean. But the most important is to have well trained staff that can deliver excellent customer service.

The money changing business offers the prospective entrepreneur a solid business opportunity. The demand for this service will most probably continue to grow. (Source: Business Coach Column by Ruben Anlacan, Jr. (President, BusinessCoach, Inc.) from the Manila Bulletin.)

5. PAWNSHOP BUSINESS

Steps to open a pawnshop business in the Philippines:

1. Call Bangko Sentral ng Pilipinas (BSP) pawnshop hotline, (02)524-8713, to check if the pawnshop name you want is already taken.

2. Register your business either at the Department of Trade and Industry (DTI), for single proprietorship, or the Securities and Exchange Commission, for partnerships or corporations.

DTI is located at the Trade & Industry Building, Sen. Gil Puyat Ave., Makati. In the provinces, DTI offices are in or near municipal buildings. Application forms are also available at DTI's website. Only Filipinos may own a pawnshop organized as a single proprietorship. For partnerships and corporations, foreign ownership should be limited to 30 percent.

3. Secure a business permit from the city or municipality where pawnshop will be located.

4. Register with the BSP. For the complete list of requirement, download the form here. These include permits from the DTI or SEC and the local government, an information sheet, personal data sheets, bank certification of at least P100,000 capital and location sketch.

5. Pay the processing fee of P1,000.

6. It will take two to three weeks for the BSP to process your application. Make sure you open your business within six months after the application is approved or your permit will be revoked.
(Source: **EntryPinoys Atpb**.)

You'll see many pawnshops in the Philippines that also have a Western Union franchise, another good way to diversify and earn some extra money. With over 10 million Filipinos working overseas sending remittances back home, a Western Union outlet offers a good money-making addition to any pawnshop.

6. MICROLENDING BUSINESS

The lending industry thrives better in times of financial crunch. To cope with the crisis, people try to stretch their budget and augment their income. Many households put up sari-sari stores; family members look for sidelines, try working abroad, or simply try to borrow money. To raise the money to finance these activities, many of them go to lending firms instead of the commercial banks. This is because lending firms are more lenient in their requirements, offer lower interest rates, and process loan applications faster.

Entrepreneurs can set up a lending business to take advantage of this demand for easier credit.

~~A lending business can be set up as a single proprietorship, partnership, or corporation.~~ Per Republic Act no. 9474 or the Lending Act of 2007 lending business should be set-up or organize under a corporation. However, you can't use the word "lending" or "finance" in your business name if you choose to set up your lending business as a single proprietorship or partnership. You can only use those words if your company is a corporation. In fact, a corporation has advantages that a single proprietorship or a partnership doesn't have.

In setting up a **microlending business**, you need to raise the required minimum capital of P1 million and then register your business with the Securities and Exchange Commission or SEC (www.sec.gov.ph). The usual permits and documents required in setting up a business will be required, like the Mayor's permit, certification from the Bureau of Internal Revenue (BIR), and Social Security System, Philhealth, and Pag-IBIG coverage for the people you will be employing in the business.

In microlending without quasi-banking activities, you may cater to employees, pensioners, sari-sari store owners, market stallholders, and OFWs. OFWs usually require bigger loan amounts that start at P50,000, but it is advisable for startups to lend smaller amounts with short payment terms. This will make repayments faster and enable you to loan out money to more borrowers. Loans could start from P5,000 to P15,000, with 3 to 5 percent interest per month. Payment terms can be from two months to six months. The advisable payment schemes are daily or weekly; for employees and pensioners, though, payments can be scheduled every payday or once a month.

To build a client base, you could partner with the human resources and accounting departments of your target companies. As an incentive to endorse you to their employees, you could also offer to the client-company a commission of a certain percentage of the loan interest you will be charging.

If you will be charging 5 percent, for example, you might want to give 1 percent to the company as a commission.

Microlending usually doesn't require co lateral from the borrower. It only requires the borrower and the comaker to sign a promissory note and submit other documents. However, for loans of P50,000 and higher, you should ask for collateral from the borrower. Any item that is of value can be used as collateral, such as jewelry, real estate, or vehicle, for as long as the borrower owns it. If the borrower doesn't own the item put up as collateral, you have to ask him or her to submit an authorization letter or special power if attorney from the owner consenting to the use of the item as collateral.

You can start this business with three employees: one to take care of releasing loans, a second to collect payments, and a third either a bookkeeper or accountant on retainer. It is advisable for the owner of the lending business to talk to potential borrowers directly to make a good assessment of their character and integrity. It is also advisable to build an internal security system and a clear accounting system that can track each borrower's account and the flow of money in the business.

Aside from the interest, you should also charge another 5 percent as a service fee to borrowers to cover your overhead costs. You may automatically deduct this from the loan amount upon release of the loan, or you may just add this to the interest rate. A penalty charge should also be imposed on delinquent borrowers.

The longer it takes the borrower to pay his outstanding balance, the smaller is your chance of getting him to pay it back. You therefore need to allot a 1 percent provision for bad debts.

(Source: This article is the advice of Mr. Edgardo Tipa, a financial trainer with BusinessCoach Inc. (www.businesscoachphil.com), as interviewed by Mishell M. Malabaguio, entrepreneur.com.ph.)

Here's one microlending business to avoid, 5/6 loans. Here's a recent article I did about Indian loan sharks operating in our home province of Guimaras:

Indian Loan Sharks in Guimaras

Had lunch at my favorite talabahan in Guimaras the other day. My asawa went up front to order her usual two bowls of oysters at P30 each. I requested a grilled chicken along with four sticks of pork BBQ. And a bottle of Pilsen, of course.

As I was stripping a tasty pork BBQ morsel from the sharp skewer I had just stuck in my mouth, I noticed an Indian walk in. Not Native American. No, he wasn't wearing a headdress like some Victoria's Secret's runway model. But a guy from India. He was accompanied by a female Indian.

I've never seen someone from India in over three years of living in and visiting Guimaras. Seen a few in Iloilo where they even have a Sikh temple. My asawa has spied some before on the pumpboats, their motorcycles used for their daily collections, on board. The couple immediately caught my attention.

He was a Bombay loan shark. He stuck his head into the kitchen window. I saw three Filipina workers inside peeling off P100 bills and handing them to the man. No doubt for a 5/6 loan.

5/6 simply means the amount you borrowed must be returned with 20% interest added. Example: If you borrowed P1,000, then you should pay it back with 20% interest: 1,000 x .20 = 200. You have to pay P1,200 in return.

The pretty pinays stepped inside the restaurant area and pointed out the menu dishes for the day to the lender. I had no doubt he would be helping himself to a free lunch. The workers were tripping over themselves to make sure the man had plenty of food. He was receiving the full-blown rock star, celebrity treatment many foreigners encounter in the Philippines. A foreigner that gives you money attains almost god-like status.

Soon another Indian man, larger than the first, came inside the talabahan. He took off his motorcycle helmet and sat down to eat with his friends. I nudged The Sainted Patient Wife who was seated next to me. She, too, had seen the money exchange and of course, knew immediately that the workers were paying back a 5/6 loan.

The Indians are known as "last resource lenders." Indian moneylenders are also sometimes preferred by Filipinos over their local counterparts. Indian lenders, most of whom are men and are more discreet, according to borrowers. The locals say that Filipino lenders are usually women who tend to gossip about their clients.

In 5-6 transactions, while legal documents are not signed, lenders get their customers' signatures in notebooks, calendars, or even on a piece of paper. They make entries in their own handwriting so the customer cannot tamper with the record.

The Sainted Patient Wife reports that none of her family has used any of the Indian lenders. And yes, perhaps that was due to the fact that my own spouse has personally loaned out thousands of pesos to some relatives (though never charging any interest.)

Is 5/6 loan sharking legal in the Philippines? Here's what the law states: Central Bank of the Philippines issued C.B Circular No. 905-82 adopted on December 22, 1982 but which took effect on January 1, 1983 effectively removing the ceiling on interest rates both for secured and unsecured loans regardless of maturity. *The news of its passage turned out as good news for loan sharks.*

The Supreme Court ruled in the case of *Florendo vs. Court of Appeals*, that "**by virtue of CB Circular 905, the Usury Law has been rendered ineffective.**" "**Usury has been legally non-existent in our jurisdiction. Interest can now be charged as lender and borrower may agree upon.**"
(Source: PhilippineBlaw.com)
An article in the Inquirer News last year reported that the Bureau of Internal Revenue (BIR) planned to go after Indian nationals involved in money lending activities. They admitted that it would not be easy to collect taxes from them.
Venerando Homez, revenue district officer for Kidapawan City, said at least a dozen Indian nationals were suspected of involvement in money lending activities, mostly to small entrepreneurs there.

Homez said they were certain the Indian nationals were not paying taxes and did not have business permits.

At least a dozen Indian nationals lending capital to small business establishments, particularly restaurants, sari-sari stores and vegetable vendors can be seen roaming around the major thoroughfares in the afternoon to collect the daily payments from the debtors, he said.

But Homez has a problem. How to build up cases against these Indian nationals. **"Only the Economic Intelligence Investigation Bureau (EIIB) based in the BIR main office has the authority to reprimand or invite foreign money lenders operating in various places in the country,"** he said. But that office has been eliminated, Homez reports.

Homez said that the BIR would have to get the testimonies of those who had borrowed money from the Indian money lenders, but admitted that would be a difficult task.

(Photo Source:Philippine Center for Investigative Journalism)
Aside from dodging the BIR, Bombay loan sharks have to occasionally dodge bullets as well in the Philippines. A recent article in **The Daily Guardian**, an Indian newspaper, reports that over 150 Indians, many of them, Punjabis, have been killed in the Philippines.

But you won't find the Philippine government agreeing with those statistics. Although, the Philippine National Police (PNP) admits its records are inaccurate there is a wide disparity from figures the Indian government reports versus the official Philippine government statistics. (Source: **Philippine Center for Investigative Journalism**.)

Still, police records and news reports strongly indicate that the attacks against Indians are indeed on the rise, and range from holdups to kidnapping to outright ambushes, and occur even outside of Metro Manila. Police records alone show that in 2005, there were only three crimes against Indians, but the figure shot up to 13 in 2006. From January to June 2007, the PNP had already recorded eight cases with Indians as victims.

The Daily Guardian reports that the resentment against the Bombay lenders also showed in adverse publicity in the Philippines. In fact in 2006, the Punjab Revenue and Rehabilitation and NRI Affairs Minister had cautioned the people of Punjab against indulging in money lending in Philippines, noting that Punjabis were joining mafia gangs with Chinese and Filipinos engaged in organized extortion and kidnapping.

"Killing of Punjabis is on the rise in Manila because there has been no remedial action," said former Union minister and Akali leader Balwant Singh Ramoowalia. He has called upon the Centre to take up the issue with the Philippines government to ensure the safety of the Punjabis in Philippines.

As I downed another bottle of cold San Miguel Pale Pilsen, the coldest bottle of beer I've ever had at this talabahan, and served by a 14-year-old waitress, I saw the Bombay loan sharks leaving. I'm sure they had more rounds to make in the sleepy little capital of Guimaras and would no doubt be adding even more pesos to their wallets. It's a dirty job, sometimes risky, but I suppose somebody has to do it.

7. TRICYCLE BUSINESS

Some expats in Dumaguete, for example, are making P20,000 a month, 476 US Dollars. Make sure you have trust worthy drivers but this is possibly a good business opportunity as demand for trike rides is usually good.

Depending on the trike, they usually run with 150cc bikes. A new one costs around P105,000-P110,000 (2,500-2,620 US Dollars) including licensing fees. You should go to a welding shop which makes sidecars and ask them for your own design.

Don't forget the additional cost of the line or permission to work a particular section of town. As one online observer noted **"you can't simply buy a trike, paint a number on it and jump in a queue. Good way to get beat up or worse!"**

Do a bit of research and see if the area you want to operate the trike has line spots available (sometimes a certain line is full and no more line permits are being issued) and if there is possibly someone on the line willing to "retire" for some money. You could then buy a used trike and his line permit.

8. INTERNET CAFE BUSINESS IN THE PHILIPPINES

Despite the proliferation of internet cafes you might find in the Philippines it is still possible to operate an internet cafe if you research the right location and other factors. While more and more Filipinos are buying computers, many still do not have the financial means to purchase one let alone pay the monthly broad ban fees from their local internet service provider.

A survey recently conducted by SocialBakers revealed how prevalent Facebook usage is in the Philippines. According to their study, one of every 4 Filipinos has a Facebook account, and there are over more than 27, 720, 300 Facebook users in the Philippines. That is about 27.75% of the 90+ million Filipinos and 93.3% of the users using the internet.

Currently Philippines ranked 8th among the so-called Facebook countries, with over 1.2 million (1,226,960) users added over the past 6 months. This would mean that there are 6,816 doing FB a day, or 204,493 a month, 284 users every hour and 4.7 users every minute.

Go to this **link** and get your own free download for your own personal internet cafe business plan in the Philippines. (You will need a Facebook account for this download from the **ICAFE** project.

9. FURNITURE BUSINESS

If your job skill back in your home country was in the carpentry field, chances are you're not going to get hired over a local Filipino working for maybe six US dollars an hour. But since carpentry is your field of expertise, why not establish a furniture business in the Philippines?

One of my wife's relatives in Guimaras, who along with being a police officer, also has a furniture shop where handcrafted cabinets, beds, dressers, mahogany doors and other furniture is made on site. He has some very skilled workers that do quality work. His shop made the solid mahogany wood doors for our home in Guimaras and they're some of the best craftsmanship I've ever seen.

There are very few furniture companies that offer a made-to-order or personalized sofa or furniture in our area. Do some market research and find out what's available in your locale in the Philippines. Why not set the trend?

My American expat friend in Guimaras, Tom, also makes furniture from bamboo, mahogany and mango trees. Some of his handiwork is shown in the above photo. He has a local caretaker that does some of the woodworking chores.

10. OPEN A SARI SARI STORE

It's estimated that one out of four households in the Philippines have a sari sari store at some time. My brother-in-law in Guimaras is working on building one that is attached to their nipa hut (see photo above.) While there are already two stores down that muddy, cow-poop laden subdivision road, my brother-in-law figures that that he has quite a few potential customers that stop by their home on a daily basis.

His wife, my sister-in-law, has a private preschool located at the back of the main house and has close to 30 students enrolled in all of her classes. When you factor in the parents or grandparents that stay and wait for their child or grandchild, he has a built-in clientele. And there's a steady stream of trike drivers who bring the kids back and forth for the three different classes not held at the school.

The students and other visitors currently go down the road for soda and snacks. Makes sense to operate a sari sari store for him as long as he follows one of the golden rules in that business: **DON'T OFFER CREDIT!**

Start up costs are relatively cheap. From P5,000, 120 US Dollars to P15,000, 360 USD. Research your area and see what the other sari sari stores don't have that you could offer.

How to Start a Sari Sari Store Business

Create a niche.

If there are already three such stores on your street, it would be good to specialize in something. Miriam's sari-sari store in Quezon City flourished because she was the only in the area that sold nail polish, pad papers for different grades, ballpens and Campbell's soups. Look at the merchandise of your competitors and buy what they didn't offer. Christine, who studied making tapa, tocino and longganisa, started selling her cured meats at her sari-sari store in a non-affluent area of Makati City and they were a big hit. Christine would cook a few pieces and offer them to her customers. Some of her neighbors would even order four to five kilos of tapa and tocino at a time.

Make it legal.

A sari-sari store is a micro-enterprise but that does not mean you do not need a business permit to operate it. You also need to talk to your utility providers because the charge for business and residential areas are different and having a store does not fall under residential.

Look for the cheapest prices. There are a million wholesalers out there, all vying to be your store of choice but just because you have a suki does not mean that you should get all your merchandise from him or her. Look for other suppliers and don't stop searching for the best bargains.

Keep records.

Even if you're not an accountant, keep records of all your transactions. Some store owners simply add the day's sales and apply a mark-up on what they sold to compute their net profit. But unless you're really good with numbers, it is better to record all transactions in a ledger.

You need cash. Many sari-sari store owners have lost money because they extended credit to people who couldn't pay them back. This is what happened to Delia of Quezon City, who extended credit lines to her neighbors and relatives. Unfortunately, these creditors did not pay their debts and Delia was left with nothing.

Registration Requirements

1.Business   name   registration   (www.bnrs.dti.gov.ph)
2.Mayor's/Business   Permit   (check   your   local   municipality/city)
3. BIR TIN (www.bir.gov.ph)
Financing Facility

(sources: dti.gov.ph, wikipedia, manilastandardtoday)

11. CATERING BUSINESS

Food catering is a great business opportunity during special occasions like Christmas, birthdays, anniversaries, weddings, parties, etc. This could be a lucrative business for anyone that loves to cook. And if you have a Filipina wife, girlfriend or lola (grandma) in the family that is know for her cooking, why not consider this business option?

The main advantage of catering business is that capital requirement for this business is quite low. In fact if you have a good chef with you then you can rent the catering equipments and appoint some people to join you in daily payment business initially. Later you can have a stable catering set-up including the manpower and the equipments for your business. When considering entering this field of work, consider the following factors when establishing a plan for your new business:

Hiring Staff

In the beginning, some self-catering businesses involve relatives and friends, but often times, there is a need to figure in the possibility of hiring staff to help with service, production, and cleanup.

Create Contracts

Professional caterers need to create contracts, which clearly state the terms of an agreement. Some of the main details include time of event, location, room set-up, duration of event, estimated attendance, and pricing arrangements. A deposit is also required, which ranges from 25% to 50% of the total event cost, which is due when the contract is signed.

Additionally, when starting your own food catering business – remember to include insurance costs (product and personal liability), record keeping, and food safety. In order to gauge final charges for your catering business, you will need to incorporate materials (cost of food and drink), overhead expenses (variable and fixed expenses), labor costs (food preparation and service), and anticipated profit in order to come to a suitable figure. In the end, final prices should reflect the amount you need to charge so you can maintain your business, as well as reap benefits.

To be a successful foodcaterer, you must be able to prepare delicious, hygienic and wholesome food. You should maintain high quality standards while preparing the food. When well planned, having your own food catering business can be personally and financially rewarding.(Source: **Pinoy Bisnes Ideas**)

12. VISA SERVICES

Here's what one expat is doing in Cebu, offering services to extend your visa in the Philippines and saving you time and frustration at the local Bureau of Immigration. Here's some information form his website:

Free Pickup and Delivery

I will pick up your passport from your hotel/home, obtain the visa extension in Cebu and deliver it back to you usually either the same day or the next working day. Most travel agencies charge a similar fee to what I am charging, but you have to take it to them and then pick it up – sometimes up to 4 days later. Plus you don't really know who actually handles your ever important passport.

Fee Schedule

The basic fee for this service will be 1200php plus the appropriate Cebu Bureau of Immigration fees for the extension or renewal.
•Recent events and the appointment of a new Commissioner have led to a much stricter set of rules for the processing of visa renewals by agents,

including the need for a special power of attorney. This has meant that my fees for this service have had to increase.

•Receipts for the amount paid to Bureau of Immigration will be provided.

•Remember you can renew a few days/weeks early and still get 59 days from the expiry date of your current visa.

•I explain to all my clients that renewing your visa yourself is not hard and the people at the Bureau of Immigration are pleasant and helpful. If you would like me to go with you the first time to walk you through the process and hold your hand, I would charge you 900 php.

The website for this information is from **Cebu Expat Services**. Another business opportunity in the Philippines.

13. OPEN YOUR OWN TIANGGE

Photo Source: atrez.com

Tiangge, a type of "flea market" or "bazaar" is used to mean "market," in general, whether wet market or dry goods. The current use of Tiangge describes a group of stalls inside a building. They sell only dry goods which include foodstuff.

The Tiangge that is well-known for having the cheapest price is called "168" which in Chinese means unending wealth/fortune or words to that effect. You could open your own stall in an existing tiangge to start up your business.

Like all tiangges, Tiendesitas is a treasure trove of goods you can't normally find in regular shopping malls.

And though the average pricing in Tiendesitas may be somewhat higher, the deals waiting to be made are still better (read: cheaper) than regular malls can offer. Because, like in all tiangges, haggling is the name of the game.

This is the tiangge advantage for the consumer: if you're looking for the best quality goods at the best (i.e. lowest) possible price, you can usually find them in a tiangge.

And if you're a seller looking for a stall spot that costs less than those in a regular mall but still has an excellent amount of foot traffic, then a tiangge is a good option for you.

Now, what would it take to start selling in a tiangge?

Simple start up

First, of course, you need capital. The startup cost of selling in a tiangge is minimal compared to buying a full-fledged franchise. Village and school tiangges offer the cheapest rates, while hotels and other prestigious flea market haunts can cost you more.

The startup cost includes your per-day payment of the space, which can range from Php500 to Php20,000—the amount will depend on how long the tiangge will run.

If you want something more long-term than a few weeks, you could check out the more permanent tiangge fixtures, such as Tutuban Mall's night market, Greenhills Shopping Center, and St. Francis Square.

Legally speaking

Because the tiangge format is so casual, tiangge owners sometimes don't even bother to do their legal paperwork. In some places like Quiapo and Baclaran, many stall owners don't carry business permits.

However, it is always much more prudent to secure your papers before starting to sell, even with an "informal" tiangge stall.

Another thing you should be wary of is the danger of transacting with the wrong people. It can happen—and has happened—that a stranger would pose as an authority at the venue, collecting fees without the owner's knowledge. Needless to say, if you pay your rental fee to unauthorized people, you can say good-bye to your money.

To prevent this, make sure you personally meet the venue owners and always transact directly with them or, if that is too inconvenient, with a representative they have personally introduced to you. Some high-end tiangge venue hosts also give their stall owners and all representatives IDs for heightened safety. This way, you can be sure that you are paying your dues to the right person.

Sell-anything mode

Now the big question: what do you sell? Most tiangges have a motif: second-hand clothes, mobile phones, handicrafts, etc., and you would, of course, be best advised to stay within or near that motif.

In fact, some tiangge organizers require that you provide them with sample products and be reviewed as an applicant before actual start of the tiangge. But as we've mentioned before, tiangges do allow you more leeway in choosing your products than regular malls do. You can generally sell the most outlandish things, from 80s clothes to frogskin wallets to antique LP (long-playing) records. Again, your main consideration would be the venue (would the most likely patrons be able to afford or would find interest in your items?) and the motif (don't try to sell your 80s clothes in a cake-bake tiangge, but you may be able to find patrons at an organic food one).

It will be most helpful if, for a month or so before you sell, you research on the area and see what particular items are crowd favorites there. Thinking of your consumer ahead of time will increase your chances of getting the revenues that you want.

Tiangge selling can last from days to weeks, and in short-term setups, it is best to sell items that are not too perishable in case they do not get sold.

Managing your tiangge business

If you have chosen a tiangge at an accessible location, and if you have secured a nice spot to lease in it, you are instantly assured of consumer traffic. There are always buyers in a tiangge, especially when major holidays, such as the Christmas season, are approaching.

Of course, it's highly likely that your fellow sellers will have almost the same wares and almost the same prices in their stall. Therefore, you should have a plan on how to make your stall stand out and get noticed.

When the sales start to come, it is highly recommended that you have a spreadsheet where you can record and compute all the incoming and outgoing money from the business. As much as possible, make the money revolve and get most of your latter expenses from your earlier income.

One last thing: you may be thinking of hiring somebody else to man your stall for you. While this is a good option for regular mall stalls, it is best that you man your tiangge stall yourself. Not only will you not have to pay another person to watch over your goods, you will also have better control of how low a haggle your customer can make.

You can even further lower your price if the buyer is buying in bulk. These are decisions that a hired person could find great difficulty in making.
And because you are not paying anybody else to man your stall for you, you can lower the price even further for your customer.

Now remember, Filipinos are suckers for the last price, so make sure that the pricing signs you place on your items are not really your final price. That way, you could make satisfactory adjustments for hagglers later on without losing your profit.

Finally when you've set up a tiangge stall, don't forget to market it. Tell the world about it in blog and forum posts; tell your friends and relatives about it on Twitter and Facebook.

You can make the most of your stall by selling your wares online as well. Take pictures of your inventory and post them on eBay.ph, Facebook, and Multiply.

Online or offline, people love tiangges
And for entrepreneurs, with their low start up costs, quick setup, wide product choices, and easy marketing, a tiangge stall is great for jumpstarting business.

So what are you waiting for? If you could use a little extra dough for Christmas, start planning your tiangge stall now! (Source: http://www.talktalktilaok.com)

14. CELLPHONE LOAD BUSINESS

Filipinos are one of the top cellphone texters on Earth. Cellphone load is *always* in demand. Filipinos are one of the top users of Facebook in the world. Many of them use mobile phones now to access their FB accounts. Many Filipinos play online games on their mobile phones now and require loads to do that. The majority of folks here do not have a monthly postpaid plan, but rely on going to sari sari stores or other outlets to purchase their loads.

15. OPEN A BAKERY

Baking, cakes, pastries, putos, leche plans etc.,You can sell this to your friends, their friends and to the friends of their friends' friends. Make sure to bake the best to achieve an effective word-of-mouth marketing among your consumers. Pan de sal is a staple in most Filipino's diet and eaten throughout the day. I know of one American expat that is operating a bakery in the Philippines along with his Filipina wife. He also has other business ventures in conjunction with the bakery business as you will find is the case with many Filipino's. It is always wise to diversify.

EXPAT JOBS IN THE PHILIPPINES

RESEARCH

I've always been a big proponent of research. I spent hundreds and hundreds of hours checking out all the information I could about moving to the Philippines before moving here over three years ago. The research greatly aided me in our move. You're already a step ahead with the purchase of this eBook.

Start your search ahead of time, don't wait until a month or two ahead of your planned arrival in this archipelago. Contact global corporations that have set up shop in the Philippines. Getting hired from abroad and having the company sponsor you makes the process of acquiring a work permit that much easier. Here's some websites that will help you in that search:

- **jobsdb**(www.jobsdb.com)
- **Jobstreet**(www.jobstreet.com)
- **Recruit.net**(www.recruit.net)
- **Mynimo.com**
- **ExpatJobster**(www.expatjobster.com)

NETWORK

You *can* find work in the Philippines and you *can* do business here, but you need to "think outside the box." You need to *network* with other expats and Filipinos you can trust. If you find friends, expats or locals, that can help you achieve your goals, why *not* ask them for help or suggestions?

How do you find those expat friends? I'm sure many of you reading this eBook have communicated with some people already living in the Philippines. Maybe you've exchanged messages on expat forums or left comments on blogs dealing with living in the Philippines. I've met quite a few people that have followed my website that have made the trip to Iloilo or Guimaras to visit with my asawa and I.

I always appreciate those visits. One of my new expat friends came over a couple of months ago from the States. He's very self-sufficient. Rides the jeepney, takes the time to learn some of the local language here, Ilonggo , Hiligaynon. If you're coming here looking for a job, it will really help you if you can learn a few basic phrases. This will endear you to the locals and could impress potential employers.

Another good place for meeting some foreigners is to check out what places they might hold regular meetings at. I've met a huge amount of expats at gatherings that are held at one of the local "watering holes" in Iloilo City. You'll make new friends and gain some valuable connections in the process. And quench your thirst with a nice cold one in the process.

But go beyond "networking" with expats and establish solid friendships with Filipinos. Make a real investment in relationships. Most Filipinos are warm and friendly so it's really not that difficult.

WHAT DO **YOU** NEED TO WORK IN THE PH?

WHAT REQUIREMENTS DOES A FOREIGNER NEED TO WORK IN THE PHILIPPINES?

Pre-arranged Employment

Pre-arranged employment visas under Section 9 (g) of the Immigration Act are issued to foreigners proceeding to the Philippines to engage in any lawful occupation, whether for wages or salary or for other form of compensation where legitimate employer-employee relations exist. They may be professors and teachers for educational institutions, doctors and nurses for hospitals, scientists, professionals and other workers for banking, commercial, industrial, agricultural and other business enterprises. Special information pertaining to 9(g) visas for missionaries is available from BI here.

A pre-arranged employment visa is issued only upon receipt, by the Consular Office having jurisdiction over applicant's place of residence, of authority to issue such a visa from the Philippine Department of Foreign Affairs (DFA) in Manila. This authority is secured on petition, under oath, filed by the prospective employer in Manila with the Department of Labor and Employment for the contracting of services of the American employee. When DOLE's requirements are met, it endorses the matter to the Philippine Bureau of Immigration for the entry into the Philippines of the American employee. If meritorious, the Commissioner of the Immigration transmits his approval to the DFA. The DFA then authorizes the appropriate consular officer to issue the visa.

The applicant must appear personally at the Consular Section of the Philippine Embassy or Consulate (list of consulates) concerned and submit the following:

Passport valid for at least six (6) months;

1.Two completed application forms;

2.Four (4) identical pictures (passport size) of the applicant signed on the front bottom of each;

3.Medical and physical examination report by an authorized physician. It must also include the chest x-ray film, laboratory reports and a certificate that the applicant is free from AIDS. The medical examination report is acceptable only if submitted to the quarantine officer at the port of entry in the Philippines, together with the visa application, within six (6) months from the date the examination is conducted;

4.Police Clearance, issued by the police authorities of the place where the applicant resides. (Police Certificate based on fingerprint check); and

5.Visa Application Fee

6.If the spouse is accompanying or joining the principal in the Philippines within six (6) months from the date of the principal's admission, the spouse must submit their marriage certificate.

7.Unmarried children under twenty-one (21) years of age accompanying or joining their parent in the Philippines within six (6) months from the date of the parent's admission, must submit their birth certificates showing the names of their parents. (Source: **Embassy of the United States in Manila**)

Working in the Philippines

Non-Resident Aliens Who Intend to Work in the Philippines

8.All foreign nationals seeking admission to the Philippines for the purpose of employment, all non-resident foreign nationals already working in the Philippines, and all non-resident foreign nationals admitted to the Philippines on on-working visas, who wish to work in the Philippines, regardless of the source of compensation and duration of employment are required by the Philippine Department of Labor and Employment (DOLE) to secure an Alien Employment Permit (AEP).

Where to Apply

Foreign nationals can apply for an AEP at the nearest Philippine Embassy or Consulate. Local employers who wish to hire the services of a foreigner can apply on behalf of the foreign national at the nearest Regional Office of the DOLE. Foreign nationals who are already in the Philippines should apply through their prospective employers with the nearest Regional Office of the DOLE. A DOLE AEP frequently-asked-question sheet is available here.

Validity of AEP

The period of validity of an AEP will depend on the nature of the position occupied by the foreign national, whether elective, technical, advisory or supervisory.

Exemptions

All members of the diplomatic services, foreign government officials accredited with the Philippine government, missionaries engaged in missionary work only, members of international organizations such as the Asian Development Bank (ADB), International Rice Research Institute (IRRI) and specialized agencies of the United Nations are exempted from securing an AEP.

NOTE: In support of the UN Spouse Employment Policy, the Philippine government has also exempted the spouses of members of international organizations from securing an AEP. Spouses however, are required to file an application for a Certificate of Exemption from the DOLE's Bureau of Local Employment (BLE). Missionaries or religious workers who intend to engage in gainful employment are not exempted from securing an AEP.

Penalties

Aliens who are found working without an employment permit as required by law, are penalized with a fine ranging from one thousand pesos (P1,000.00) to ten thousand pesos (P10,000), or imprisonment ranging from three months to three years, or both. In addition to such penalties, any alien found guilty shall be summarily deported upon completion of service of sentence.

Resident Aliens and Immigrants Who Intend to Work in the Philippines

Resident Alien - refers to any foreign national who is allowed by law to reside indefinitely in the Philippines. All foreign nationals admitted to the Philippines as immigrants, who wish to seek employment, and all resident aliens already working in the Philippines, irrespective of the source of compensation and nature and duration of employment are required to secure an Alien Employment Registration Certificate (AERC) from the DOLE's Regional Office.

Where to apply - The resident alien or the employer shall apply at the nearest Regional Office of the DOLE where the employer-establishment is located. Requirements for application of an AERC can be found at the Bureau of Local Employment website:www.ble.dole.gov.ph.

Validity of AERC

An AERC issued shall be valid only for the position and employer which it was issued, unless otherwise canceled or revoked for cause. (Source: **Embassy of the United States in Manila**)

Here's a copy of an Alien Employment Permit, AEP, which can be downloaded at the Department of Labor Enforcement, DOLE, website. Check this **link** if you wish to download the form now.

Republic of the Philippines
DEPARTMENT OF LABOR AND EMPLOYMENT
REGIONAL OFFICE NO._____

2 X 2
PICTURE
in white background

ALIEN EMPLOYMENT PERMIT (AEP) APPLICATION FORM

(Please supply all required information. Misrepresentation, false statement or fraud in this application or in any supporting document is ground for denial/ revocation/cancellation of the permit.)

TYPE OF APPLICATION: [ ] NEW   [ ] RENEWAL

PERSONAL DATA

NAME: _____
             (Last name)   (First name)   (Middle name)

SEX:_____ CITIZENSHIP:_____ TIN: _____
CIVIL STATUS_____ DATE OF BIRTH _____ PLACE OF BIRTH _____
HIGHEST EDUCATIONAL ATTAINMENT/COURSE FINISHED: _____
ADDRESS IN THE PHILS. _____
_____ E-MAIL _____
PERMANENT ADDRESS ABROAD _____

PASSPORT NO._____ PASSPORT VALID UNTIL_____
PLACE OF ISSUE_____DATE OF ISSUE_____
VISA _____ VALID UNTIL _____

EMPLOYMENT HISTORY IN THE PHILIPPINES: (Please attach additional sheet if necessary)

Employer's Business Name and Address	Position	Duration of Employment

PRESENT EMPLOYMENT:

POSITION _____
NATURE OF ASSIGNMENT: [ ] INVESTOR, [ ] INTRA-CORPORATE TRANSFEREE, [ ] SERVICE SELLER, [ ] PROFESSIONAL, [ ] CONTRACTUAL SERVICE SUPPLIER, [ ] SPECIALIST
PLACE/S OF ASSIGNMENT _____
NAME AND ADDRESS OF EMPLOYER _____

E-MAIL ADDRESS_____ TEL _____
NATURE OF BUSINESS _____
TOTAL EMPLOYMENT (Exclude Foreign Nationals) _____ NUMBER OF FOREIGN NATIONALS _____

Have your application for AEP been previously denied? [ ] yes [ ] no   When? _____
Have your AEP been previously cancelled/revoked? [ ] yes [ ] no   When? _____
Please state reason for denial/cancellation/revocation: _____
_____
What actions have you taken? _____

_____   _____
SIGNATURE OF APPLICANT   DATE FILED

INDORSEMENT BY THE EMPLOYER:

_____   _____
NAME AND SIGNATURE OF COMPANY OFFICER   POSITION IN THE COMPANY

        SUBSCRIBED AND SWORN to before me this _____day of _____20____. Affiant exhibited his/her Passport No. _____ issued at_____
on_____20_____.

NOTARY PUBLIC

1

Here's a copy of an Alien Employment Permit, AEP, which can be downloaded at the Department of Labor Enforcement, DOLE, website. Check this **link** if you wish to download the form now.

More on Philippines 9G Visa and Work Permit (ACR)

Obtaining proper Philippines employment permits and working visas (9G) for you and your foreign employees is a must and should be done prior to commencing employment.

Philippines Working Visa (9G) & Permit Process

Any foreign national wishing to work in the Philippines must obtain a work visa (9G). A "9(g)" is a Philippine working visa for foreigners entering the Philippines to engage in a lawful occupation. In general, it must be shown that the services of the alien are indispensable to the management, operation, administration, or control of local or locally based firms. The companies must petition their employees to obtain this visa. If the duration of the assignment is less than six months, a Special Work Permit application may be submitted to the authorities. If the assignment is for more than six months, the assignee may apply either in the Philippines or via a Philippines Consulate.

An application for a separate Philippines Alien Employment Permit (ACR) is required as an accompaniment to the principal work visa application. This is not a travel document. It is issued by the Philippines Department of Labor and Employment.

A Special Return Certificate may be required as an accompaniment to the employee and dependent's applications. It is mandatory requirement for travel outside of the Philippines.

A Philippines Alien Certificate of Registration (ACR I-Card biometrics registration) may be required as an accompaniment to the employee and dependent's applications. This is a mandatory requirement for travel outside of the Philippines.

More on the Philippines Alien Employment Permit (AEP)

An Alien Employment Permit (AEP) is a document issued by the Department of Labor and Employment that allows a foreign national to work in the Philippines. This is normally applied in tandem with a 9(g) pre-arranged employment visa and applies to foreign nationals seeking employment in the Philippines, foreign professionals allowed to practice their profession in the Philippines, and Holders of SIRV, SRRV, Treaty trader visa 9(d), Special Non-immigrant Visa for executive, advisory, supervisory, or technical positions. An employee must be petitioned by his/her company and it must generally be shown that no person found in the Philippines is willing or competent to perform he service for which the foreign national is hired.

AEPs are valid for a period of one (1) year, unless the employment contract, consultancy services, or other modes of engagement or term of office for elective officers, provides for a longer period. Permits of resident foreign nationals shall be valid for multiple employers provided they report changes in their employment status and the identity of their employers to the DOLE Regional Office which issued the permit.

Philippines Provisional Permit to Work

In addition to the Alien Employment Permit foreign nationals must obtain a provisional permit to work pending the approval of the 9(g) visa. This permit is issued by the Bureau of Immigration and is normally valid for a period of 3 months from issuance. The Bureau of Immigration will not issue a 9(g) working visa unless and until the AEP from the DOLE is obtained. (Source: **Kittelson & Carpo Consulting**)

DETECTING EMPLOYMENT SCAMS

People are always looking for jobs. It could either be due to unemployment or a want for a better career. Job hunting will always be an ongoing activity.

Employment scams or commonly known as job scams have been prevalent lately. This usually involves a supposed employer offering an applicant an attractive opportunity which require money in advance. This opportunity usually is in another country and that the money collected will be for visa application and travel expenses. Once the victim has completed payment, the employer disappears and is never heard of again. The incidence of cases such as this has increased these last couple of years, mostly in the form of illegal recruiters. That is why people should be wary before pursuing any job offer. These warning signs and tips will definitely help you determine whether a job is a scam or not.

Research about the Company as well as the position offered. Do a background check of the company. You should be able to find information about them, compare if it is consistent with what the person you've met with said. If you haven't heard of the company before, make sure that you have reliable people you know who do. Consider it as a warning sign if they don't have a website and if you cannot find them on the Internet. Legitimate companies do not have anything to hide.

Doubt emails

Job scams usually spread faster because of the Internet. Money-making scams especially thrive through spam. You should be wary of spam emails that offer you jobs without properly giving information about their company. These industries would ask you for your personal bank account as part of "getting to know you". Be mindful of these kinds of hint. You should be able to know the difference between a legitimate job offer email and a spam.

Consult Scam Lists

Countless campaigns have been put up to stop scammers. On the Internet alone, you will be able to see lists of illegitimate companies and websites. If they have a hotline, you can call and ask some question. You can relay the nature of your problem and ask them for advise. Make sure to check these sites out for reference.

Be wary

If an offer sounds "too good to be true", chances are it is. There is no shortcut to success and if the employer is offering you a ridiculously high salary for a starting position, don't dive right away. Sometimes scammers take on subtle ways of deception. Read and re-read job offers carefully. Have someone you trust look through any document and listen to outside opinion before you sign anything. Lastly, always remember that the company will hire you, you don't have to pay them anything at all. (Source: **Trabaho Philippines**)

EXPAT JOB OPPORTUNITIES IN THE PHILIPPINES

First realize that as a foreigner, you might think you will be offered a better salary than what is offered to local Filipinos because English is your first language, especially for the majority of Americans. But if you expect that, you'll more than likely be disappointed. In certain fields that require a specialized degree, that could be true. But for the most part, my research on this topic indicated that your wages will be on par with your Filipino co-workers.

Let's take a look at jobs in the Philippines which offer employment opportunities for expats:

1. CALL CENTER AGENT/SUPERVISOR

The Philippines has surpassed India as the top call center destination in the world. The Philippines employs 400,000 in the industry against India's 350,000.

This trend doesn't owe a single bit to the rising salaries in India. In fact, a call center executive in Philippines is paid more than his counterpart in India. Then what gives? Accent and hospitality.

According to an article in the November 2011 issue of the **asian correspondent.com**, the Philippines has a **"unique combination of Eastern, attentive hospitality and attitude of care and compassion mixed with what I call Americanization,"** said Aparup Sengupta, CEO of Aegis Global.

For all the prowess acquired over the years, Indian English isn't American enough. And Americans are comfortable speaking to a Filipino because they are more Americanized than Indians.

So if Americans are more comfortable talking to Filipino's, it would stand to reason that they would be more at ease speaking to another American or English-speaking Westerner on the other end of the line also, right?

The call center phenomenon in the Philippines.

The call center phenomenon in the Philippines started in 2000 wherein it has been recorded that four contact centers started to do outsourcing business. After five years, potential investors started to outsource their business here until it continues to expand. The ability of the Filipinos to do better in customer service is a good advantage. Likewise,the Philippines geographic location which is the gateway to the other Asian nations maintain the interest the investors.

Today, the Philippines is the world's top player in offshore call center business together with China and India. Investors are likely to place more contact centers because of the lower cost of labor compared to the other Asian countries and better infrastructure including the state-of-the-art technology.

The Philippine call centers continue to caters clients from the US, United Kingdom and Australia. The hired customer service representatives are obliged to learn foreign accent (as an American or other Westerner, you've already got the edge) and study the geography and cultural mores of these foreign countries and work on a graveyard shift. Being the third largest English speaking country in the world and with a high literacy rate, the Philippines is considered as one of the most competitive call center destinations in the world.

When it comes to the benefits, call center workers enjoy the premium salary package. They are also entitled to receive benefits like SSS, Health Insurance and salary loans. Aside from these, they also enjoy commissions, night differential pay, bonuses and freebies from the company.

Working in a call center in the Philippines will not require an age limit, as long as the applicants can communicate English. The contact center companies also encourage fresh graduates from the universities and colleges to apply at them anytime. The successful candidates also learn the update of their application whether they pass or failed to make it on the list.

A call center in the Philippines continues to be acknowledged as the sunshine industry because of the massive developments brought to the country. Not only, Metro Manila specifically Tortillasis housing the famous contact centers. It also has expanded to the other provinces such as Baguio, Cebu, Iloilo, Bacolod, Davao, among others. Call centers in Philippines continue to gather support from the government. (Source: **http://www.uniqueinteraction.com/**)

Iloilo City, where I reside, recently emerged as one of the cities in the top 100 emerging locations from the six highly competitive Southeast Asian countries to accelerate in the Information Technology-Business Process Outsourcing (IT-BPO) industry.

Mayor Jed Patrick Mabilog said the city's current 2012 IT standing was ranked by India-based Tholons, an advisory, investment and research firm. Tholons is a leading full-service strategic advisory firm for global outsourcing and research that provides strategic actionable advice backed by solid location analysis and strategic growth and expansion services.

Iloilo is ranked number 92 in 2012, a significant increase from 98th in 2011. Other Philippine cities within the top 100 cities are Manila National Capital Region as fourth, Cebu in the ninth spot, Davao at number 69, and Sta. Rosa Laguna at number 86. (Source: **Sun Star Iloilo**)

Due to the BPO boom in the Philippines in the last few years, the country has attracted American and other foreign management talent to work in these industries. Call centers are either **inbound,** taking calls for customer service, online sales, requests for catalogs and information, etc., or **outbound,** usually in the telemarketing sales areas.

Outbound call center agents call businesses to solicit space in directories and set appointments for sales calls. Working in an outbound call center would not be for the faint of heart, but remember, this is a "Philippines Survival Guide." You've got to suck it up and do what you have to do to make it.

Foreigners are usually sought as language coaches and trainers. They may advance to team leaders and other second-level supervisory positions.

Average wages of call center employees in the Philippines.

Entry level Customer Support Agents	$300 USD
Experienced Customer Support Agents	$450-500 USD
Team Lead Agents	$550-700 USD
Project Manager or Assistant Manager	$900-1400 USD
Manager	$1500-2500 USD

BPO Wages

Entry Level BPO Staff	$200-250 USD
Experienced BPO	$350 USD
Team Lead Agents	$500-700 USD
Project Manager or Assistant Manager	$800-$1,200
Manager	$1,300-$2,500

(sources: **Kittelson & Carpo Consulting**)

CALL CENTER JOBS IN ILOILO

There are many call centers in Iloilo that are currently hiring. **TeleTech** is one of those establishments. TeleTech's salaries begin at P18,000 a month, or around 428 US Dollars, for an entry level customer support job.

Both my twin nieces applied for jobs at a call center in Iloilo, **SPI Global**, and told they had passed their initial interviews and would be called back. They haven't heard anything back from them. The starting pay scale for SPI is lower than TeleTech, P15,000 a month, about 357 USD. Could you survive on that in the Philippines? Yes, if you adopt a "native lifestyle."

TeleTech is one of the premier call center operations in the Philippines. Their center in Iloilo City is located in SM City. I've posted some jobs available with their company in the following section:

Customer Service Associates Ioilo, Western Visayas, Philippines

TeleTech is now hiring. Join our team of upbeat, friendly Customer Service Associates. If this describes you ... *Customer-service oriented, Outgoing &Kind, Passionate & Motivated...* then, **APPLY TODAY**!

Being a TeleTech Customer Service Associate can be an exciting, fast-paced career where you can go as far as your ambitions will take you. TeleTech is looking for people who LOVE making customers happy. We are a company filled with high energy people with a willingness to put the customer's needs first.

In this position, you'll be fielding questions from customers of Fortune 500 brands. You'll be assigned to an account and have full training on the product or service which you'll be assisting customers with. As a Customer Service Associate, you get to hear the satisfaction from your customer after you've been able to help them get the most out of their products or services.

Become a Member of the TeleTech Team. TeleTech has a 30-year history of hiring great people just like you! In fact, our team includes more than 40,000 employees in over 17 countries worldwide, handling approximately 3.5 million customer transactions daily. Its people just like YOU that make TeleTech a great place to work.

What we offer:
And here's the important stuff…TeleTech provides our associates with:

   ·Competitive salary + bonuses
   ·Advancement and Career Opportunities
   ·Tuition Reimbursement & Retirement Savings
   ·Employee Rewards and discounts

What we're looking for:
Motivation, Passion, Integrity. Those are just some of the attributes valued at TeleTech. Of course, there are some other requirements too. These include:

   ·at least 2 years in College or has finished 72 units
   ·6 months or more of customer service experience
   ·Competency using Microsoft Windows
   ·Exceptional Communication & Verbal skills
   ·Ability and desire to excel in a fast-paced work environment

For more information on the world of opportunity that awaits you at TeleTech visit our career website at http://www.TeleTechJobs.com.

Eligibility note: It is unlawful to employ a person who does not have permission to live and work in the Philippines. Unless the advert states otherwise, please ensure you have this permission before applying.

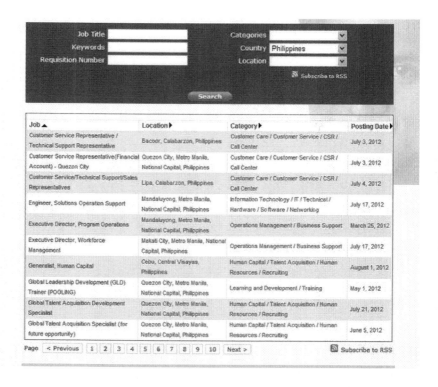

Job ▲	Location ▶	Category ▶	Posting Date ▶
Customer Service Representative / Technical Support Representative	Bacoor, Calabarzon, Philippines	Customer Care / Customer Service / CSR / Call Center	July 3, 2012
Customer Service Representative(Financial Account) - Quezon City	Quezon City, Metro Manila, National Capital, Philippines	Customer Care / Customer Service / CSR / Call Center	July 3, 2012
Customer Service/Technical Support/Sales Representatives	Lipa, Calabarzon, Philippines	Customer Care / Customer Service / CSR / Call Center	July 4, 2012
Engineer, Solutions Operation Support	Mandaluyong, Metro Manila, National Capital, Philippines	Information Technology / IT / Technical / Hardware / Software / Networking	July 17, 2012
Executive Director, Program Operations	Mandaluyong, Metro Manila, National Capital, Philippines	Operations Management / Business Support	March 25, 2012
Executive Director, Workforce Management	Makati City, Metro Manila, National Capital, Philippines	Operations Management / Business Support	July 17, 2012
Generalist, Human Capital	Cebu, Central Visayas, Philippines	Human Capital / Talent Acquisition / Human Resources / Recruiting	August 1, 2012
Global Leadership Development (GLD) Trainer (POOLING)	Quezon City, Metro Manila, National Capital, Philippines	Learning and Development / Training	May 1, 2012
Global Talent Acquisition Development Specialist	Quezon City, Metro Manila, National Capital, Philippines	Human Capital / Talent Acquisition / Human Resources / Recruiting	July 21, 2012
Global Talent Acquisition Specialist (for future opportunity)	Quezon City, Metro Manila, National Capital, Philippines	Human Capital / Talent Acquisition / Human Resources / Recruiting	June 5, 2012

Page < Previous 1 2 3 4 5 6 7 8 9 10 Next >   Subscribe to RSS

I have also found that **Convergys Philippines** is reportedly hiring foreigners. Here's their website link: http://convergysphilippines.com/

All of my research indicates that call center jobs offer some of the best job opportunities for foreigners. It makes sense that a company fielding questions and offering services to people in English-speaking countries such as the United States would need people fluent in English and understand the slang and culture that goes with that country.

Since I worked for AT&T for 30 years and for the last ten years of my employment I called different call centers all over the world, including the Philippines, I think I can offer some insight on this topic.

If you are *serious* about moving to the Philippines and finding a job, I honestly believe that a call center is an excellent place to start your job search. Many companies are even offering bonuses to join their call center staff. Business is booming! As an American or a foreigner from Canada, Australia, New Zealand or the U.K., you've got more than a fighting chance to land a job.

Listen, I hear a lot of negative chatter out there on the web about expats finding a job in the Philippines. And as I've said before, I was one of them. Not anymore. I *want* to see you succeed. I *want* you to able to join that loved one in the Philippines.

I want you to able to retire to your own little slice of "paradise" before you're old geezer like me. **YOU CAN DO IT!** The only person holding you back is....*YOU*. But the fact that you've purchased this eBook and plunked down your hard-earned cash, indicates to me that you're serious about moving here and you're *not* a quitter.

2. TEACHING ENGLISH

International ESL Jobs (English as a Second Language) teaching English to Korean and Japanese students provides some *excellent* job opportunities for foreigners living in the Philippines

ESL stands for English as Second Language. It refers to teaching English to a person whose native or primary language is one other than English. The ESL Program is a tourist activity in which the study of English as a Second Language forms part of a structured tour package.

In the Philippines, ESL schools continue to be one of the best places to learn English as far as the Korean student market is concerned. The Department of Tourism shared that over 100 thousand Koreans flew to the country last year for various English as a Second Language (ESL) programs and other study tours.

Philippines ESL programs from schools based in Baguio, Manila, Iloilo, Cagayan Valley and Cebu are currently the most popular.

These schools have become popular with Koreans and Japanese because of the small class size. As a native speaking English teacher your class size will usually be a maximum of 6 to 8 students. The ESL jobs industry in the Philippines has been growing rapidly recently. There is currently a *demand* for American teachers seeking Philippines jobs who are qualified and competent professionals.

The international ESL jobs at schools in the Philippines for Korean and Japanese students are good jobs for expats. The schools are heavily advertised in Korea and Japan, but not widely known to advertise any open positions for native English speaking ESL teachers. In Iloilo City where I live, there is a *large* contingent of Korean students and they've come to Iloilo primarily to learn English.

Many of the students *prefer* having an American or other Westerners teach them. I've turned down a job offer teaching English here at a private school. And I have no teaching degree.

You don't have to give formal lessons. Many of the students want to learn "conversational" English and slang. They may chat with you in the local McDonald's or a place of your choosing.

I met two Korean ladies while at Raymen Beach in Guimaras the other Sunday on an outing with my wife and our relatives. One was there for three months specifically to learn English. The other young lady was vacationing there. There was a large contingent of young Koreans on the beach. Again, there are *plenty* of opportunities in our area as this trip to the beach indicated.

Check out the Filipina from Iloilo and her ad below on "FindMyFavouriteTeacher.com." She's asking P100-P120 an hour. That's 2.38-2.85 per hour. As an American or foreigner from a Western country, you should be able to get at least P200 an hour, about 4.75 USD or more. Now when you consider my niece, April, who will be working at SM City will only be making around six US Dollars a day, 200 pesos an hour is a good wage in the Philippines.

Home   Our Service   Learning Tips   FAQ

Find private English language schools, courses, lessons & tuition in Iloilo City.

rae.l is a professional English teacher, tutor /or school in Iloilo City, Philippines!

JobStreet.com

Sign Up and Apply Now!

| Back to Search result | Add to "Favourite" | Email | | Report abuse |

Date of last access	23, July 2011
Nickname	rae.l
Gender	Female
Age	18
Current availability	Open
Country of residence	Philippines / Any / Iloilo City
Nationality/hometown	Philippines / Surigao City
Native language	Cebuano
Languages spoken	English,

Message to students!

I am Rae, currently a mass communications student in University. I have past experiences in English tutorials with Koreans of various ages. I also have Korean friends, and i enjoy being with them. I am also open to tutor people from different countries around the globe via skype. I am bubbly, fun to be with, and i enjoy learning and sharing what i have learned. I look forward to meet my future student soon. :)

Offering language lesson	English
Lesson fee / hour	Philippine peso 100-120
Trial lesson fee / hour	Philippine peso 80
Group lesson fee / hour / person Up to 5	Philippine peso 60
Possible teaching area	Iloilo City
Teaching place	Quiet café, Student's office
Type of lesson	General conversation, Vocabulary building, Pronunciation practice, Listening practice, Children's lessons, Lesson via SKYPE, Survival travel conversation
Teaching qualification	
Teaching experience (years)	Less than 1

Available days and time	AM	PM	Evening
Monday			✓
Tuesday			✓
Wednesday			✓
Thursday			✓
Friday			✓
Saturday	✓	○	✓
Sunday	✓	○	✓

This is an extremely viable employment opportunity for expats in Iloilo and other cities in the Philippines. I personally know American expats that are teaching English in private schools and online that are doing this.

As I said before, I was extremely skeptical of any foreigner coming to the Philippines and finding a job. It was easier for me to follow the prevailing negativism out there and agree that it was virtually impossible. I would keep harping on the fact that a person would need a guaranteed source of income like a pension to make it here. I was wrong.

DO YOU NEED A DEGREE?

It is possible to find a teaching job without a degree and/or a certificate. As I said before, the job opportunity I had in Iloilo through a contact, could have had me teaching English without any degree at all. However, some people will advise you to obtain a certificate of some kind (TEFL/TESOL) - simply because it will benefit both, you and the school/students. It will also aid you in your job search and possibly provide you with more pay. Courses can range anywhere from $150-$1500 USD, and be anywhere from a few days to 4 weeks or longer. Some of them can be taken online, locally or abroad. TEFL - Teaching English as a Foreign Language. TESL - Teaching English as a Second Language.

TEFL AND TESL COURSES

If you haven't made your move to the Philippines yet and are considering teaching English as a job, here's some information from a company that offers job searches for people looking to teach English in a foreign country. They also offer the necessary training for those jobs. I do not receive any compensation from this company if you sign up for their course.

I have to tell you that if you're your serious about moving to the Philippines and finding a job, I would recommend that you consider getting this training. For a small investment, such a training certificate could boost your job chances considerably.

Here's some tips from **www.online tefl.com:**

Make the decision. Be sure that this is the right thing for you. Teaching is amazingly rewarding, but not for the faint-hearted! Make the decision to go and set a date to make it happen!This may seem obvious but half-hearted attempts are doomed to failure, so make the decision and go for it! Decide where you want to go – different countries offer different salaries and experiences. Check out the TEFL jobs section at www.onlinetefl.com/tefl-jobs-abroad or chat to other TEFLers on Chalkboard (www.onlinetefl.com/teflchalkboard) to get an idea of where would suit you

Get some training. Boost your earning of 120 hours of TEFL training or more. Take your TEFL course with an internationally-recognized and accredited provider. Make sure you do a course that suits your plans. Request a consultation with a TEFL expert to get advice on the right course for you: www.onlinetefl.com/consultation. Don't make it up as you go along in the classroom. Your students deserve more than that. Don't just take any old course! Sadly there are a lot of cowboy course providers out there, so check your certificate will be worth the paper it's printed on before signing up.

Find your dream job. Consider a paid teaching internship (www.onlinetefl.com/teaching-overseas.) They're a great option if it's your first time teaching overseas, as you'll get full training, a reputable five month placement and 24/7 in-country support. Let your course provider do the leg-work for you. Many have free job-placement services or relationships with schools overseas. Make the most of these! Use your mouse. Job sites like www.tefl.com and www. eslemployment.com list vacancies from schools all over the world. It's also worth joining TEFL communities like TEFL Chalkboard (www.onlinetefl.com/tefl-chalkboard) and Dave's ESL Cafe (www.eslcafe.com) to network with other teachers. Take a look at our TEFL Jobs Board (www.onlinetefl.com/tefl-jobs-abroad/jobs-board). There are hundreds of jobs worldwide and we make sure that there are lots of opportunities for first time teachers like you. We check every listing and every school too, so you can rest assured that all jobs advertised are with reputable schools that won't rip you off!

Try looking for a job when you get there. Pavement-pounding and using the local English-language newspaper are both good places to start, but you will need guts, and a bit of a financial buffer in case your job hunt isn't initially successful! Check your school out thoroughly before you apply. There are lots of sharks out there who seem unable to pay on time and love to over-work their teachers! Keep your expectations realistic when applying from your home country. Many schools experience lots of no-shows from teachers, so they may offer the same position to many applicants just to be sure that one turns up at the beginning of term.

So there are opportunities for teaching English all throughout the Philippines. But if you are here on a tourist visa you are working illegally and you have no real rights for getting your money if your student would refuse to pay you. But some people have existed for years here on tourist visas while teaching English. I met an American at the local SM Hypermarket who has been living in Iloilo for over eight years with an expired visa. He teaches online via Skype. Where there's a will, there's a way, goes the old cliché. How do you get paid online? You could just open up a free PayPal account.

Here's a link to a complete online list of English schools in the Philippines.
(source: http://cebu-philippines.net)

3. FREELANCE CALL CENTER ADVISOR

I found this interesting article online about a guy that decided to take matters into his own hands and find his own job opportunities in the Philippines.

He emailed several call centers in the area and offered his services as an English advisor and monitor. For five hours per day, five days a week, he would monitor, manage and enhance their agents' English skills and set skills for 40-50,000 pesos per month salary. That's 950-1,190 US Dollars a month.

He had three replies straight away asking if he could come in the next day! He doesn't understand it when people say there are no opportunities in the Philippines. He said you need to stop thinking like a westerner.

He went on to remark that if your employer asks you for a visa, just tell him not to to worry about it, it's being taken care of. If you need to get one right away, and I agree that you should always keep your visa current, you will be able to find someone to expedite the situation for you without any problem.

4. KPO (KPO (Knowledge Process Outsourcing) Jobs

Gurus of KPO

Bill Pfluger
General Manager (fmr)
Chevron Shared Services
(Philippines, Argentina)

Erik Nielsen
Managing Director
Maersk Global Services
(Philippines, China)

Rosario Bradbury
Managing Director
SGS
(Philippines, Guam)

(photos from Asia CEO Forum)

KPO describes the outsourcing of core business activities, which often are competitively important or form an integral part of a company's value chain. Therefore KPO requires advanced analytical and technical skills as well as a high degree of proprietary domain expertise. Reasons behind KPO include an increase in specialized knowledge and expertise, additional value creation, the potential for cost reductions, and a shortage of skilled labor. (Source: **Wikipedia.**) KPO is the next outsourcing wave and it has arrived in the Philippines.

From the Sun Star Cebu: Professionals asked to stay in country, take advantage of growing KPO industry

PROFESSIONAL nurses, lawyers and accountants need not go abroad in search of high-paying jobs, an official said. They can stay in the country and maximize the business opportunities offered by the growing knowledge process outsourcing (KPO) industry, Cebu Chamber of Commerce and Industry (CCCI) BPO/IT committee chairman Jerry Rapes said.

He said professionals can find a variety of career and business opportunities with KPO, especially with "cloud computing."

Rapes said experienced professionals such as nurses, lawyers, radiologists, medical doctors and accountants can start a KPO business of their own by forming a group that offers expertise and provides various services via the cloud in the field of health services, finance, legal services, data management and human resources.

Demand for nurses

He said nurses, for instance, are in demand for KPO services because of the growing offshore services in the medical industry. He said this also offers alternative jobs for unemployed nurses.

"In this way, nurses need not leave the country and search for high-paying jobs but rather stay here and earn the same pay," he said.

While Cebu has started taking advantage of the opportunities provided by KPO, Rapes said professionals providing these services here are still "loosely-organized."

Unlike the usual outsourcing activities that involve concerns of customers, a KPO service deals with knowledge-based services or those that involve high-value work carried out by highly skilled staff.

The US is not only the lone market for KPO services, as the industry is maturing and the services have expanded to many other countries. India is currently the major hub for KPO activity but the Philippines is seen as an emerging KPO service location, according to international research firm Ovum in its report last November.

Ovum said that along with China and Sri Lanka, the Philippines is also becoming an increasingly important player in the KPO market.

Niche

"It (Philippines) has started to carve out a niche for itself in a number of key areas, including health care outsourcing (providing industry-specific services to hospitals and health care providers). This market is expected to grow significantly during the next few years, with a notable increase in demand coming from the US as a result of the recent reforms in health care regulations," it said.

Industry players, meanwhile, recognized KPO as another important industry that can protect the business process outsourcing (BPO) industry from the possible impact of the pending US bill on outsourcing.

"Moving up on a higher value chain where knowledge and skills are present will help preserve employment and sustain the BPO industry, particularly here in Cebu," said Cebu Educational Development Foundation for Information Technology (Cedf-it) chairman Francis Monera. (Source: **Sun Star Cebu**)

TOURISM INDUSTY

There are jobs for expats in the tourism industry such as chefs in major hotels. Many clubs and upscale restaurants in the Philippines are looking for **Bar and restaurant managers** with salaries around 500-600 US Dollars a month.

My research indicates that Angeles City is a good place to look for such jobs. Just walk down Fields Avenue and enter any club and you will find foreigner bar managers. But that lifestyle would probably too hectic for many. However, if you're looking for some adventure, this might be the job for you.

6. SALES. Foreigners Can Also Apply.

While doing research for this eBook I was constantly running across **"Yats Leisure"** as a company that was looking for great salespeople. They welcome foreigners to apply for the sales positions. Here's what what one website had to say about employment at Yats:

"Some people are born to be in sales while others struggle to sell even the best products in the world. Sales is not a career for everyone and not everyone is for this job. It is a challenging and demand job, one that is fraught with frustrations and rejections, stressful even for the strong willed and sturdy heads. However for the few who are born to be in sales, this is the only job that will make them happy, accommodates the urge to succeed and the only way to satisfy the killer instinct of a natural-born marketer.

Yats Leisure is inviting natural-born sales persons, male, female, young and matured to apply for a position in sales that can only be filled successfully by true professionals. Those who are not sure about their destiny of being a professional sales person need not waste time to apply.

Yats Leisure sells rental of rooms and outdoor event venues in its 13-hectare Clearwater Resort in Clark Pampanga.http://www.ClearwaterPhilippines.com

Its wine division – Yats Wine Cellars – is generally regarded as one of the leading suppliers of fine vintage wines in Asia. (http://www.YatsWineCellars.com)

Yats Restaurant and Wine Bar is one of the top-dated fine dining restaurants in the Philippines, also located inside Clark Freeport, at Mimosa Leisure Estate. (http://www.YatsRestaurant.com)

These are products and services that our professional sales person will market to a suitable audience in Manila and Pampanga.

Applicants should have at least three years working experience in sales with a successful track record. Those who have been working in banquet and event sales for hotels, resorts, catering and restaurants will find it very easy to make the transition. Others who have experience dealing with corporate clients either in travel agencies or event management companies will also adopt quite easily.

Required in this line of work is a high degree of discipline. An average work day starts at 8am. The first two hours will be spent on catching up on paperwork, sending out quotations and proposals, answering questions of clients as well as dealing with operations to finalize points for a project. At the same time, re-confirmation for the day's appointments should be done. From 10am to 4pm is the prime time for client visits and a minimum of five appointments are expected to be completed each day. Upon returning to the office, the rush is on to complete the paperwork required to address the concerns and accommodate the requirements of clients, while confirming appointments for the next day.

A good command of the English language is essential. Successful candidates are expected to have the natural ability to establish rapport with clients, be articulate over the phone and in person about the virtues and features of our products and services. But most importantly, a good sales person is always a great listener, able to read between the line and grasp the key issues that make or break a deal.

Before you apply, learn as much as you can about our products and services. Interested candidates should first visit the web site http://www.YatsLeisure.com to familiarize themselves with the operations of Yats International and download resume templates through the site by clicking on About Yats and then click on Download Resumes. You can then email the completed resume to Jobs@Yats-International.com

Interviews will be conducted in Manila Office at 3003C East Tower, Philippines Stock Exchange Center,Exchange Road, Ortigas Center, Metro Manila, Philippines 1605 (632) 633-1566 0917-520-4393 Chay Tanglao or Rea Didioco.

Facebook http://www.facebook.com/#!/yats.wine

Here's another job opening for a sales person that was posted on the **learn 4 good** website:

7. U.S. EMBASSY JOBS

The United States Embassy in Manila is one of America's largest overseas posts, housing 27 agencies staffed by both Americans and Filipino national employees. The U.S. Mission in Manila provides equal opportunity and fair and equitable treatment in employment to all people without regard to race, color, religion, sex, national origin, age, disability, political affiliation, marital status, or sexual orientation. The Department of State also strives to achieve equal employment opportunity in all personnel operations through continuing diversity enhancement programs.

The U.S. Embassy Manila is currently hiring for the following positions. Please click on the link to learn more about the specific opening. If there are no job vacancies, please check back at a later date.

Here's one of the job openings that was available at the US Embassy in the Philippines at the time this eBook was published:

VACANCY ANNOUNCEMENT

AMERICAN EMBASSY
MANILA

ANNOUNCEMENT NUMBER: 2012-095
OPEN TO: All Interested Candidates / All Sources
POSITION: Cultural Affairs Specialist, LES-10, FP-5
(This position is budgeted for the Local Compensation Plan)
OPENING DATE: August 3, 2012
CLOSING DATE: August 17, 2012
WORK HOURS: Full-time; 40 hours/week
SALARY: P 708,111 per annum (Starting salary)
NOTE: ALL ORDINARILY RESIDENT (OR) APPLICANTS (See
Appendix A)
MUST HAVE THE REQUIRED WORK AND/OR RESIDENCY PERMITS
TO BE
ELIGIBLE FOR CONSIDERATION.
The U.S. Embassy in Manila is seeking an individual for the position of
Cultural Affairs Specialist in the Public Affairs Section (PAS).
BASIC FUNCTION OF THE POSITION
Advises public diplomacy officers, the Office of the Chief of the Mission,
and other Mission officers on all aspects of Public Affairs Section arts, sports,
and speaker programs, as well as trends and influences in Philippine arts,
culture, and society. Maintains direct liaison with Public Affairs target
audiences, including top-level contacts, for the purpose of determining
programming needs and opportunities. Serves as a major source of
nominations for the International Visitor Program and jointly supervises and
delegates tasks to Cultural Affairs Assistants. Identifies issues to be
addressed, appropriate target audiences and institutional partners, and
organizes all aspects of U.S. Speakers and Embassy Speakers Bureau visit
and program events and produces evaluation reports and recommendations
for follow up. Recommends influential Filipinos and organizations for
inclusion in Embassy-sponsored lectures, seminars and receptions. Liaises

daily with a wide range of Mission staff.

ANNOUNCEMENT NUMBER: 2012-090
OPEN TO: All Interested Candidates / All Sources
POSITION: Administrative Clerk (BBG/IBB/PTS), LES-6; FP-8
(This position is budgeted for the Local Compensation Plan)
OPENING DATE: July 25, 2012
CLOSING DATE: August 8, 2012
WORK HOURS: Full-time; 40 hours/week
SALARY: P 340,278 per annum (Starting salary)
NOTE: ALL ORDINARILY RESIDENT (OR) APPLICANTS (See Appendix A)
MUST HAVE THE REQUIRED WORK AND/OR RESIDENCY PERMITS TO BE
ELIGIBLE FOR CONSIDERATION.

The U.S. Embassy in Manila is seeking an individual for the position of Administrative Clerk at the International Broadcasting Bureau, Philippines Transmitting Station (IBB/PTS) located near Barangay Tinang, Concepcion, in Tarlac Province. BASIC FUNCTION OF THE POSITION Prepares travel authorizations for local and overseas travel of Station personnel and visitors. Reviews travel claims and supporting documents submitted by Station personnel for accuracy, completeness, and compliance with travel regulations and policies. Drafts for approval and submission through official channels all travel messages of arriving/departing American personnel and eligible family members, including request for education travel authorizations, direct transfer, home leave transfer, home leave and return. Maintains and updates accurate personnel records of Station's American Officers and LES official personnel folders. Drafts routine message for incoming American Officers and prepares check-in sheets. Check accuracy of all incoming personnel actions prepared by the Embassy Human Resources Office.

ANNOUNCEMENT NUMBER: 2012-091

OPEN TO: All Interested Candidates / All Sources

POSITION: Radio Technician (Trainee Level 2), LES-5; FP-9

(This position is budgeted for the Local Compensation Plan)

OPENING DATE: July 26, 2012

CLOSING DATE: August 9, 2012

WORK HOURS: Full-time; 40 hours/week

SALARY: P 307,673 per annum (Starting salary)

NOTE: ALL ORDINARILY RESIDENT (OR) APPLICANTS (See Appendix A)

MUST HAVE THE REQUIRED WORK AND/OR RESIDENCY PERMITS TO BE

ELIGIBLE FOR CONSIDERATION.

The U.S. Embassy in Manila is seeking an individual for the position of Radio Technician (Trainee Level 2) in the International Broadcasting Bureau, Philippines Transmitting Station (IBB/PTS) in Tarlac.

BASIC FUNCTION OF THE POSITION

Operates and maintains high powered shortwave radio broadcast transmitters and associated equpment. Tunes, operates, maintains and tests very high powered radio broadcast transmitters and all associated equipment in the program chain including very high power antenna switching systems. Monitors transmitter system operating parameters, logs meter readings, monitors program output for quality, reports abnormalities and corrects malfunctions. Performs duties in the Master Control Room. Adjusts program levels and modulation control, monitors satellite program for proper content and report discrepancies.

My asawa, far left, partying with the Peace Corps in Guimaras

8. THE PEACE CORPS

Remember, think "outside the box." While a regular full-time Peace Corps Volunteer cannot *choose* the country they want to be assigned to (they can request, however, the country they would *like* to volunteer in), short term vacancies are available in the Philippines. Here's three jobs that were open at the time of the publication of this eBook. Check this **website** for further updates.

Job details

| Apply to Peace Corps Response position | Send to friend | Save to cart | View similar jobs |

Title	Information Systems Analyst (Philippines)
Country	Philippines
Who May Apply	Open to All
Projected Start Date	01-Jan-2013
Duration (months)	6
Language Qualifications	English
Program Area	Information Technology
Partner	Ugat ng Klausugan, Inc.
Description	A Peace Corps Response Volunteer is needed to serve as an Information Systems Analyst for Ugat ng Klausugan, Inc. (Roots of Health). UNK's mission is to empower women and girls of the Philippines to secure their rights to health and freedom from violence. They believe that health is a human right that is best preserved using community-based approaches. UNK has been collecting data from the community since their services began over two years ago. There are large amounts of data regarding unmet contraception needs, number of family planning receptors, weights of infants and children, and basic socio-demographic indicators. Currently, the organization lacks the capacity to access the data easily and analyze what the data represents.

The Information Systems Analyst will enhance the work of UNK by creating an appropriate data management system for the organization to refine its programs. The Peace Corps Response Volunteer will also design a survey questionnaire on health and socio-economic information to use with its clients in the community. The Response Volunteer will review and assess UNK's existing data banking system and conduct consultation meetings with UNK staff. He or she will establish a computer generated system for health information data management and specifically design a survey questionnaire to allow for optimal data collection. Finally, he or she will train counterparts in how to utilize the data management system. |
| **Academic Qualifications** | Bachelor's Degree |
| **Mandatory Qualifications** | Degree in computer science, engineering, or another IT-related field
Two years' background experience in research and survey designs of health systems
Two years' experience in data management systems and data collection, preferably on health information |
| **Desired** | Tagalog language skills helpful |

Qualifications

Title	9.Web/XML Applications Developer (Philippines)
Country	10.Philippines
Who May Apply	11.Open to All
Projected Start Date	12.01-Jan-2013
Duration (months)	13.6
Language Qualifications	14.English
Program Area	15.Information Technology
Partner	16.Department of Social Welfare and Development (DSWD)
Description	17.A Peace Corps Response Volunteer is needed to serve as a Web/XML Applications Developer for the Department of Social Welfare and Development (DSWD). The World Bank has deemed the Philippines to be one of the most hazard-prone countries in the world. Disasters have destroyed human, social, and physical capital and derailed social and economic development. The need to assess the value of the department's work in disaster risk reduction and management is an emerging priority. There is a continuing need to analyze the timing, relevance, efficiency, and effectiveness of services and interventions. Providing accurate and timely data to the public is of foremost concern and requires a strong database and information management system.

18.A PCRV skilled in web development and disaster management will assist DSWD to strengthen the internal and external coordination and information management through its Disaster Risk Reduction and Management Information System. The Web/XML Applications Developer will review the Disaster Management Computerized Information System (DMCIS) design documentation to determine which customer data service components to develop. The Response Volunteer will then analyze the current disaster management information systems business process flows. He or she will also develop the code for a department-wide re-engineering pilot system based on the DMCIS design. Finally, the Volunteer will perform operational readiness testing of the pilot system in certain functional and geographic areas of the Philippines.

Academic Qualifications	19.Bachelor's Degree
Mandatory Qualifications	20.Five years of extensive experience in ICT web services enterprise applications development and implementation
	21.Proficiency in customer data service components in at least one of the following – POJO, Spring Bean, Java Bean, or HTTP/XML applications – for use with the mule ESB and LAMP-based Free and Open Software Source (FOSS)

22. Basic knowledge of ICT implementation in disaster risk reduction and management (e.g., Geographic Information Systems (GIS), SAHANA Disaster Management System, etc.)

Title	24. Occupational Therapy Specialist (Philippines)
Country	25. Philippines
Who May Apply	26. Open to All
Projected Start Date	27. 01-Jan-2013
Duration (months)	28. 6
Language Qualifications	29. English
Program Area	30. NGO Development
Partner	31. Norfil Foundation, Inc.
Description	32. A Peace Corps Response Volunteer is needed to serve as an Occupational Therapy Specialist for Norfil Foundation, Inc.—a local nongovernmental organization specializing in the care and rehabilitation of disabled, neglected, and abandoned children through community and family-based programs. Norfil uses a community-based rehabilitation strategy for rehabilitation, equalization of opportunities, poverty reduction, and social inclusion of children and youth with disabilities. For the past few years, the foundation has been successful in training parents, community volunteers, and public school teachers on special education and integration of children with disabilities into regular schools. However, the foundation needs to improve in the areas of physical and occupational therapy. Specifically, Norfil needs a technical consultant to provide intensive training to community volunteers on different therapeutic strategies for improving the fine and gross motor skills of children with mobility challenges. The foundation also sees a need to train young adults on vocational rehabilitation for livelihood opportunities and employment. 33. A PCRV skilled in physical or occupational therapy will develop a training manual for staff, community volunteers, and parents that will equip them to: (1) assist children and youth with motor problems to maximize their abilities and become more independent; (2) promote the prevention of secondary complications as a result of physical disabilities; and (3) ensure that children and youth with motor problems have access to and equal opportunities for education, employment, and other activities of mainstream society. In addition to developing the training manual, the Occupational Therapy Specialist will provide training to caregivers and

demonstrate techniques and strategies for handling children with motor problems and delays. The PCRV will develop a checklist to be used by staff and volunteers for monitoring parents in the implementation of a home program for children with motor problems. The Volunteer will also assist Norfil in establishing linkages with other organizations serving children with motor problems and delays. As time permits, the PCRV will design and implement training on vocational rehabilitation and employment for young adults with disabilities.

34.Academic Qualifications	35.Bachelor's Degree
36.Mandatory Qualifications	37.Degree in physical or occupational therapy 38.At least two years of experience working with community-based rehabilitation programs 39.Broad experience in handling motor dysfunction and motor delay in children with disabilities 40.At least two years of experience working in vocational and sheltered workshops for persons with disabilities

9. CREATE YOUR OWN ONLINE JOB

Instead of a traditional Philippines job, why not try a job online? In today's world of high speed DSL internet access a lot of jobs are being created using the instant communication features of the internet. That's what I did three years ago after moving to the Philippines.

It was a challenge just getting my broad ban connection set up from Smart Bro. Our home in Guimaras sits quite lower than the main road. A nearby business not far from us, Albert's Motorcycle Shop (now there's a smart businessman; 86% of all registered vehicles in our rural province are motorbikes) sat on the main road and was able to get his signal from the tower with just the standard rooftop antenna.

But when Moises, the tech from Smart Bro came out to our residence he said we would require a 50 foot tower at a cost of 18,000 pesos, 428 US Dollars. At the time, I didn't care. We had only been here a month and I was going crazy from boredom. Plus, I had a magicJack phone that I needed to hook-up to a high speed internet connection to call my Dad back in Vegas. It was too expensive to buy a phone card for my cell phone which burned up international calls in just a few minutes.

My relatives at our home, including my wife, felt I was getting ripped off. A contractor that had our new CR, Comfort Room, built and put on a new roof for us, informed me he could have done it for P10,000. But I had already given Moises half the money down as a deposit and since he was the one that was going to be hooking up the internet service, I stayed with him. In the Philippines, as is the case in America, someone will always tell you they know somebody that could have done it cheaper. Cheaper doesn't always mean better.

Two weeks later the antenna went up. You can see the base of the tower in the picture above located right in front of our front porch. I was told it was the highest tower in Guimaras at that time.

Starting your online business

I had worked with a personal computer at home and on my job with AT&T as a Marketing Support Specialist. I was by no means a "computer geek," but after one boring afternoon of playing another round of "Final Fantasy" on my Playstation 2, an epiphany struck me. Why not blog? But how in the world do I do that and what in the world is a "blog" in the first place?

Darren Rose, from **ProBlogger**, one of the most successful bloggers in the world, describes his definition of a "blog": "**To put it as simply as possible –a blog is a type of website that is usually arranged in chronological order from the most recent 'post' (or entry) at the top of the main page to the older entries towards the bottom.**"

Darren goes on to state that "Blogs are usually (but not always) written by one person and are updated pretty regularly. Blogs are often (but not always) written on a particular topic – there are blogs on virtually any topic you can think of. From photography, to spirituality, to recipes, to personal diaries to hobbies – blogging has as many applications and varieties as you can imagine. Whole blog communities have sprung up around some of these topics putting people into contact with each other in relationships where they can learn, share ideas, make friends with and even do business with people with similar interests from around the world."

Darren Rose is one of the masters in the business. Check out **ProBlogger** for more tips on starting your own website or blog.

Creating a job and building an income online *can* be done. It requires effort, some time, and a learning curve, but what job doesn't? I would highly recommend writing about something you are passionate about.

Google Search is your best friend

I'm working on a new eBook that will go into great detail on how to start your own website and how to make money from it. Almost 90% of those that start a blog or website do not succeed in making any money from their online ventures. It takes time and a lot of work. I've found most of the solutions to any questions I had about starting, maintaining and making money with a website by using Google.

How much can you make with a website?

From zero to millions. It's all up to you. Some of the "big dogs" easily make over 100 grand a year and more. And I'm not talking about pesos. I'm approaching my goal of 1,000 US Dollars a month. I have a supplemental income, my retirement IRA, that provides me with a guaranteed source of income. I would not recommend coming to the Philippines hoping to make your money living off the internet unless you've had some prior experience. But you can do it. And yes, there are plenty of guys making a living in the Philippines off the web. No reason you can't be one of them. But it takes work. Lots of it.

10. JOBS ON CRAIGSLIST

Craigslist offers many opportunities for those expats seeking a job in the Philppines. Here's a list of available jobs I copied from their website offering employment in Iloilo, where we live.

jobs

accounting+finance
admin / office
arch / engineering
art / media / design
biotech / science
business / mgmt
customer service
education
food / bev / hosp
general labor
government
human resources
internet engineers
legal / paralegal
manufacturing
marketing / pr / ad
medical / health
nonprofit sector
real estate
retail / wholesale

sales / biz dev
salon / spa / fitness
security
skilled trade / craft
software / qa / dba
systems / network
technical support
transport
tv / film / video
web / info design
writing / editing

Here's one of those job postings:

Talkfriend Inc. is an on-line English institution providing online programs to students in KOREA. We are looking for passionate and dedicated teachers with experience in the PHILIPPINES. The lesson plans and teaching materials will be provided.

Starting Date: August
Working Hours:
Full-time: Mon-Fri 4pm -11pm(KST)
Part-time: Flexible hours
Types of Students: Elementary to Adults
Compensation: Up To 20K (PHP) / Month
Benefits: 7 Days Paid Vacation + Bonus

Requirements:
Bachelor's / College degree
English (with very mild accent or no accent)
At least one year(s) of teaching experience

Please email us with following documents and information:

Resume // Photo(passport photo) // recording sample (2-3 mins of self-introduction)

11. MEDIA RELATED JOBS

My American expat friend in Guimaras, Tom, has an online graphic design business he operates. You can start them up in your home country, like Tom, did and continue to pursue your business in the Philippines. All you need is a computer or Internet cafe. Tom doesn't have an internet connection at this location so he brings his laptop computer over to a local hotel lobby and uses their free WI-fi connection. Here are some media related jobs available that you can do from home.

Online publications
Proofreading
Magazines
Desktop publishing
Resume writing
Web and graphic
Photography

12. ACE COACH

If you have a Bachelor's degree in English you could find work at a call center as an ACE (Accent and Conversational English) coach. The salary of an ACE coach is bigger than that of an average call center agent. An ACE coach can earn 20,000 - 40,000 pesos (475-950 US Dollars a month.)

The ACE coach teaches and trains and monitors the agents with their English skills: grammar, conversational skills, accent reduction and neutralization, etc. The ACE coach also evaluates agents and do coaching to help agents who are having difficulties with their speaking skills. An ACE coach has the opportunity to get promoted to supervisor of the ACE department.An ACE coach can also work with the Quality Services department (Quality Assurance Specialist) which is considered to be a supervisory position. A Quality Assurance Specialist evaluates agents, does coaching as well, monitor agents' calls and ensures that the agents are following the protocol in handling customers. Salary is around 15,000-25,000 pesos per month.

BEST PLACES TO LIVE IN THE PHILIPPINES ON A BUDGET

Most expats will tell you that if you don't have a specific location in mind when moving to the Philippines, check out several places. Live in them for a few months until you get the feel of the place and see how you like it.

My number one rule for any expat moving here is not to live too close to your asawa's or girlfriend's relatives. You're more likely to get frequent visits from cousins and other long lost relatives your wife hasn't seen in decades looking for "loans." Take my advice and the advice of other expats out there. Live at least three hours away from the relatives. You'll find you'll have more pesos in your pockets at the end of the month.

It *is* cheaper to live in the Philippines for the most part, but no one can tell you the cost of living for your situation. We all have different needs and comfort levels.

We all have different lifestyles. If you're a person that needs the most western amenities you will not nearly save as much as those that can adapt, or survive, in the culture. Some guys are happy on $500 a month. Others can't make it on $3,000 a month, a king's ransom here.

That said, here's a list of places in the Philippines that I think might be some of the best places to live on a budget. I'm not ranking which is the best, because, of course, that's subject to a person's own interpretation. Of course there are thousands of other choices that could be made, but this is just a sampling of possible options. You will generally find it is cheaper to live in the provinces or rural areas rather than the Metro Manila area. I personally love living in Iloilo City, our present home, and will be covering Iloilo on this list.

Olango Island

Cabilao Island / Olango Island Philippines

Jan. 18, 2012, **Olango Island, Philippines**, qualifies as one of the cheapest places in the world to retire overseas in 2012.

Dear Live and Invest Overseas Reader,

"As I young adult," writes Philippines Correspondent Victoria Clair, "I often dreamed of the kind of place where I would like to live...and it never involved snow storms. I dreamed of a tropical paradise where the sun was almost always shining, it never got cold, and I could swim in the ocean whenever I liked. I dreamed of breakfasting on tropical fruits and of sipping mango lassies while feasting on curry at a beach side restaurant.

"Now these dreams have come true. I live on Olango Island in the Philippines.

"Olango Island lies 5 kilometers east of Mactan Island, between the islands of Cebu and Bohol. Olango and its neighboring islets have a total land mass area of approximately 10 square kilometers (about 4 square miles). It's a tiny tropical dream offering much to explore in the way of natural delights, from sandy beaches and rocky shorelines to beds of sea grass, forests of mangrove, and reefs of coral.

"I've lived in the Philippines for three years now, mostly in Cebu. I moved to Olango just five months ago. Olango, along with neighboring Mactan Island, is officially part of Cebu. Mactan can be reached from Cebu either by a bridge or by ferry, but to get to Olango you take a 20-minute boat ride across the sea channel.

"The Philippine Islands lie about 800 kilometers (500 miles) off the southeast coast of China, to the northeast of Borneo. More than 7,000 islands, originating from volcanic activity, form the island nation, yet the total land mass is about the same as that of the state of Arizona. Only about 7% of the islands are larger than 1 square mile, and only one-third of them have names. They form three main groups: Luzon, Visayas, and Mindanao.

"Manila, the capital of the Philippines, is the largest city, with a population of more than 10 million in the greater metro area and 1.5 million in the city proper. Cebu, the Philippines' second-largest city, has nearly 1 million residents. As of 2010, the country's total estimated population was just under 100 million.

"This is the tropics, meaning the weather is hot and humid. Cebu, Mactan, and Olango are protected by outlying islands from the fierce typhoon winds that beat on the island of Luzon most years. The rainy season runs from October through December, but it typically rains only an hour or less every day. Otherwise, the sun shines.

"Manila and Cebu draw good numbers of foreign retirees from all over the world but mostly from the United States, England, and Australia, and a few from Germany. Most all are men, from their mid-40s to their mid-60s, either retired and/or are disabled veterans. There are few retired foreign women living in the Philippines; to my knowledge, I am the only one in the Cebu region.

"Most of the single male expats come for two reasons. First, their income stretches much further here, meaning they can enjoy a more comfortable life in the Philippines than they would be able to afford in their home countries.

Second, many come to restart their lives with younger Filipinas, perhaps starting second families.

"Again, though, the biggest appeal for this part of the world is the cost of living. It can be extremely, extremely low, as little as about US$600 a month on Olango.

"Of course, you can spend more, and housing costs vary greatly. New high-rise apartments going up in Cebu designed to appeal to Westerners offer all the amenities a foreigner might expect...and come with higher price tags than the 'local' housing options. These one- to three-bedroom apartments, with separate quarters for live-in help, can cost from US$800 to US$1,500 a month.

"Or you could rent a three-bedroom, three-bathroom condo for anywhere from US$250 to US$500 a month. A 'lower-end' apartment like this will not be in the heart of the business district of Cebu and likely will not have hot water. But that's easily overcome with an investment of about US$160 in a water heater.

"Rent on Olango is considerably less expensive than in Cebu or Mactan. My apartment costs just under US$100 a month, and I pay about US$20 a month for electricity.

"Yes, there are drawbacks to living on a tiny island like Olango. Yes, my life is very simple. But I feel blessed, and, all things considered, I love my life here. It is quiet and smog-free. I live right on a lovely, private, sandy beach with yellow, pink, white, and red wildflowers growing everywhere.

"Except for those days when I need to take the boat over to Mactan or Cebu for errands or for visiting with friends over lunch, my days are free and unstructured. Olango Island is my base of tranquility, from which I explore. Here I have time, and the opportunity, to be still for a while and let my dreams come to the surface. It could work for you, too..." (source: **"Live and Invest Overseas"**)

Tagum City

photo source: en.wikipedia.org

I saw a testimonial from a foreigner that has been living in **Tagum City** for a year now. This expat loves the place. Says it's a beautiful city with plenty of things to do. Traffic isn't nearly as bad as compared to the larger nearby city of Davao and it's a very safe place as well. The expat reports that you can live comfortably in Tagum for around 700 US Dollars a month. One of the readers of my website also lives in Tagum City and raves about it, stating that it is the best place in the Philippines to live.

Tagum City, from being a predominantly agricultural area, has become Mindanao's fastest-rising urban city due to its strategic location, being in the crossroads between the rural areas of Davao del Norte and Compostela Valley and the urban Metro Davao. Blessed with a developed infrastructure, the city manages to export goods like wood chips, veneer plywood, and wood lumber. Fresh bananas, however, remain as the chief export product.

Thanks to the influx of people from the countryside of Davao del Norte and Compostela Valley the rise of human resources has helped a lot in the revenue generation of the City.

Tourism has also become of the city's main economic powerhouse lately. With fifteen festivals in the city's calendar, small and medium entrepreneurs, or SMEs, and the transportation sector have benefited with the rapid influx of domestic and international visitors visiting the various. (Source: **Wikipedia.**)

Dumaguete

Photo Source: en.wikipedia.org

The **City of Dumaguete** is a city in the Philippine province of Negros Oriental. It is the capital, principal seaport, and largest city of the province. According to the 2010 census, it has a population of 120,883 people. A person from Dumaguete is called a "Dumagueteño." The city is nicknamed *The City of Gentle People*.

Dumaguete is referred to as a university town because of the presence of four universities and a number of other colleges where students of the province converge to enroll for tertiary education. The city is also a popular educational destination for students of surrounding provinces and cities in Visayas and Mindanao. The city is best known for Silliman University, the country's first Protestant university and the first American private university in Asia. There are also 12 elementary schools and 9 high schools. The city's student population is estimated at 30,000.

The city attracts a considerable number of foreign tourists, particularly Europeans, because of easy ferry access from Cebu City, the availability of beach resorts and dive sites, and the attraction of dolphins and whale watching in nearby Bais City (Source: **Wikipedia**)

Restaurants	Avg.
Meal, Inexpensive Restaurant	1.89 $
Meal for 2, Mid-range Restaurant, Three-course	7.61 $
Combo Meal at McDonalds or Similar	3.12 $
Domestic Beer (0.5 liter draught)	0.73 $
Imported Beer (0.33 liter bottle)	1.21 $
Cappuccino (regular)	0.82 $
Coke/Pepsi (0.33 liter bottle)	0.39 $
Water (0.33 liter bottle)	0.28 $

Transportation	Avg.
One-way Ticket (local transport)	0.16 $
Taxi Start (Normal Tariff)	0.63 $
Taxi 1hour Waiting (Normal Tariff)	2.84 $
Gasoline (1 liter)	1.34 $

Utilities (Monthly)	Avg.
Basic (Electricity, Gas, Water, Garbage) for 85m2 Apartment	62.72 $
1 min. of Prepaid Mobile Tariff Local (No Discounts or Plans)	0.04 $
Internet (6 Mbps, Unlimited Data, Cable/ADSL)	47.51 $

Rent Per Month	Avg.
Apartment (1 bedroom) in City Centre	216.01 $
Apartment (1 bedroom) Outside of Centre	162.79 $
Apartment (3 bedrooms) in City Centre	358.52 $
Apartment (3 bedrooms) Outside of Centre	302.51 $

Here's a breakdown of some cost of living expenses in Dumaguete.

(Source: **NUMBEO**)

CEBU CITY

Photo Source: trekearth.com

The City of Cebu is the capital city of Cebu and is the "second city" in the Philippines with the second most significant metropolitan center and known as the oldest settlement established by the Spaniards in the country.

The city is located on the eastern shore of Cebu and was the first Spanish settlement in the Philippines. Cebu is the Philippines' main domestic shipping port and is home to about 80% of the country's domestic shipping companies. Cebu also holds the second largest international flights in the Philippines and is a significant center of commerce, trade and industry in the Visayas and Mindanao regions.

Cebu City is the center of a metropolitan area called Metro Cebu, which includes the cities of Carcar, Danao, Lapu-lapu, Mandaue, Naga, Talisay.

Metro Cebu has a total population of about 2 million people. The Mactan-Cebu International Airport, located in Lapu-Lapu City is only a twenty-minute drive away from Cebu City. To the northeast of the city are Mandaue City and the town of Consolacion, to the west are Toledo City, the towns of Balamban and Asturias, to the south are Talisay City and the town of Minglanilla. Across Mactan Strait to the east is Mactan Island where Lapu-Lapu City and an aquarium attraction are located.

I visited Cebu City, "The Queen City of the South," two years ago on business. Easy to get around, friendly people. Did some shopping at the SM City Cebu. Saw a lot of foreigner there with much younger Filipina asawas or girlfriends. The taxi cab drivers did not go off meter and I didn't have any problems on the jeepneys I traveled on.

Photo Source: kontikidivers.com

Extremely nice folks at the airport. I would recommend anyone thinking of living in the Philippines to certainly check out the Cebu area.

Here's a breakdown of some cost of living expenses in Cebu City.(Source: **NUMBEO**)

Restaurants

	Avg.
Meal, Inexpensive Restaurant	3.74 $
Meal for 2, Mid-range Restaurant, Three-course	12.44 $
Combo Meal at McDonalds or Similar	2.92 $
Domestic Beer (0.5 liter draught)	0.94 $
Imported Beer (0.33 liter bottle)	2.36 $
Cappuccino (regular)	2.11 $
Coke/Pepsi (0.33 liter bottle)	0.51 $
Water (0.33 liter bottle)	0.37 $

Transportation

	Avg.
One-way Ticket (local transport)	0.21 $
Monthly Pass (Regular Price)	14.98 $
Taxi Start (Normal Tariff)	0.94 $
Taxi 1km (Normal Tariff)	0.37 $
Taxi 1hour Waiting (Normal Tariff)	3.07 $
Gasoline (1 liter)	1.26 $
Volkswagen Golf 1.4 90 KW Trendline (Or Equivalent New Car)	27,440.91 $

Utilities (Monthly)

	Avg.
Basic (Electricity, Gas, Water, Garbage) for 85m2 Apartment	58.92 $
1 min. of Prepaid Mobile Tariff Local (No Discounts or Plans)	0.17 $
Internet (6 Mbps, Unlimited Data, Cable/ADSL)	23.21 $

Rent Per Month

	Avg.
Apartment (1 bedroom) in City Centre	306.91 $
Apartment (1 bedroom) Outside of Centre	188.17 $
Apartment (3 bedrooms) in City Centre	776.15 $
Apartment (3 bedrooms) Outside of Centre	285.83 $

BACOLOD CITY

Photo Source: paraisophilippines.com

The Cleanest and Greenest and the Most Livable City in the Philippines. The capital of the Province of Negros Occidental which is the Sugarbowl of the Philippines. Bacolod City serves as the entrance of the sugar-rich cities and towns of the Province. Visitor's facilities abound, modern means of in-land transport can take guests for business or leisure to any point in the island of Negros.

Bacolod will charm you with the genuine warmth and hospitality of her people in harmony with their lilting melodious accent. The Bacoleños will delight you with food and cuisine that is as vigorous yet as subtle as the legendary Ilonggo gentility and taste for the good life. (Source: **Bacolod City Official Website**.)

Here's a breakdown of some cost of living expenses in Bacolod City.

Restaurants	Avg.
Meal, Inexpensive Restaurant	2.59 $
Meal for 2, Mid-range Restaurant, Three-course	11.50 $
Combo Meal at McDonalds or Similar	3.45 $
Domestic Beer (0.5 liter draught)	0.58 $
Imported Beer (0.33 liter bottle)	0.98 $
Cappuccino (regular)	2.53 $
Coke/Pepsi (0.33 liter bottle)	0.83 $
Water (0.33 liter bottle)	0.35 $

Transportation	Avg.
One-way Ticket (local transport)	0.17 $
Taxi Start (Normal Tariff)	
Taxi 1hour Waiting (Normal Tariff)	
Gasoline (1 liter)	1.34 $
Volkswagen Golf 1.4 90 KW Trendline (Or Equivalent New Car)	20,204.37 $

Utilities (Monthly)	Avg.
Basic (Electricity, Gas, Water, Garbage) for 85m2 Apartment	46.01 $
1 min. of Prepaid Mobile Tariff Local (No Discounts or Plans)	0.23 $
Internet (6 Mbps, Unlimited Data, Cable/ADSL)	27.60 $

Rent Per Month	Avg.
Apartment (1 bedroom) in City Centre	126.69 $
Apartment (1 bedroom) Outside of Centre	66.36 $
Apartment (3 bedrooms) in City Centre	221.21 $

(Source: **NUMBEO**)

BAGUIO CITY

The name Baguio conjures, for both the international and domestic traveler, a highland retreat in the Grand Cordillera in Northern Luzon, with pine trees, crisp cold breezes and low verdant knolls and hillocks. Through the numerous decades Baguio has morphed from what was once a grassy marshland into one of the cleanest and greenest, most highly urbanized cities in the country.

Baguio has made its mark as a premiere tourist destination in the Northern part of the Philippines with its cool climate, foggy hills, panoramic views and lovely flowers. Being the ideal convergence zone of neighboring highland places, Baguio is the melting pot of different peoples and cultures and has boosted its ability to provide a center for education for its neighbors. Its rich culture and countless resources have lured numerous investments and business opportunities to the city. (Source: **Official Website of Baguio City**)

Restaurants	Avg.
Meal, Inexpensive Restaurant	2.43 $
Meal for 2, Mid-range Restaurant, Three-course	26.60 $
Combo Meal at McDonalds or Similar	4.58 $
Domestic Beer (0.5 liter draught)	1.11 $
Imported Beer (0.33 liter bottle)	3.07 $
Cappuccino (regular)	1.08 $
Coke/Pepsi (0.33 liter bottle)	0.84 $
Water (0.33 liter bottle)	0.37 $

Transportation	Avg.
One-way Ticket (local transport)	0.22 $
Taxi Start (Normal Tariff)	0.77 $
Taxi 1km (Normal Tariff)	0.22 $
Gasoline (1 liter)	1.06 $

Utilities (Monthly)	Avg.
Basic (Electricity, Gas, Water, Garbage) for 85m2 Apartment	69.27 $
1 min. of Prepaid Mobile Tariff Local (No Discounts or Plans)	0.20 $
Internet (6 Mbps, Unlimited Data, Cable/ADSL)	28.84 $

Rent Per Month	Avg.
Apartment (1 bedroom) in City Centre	102.29 $
Apartment (1 bedroom) Outside of Centre	81.47 $
Apartment (3 bedrooms) in City Centre	238.47 $
Apartment (3 bedrooms) Outside of Centre	180.56 $

Here's a breakdown of some cost of living expenses in Baguio City:(Source: **NUMBEO**)

DASMARINAS

The **City of Dasmariñas** is a first class city in the province of Cavite, Philippines. It is located approximately 30 kilometers (19 mi) south of Manila. According to the 2010 census, it has a population of 575,817 people, making it before the most populous municipality in the Philippines before it was converted into a city. Dasmariñas is now the 11th largest city in the country in terms of population. It has a land area of 90.1 square kilometers (34.8 sqmi).

Dasmariñas City used to be part of Cavite's second congressional district until June 30, 2010. The city has now its own legislative district, although that district is still part of the representation of Cavite.

Dasmariñas is the wealthiest local government unit in the province of Cavite according to the 2006 Commission on Audit report. In addition, prior to its conversion into a city, Dasmariñas was the only municipality in the Philippines that had both an SM and Robinsons Mall.

With the continuous expansion of Metro Manila, the city is now part of Manila's conurbation which reaches Lipa City in its southernmost part.

Dasmariñas has the biggest population in the entire province with over 700,000 people within its borders during the day. The city has 75 barangays, has more than 170 subdivisions and the biggest resettlement area in the Philippines, Dasmarinas Bagong Bayan.

Most affluent families from Metro Manila and nearby towns and provinces have chosen Dasmariñas to be their home due to its proximity to the National Capital Region. The mass exodus of people here in Dasmariñas is also brought about by the industrial boom which brought about more jobs. There are also a big number of foreign residents such as Koreans, Chinese, Japanese, Americans, Hindus, Britons and Eurasians. Because of this, Dasmariñas can be also considered as the "Melting Pot" of Cavite. (Source: **Wikipedia**)

Here's a breakdown of some cost of living expenses in Dasmariñas :

Restaurants	Avg.
Meal, Inexpensive Restaurant	5.09 $
Meal for 2, Mid-range Restaurant, Three-course	12.81 $
Combo Meal at McDonalds or Similar	1.07 $
Domestic Beer (0.5 liter draught)	0.54 $
Imported Beer (0.33 liter bottle)	1.30 $
Cappuccino (regular)	2.82 $
Coke/Pepsi (0.33 liter bottle)	0.64 $
Water (0.33 liter bottle)	0.36 $

Transportation	Avg.
One-way Ticket (local transport)	0.23 $

Taxi 1hour Waiting (Normal Tariff)	
Gasoline (1 liter)	1.00 $

Utilities (Monthly)	Avg.
Basic (Electricity, Gas, Water, Garbage) for 85m2 Apartment	56.66 $
1 min. of Prepaid Mobile Tariff Local (No Discounts or Plans)	0.09 $
Internet (6 Mbps, Unlimited Data, Cable/ADSL)	20.95 $

Rent Per Month	Avg.
Apartment (1 bedroom) in City Centre	57.97 $
Apartment (1 bedroom) Outside of Centre	65.90 $

(Source: **NUMBEO**)

ILOILO CITY

Iloilo is a province of the Philippines located in the Western Visayas region. My wife and I have lived in Iloilo since October 2011. We lived in her home province of Guimaras, just off Iloilo's southeast coast when we moved to the Philippines in July 2009. While Guimaras' beaches are great places to visit and the annual Manggahan Festival is one party you don't want to miss, it's proximity to my wife's relatives made it more desirable to move further away to Iloilo which offered vastly more shopping and healthcare facilities.

Iloilo occupies the southeast portion of Panay Island and is bordered by Antique Province to the west and Capiz Province and the Jintotolo Channel to the north. Across the Panay Gulf and Guimaras Strait is Negros Occidental. Iloilo's capital is Iloilo City though the city itself is independent and not governed by the provincial government of Iloilo. (Source: **Wikipedia**)

My wife and I absolutely love living in Iloilo City. We use jeepneys to travel around and enjoy living in our subdivision which is only a two jeepney ride from the biggest shopping mall in Iloilo, SM City.

Here's a breakdown of some cost of living expenses in Iloilo City:

Restaurants	Avg.
Meal, Inexpensive Restaurant	2.91 $
Meal for 2, Mid-range Restaurant, Three-course	11.19 $
Combo Meal at McDonalds or Similar	2.37 $
Domestic Beer (0.5 liter draught)	1.17 $
Imported Beer (0.33 liter bottle)	2.29 $
Cappuccino (regular)	1.19 $
Coke/Pepsi (0.33 liter bottle)	0.52 $
Water (0.33 liter bottle)	0.32 $

Transportation	Avg.
One-way Ticket (local transport)	0.22 $
Monthly Pass (Regular Price)	50.43 $
Taxi Start (Normal Tariff)	0.90 $
Taxi 1km (Normal Tariff)	1.11 $
Taxi 1hour Waiting (Normal Tariff)	4.39 $
Gasoline (1 liter)	1.13 $
Volkswagen Golf 1.4 90 KW Trendline (Or Equivalent New Car)	16,683.05 $

Utilities (Monthly)	Avg.
Basic (Electricity, Gas, Water, Garbage) for 85m2 Apartment	54.51 $
1 min. of Prepaid Mobile Tariff Local (No Discounts or Plans)	0.15 $
Internet (6 Mbps, Unlimited Data, Cable/ADSL)	28.48 $

Rent Per Month	Avg.
Apartment (1 bedroom) in City Centre	158.50 $
Apartment (1 bedroom) Outside of Centre	80.71 $
Apartment (3 bedrooms) in City Centre	374.89 $
Apartment (3 bedrooms) Outside of Centre	192.94 $

(Source: **NUMBEO**)

BEST PLACES TO LIVE IN THE PHILIPPINES ON A SHOESTRING BUDGET

So you want to move to the Philippines? But you don't have much money. You don't even have a guaranteed source of monthly income like a Social Security Pension. So how do you think you can survive in a Third World Country? Will you find a job? Start a business. Marry a rich Filipina lady? Is there any possible way you could move to this archipelago of 7,107 islands and survive on a shoestring budget? The answer to that question: **"YES!"**

Let's take a look at a chart that breaks down the average annual income and expenditures for families broken down by region in the Philippines. Note that this chart only has 2009 for it's latest figures, but factor in the inflation rate in the past few years, and these figures still shall be fairly close.

Average Income and Expenditure of Families by Region, at 2000 Prices:
2006 and 2009
(in thousand PhP)

Region	2006		2009	
	Average Income	Average Expenditure	Average Income	Average Expenditure
Philippines	125	107	129	110
NCR	221	183	227	197
CAR	137	108	136	108
Ilocos	102	89	116	94
Cagayan Valley	108	89	115	90
Central Luzon	147	127	139	119
Calabarzon	153	136	158	135
Mimaropa	82	70	90	77
Bicol	92	81	95	85
Western Visayas	97	86	99	89
Central Visayas	101	87	111	92
Eastern Visayas	94	78	98	78
Zamboanga Peninsula	93	73	88	73
Northern Mindanao	102	84	98	83
Davao	96	82	99	85
Soccsksargen	85	72	96	82
Caraga	86	73	88	74
ARMM	61	52	62	54

Also notice that the graph list expenditures for **families**. If you come over here as a single guy and follow the advice of this "Shoestring Report," your own expenses could be even lower.

I'll be using a Philippine Peso to US Dollar exchange rate of 42 PHP to 1 USD. At the time of this "Shoestring Report," the rate was actually 42.15 PHP to 1 USD.

But let's set aside all of that mindset of "thinking in dollars." You're not in the United States, Australia, Great Britain or whatever country you have moved from. You're in the Philippines now. Think **"PESO."**

Ok, now let's take a look at the cheapest region to live in the Philippines, ARMM, the Autonomous Region in Muslim Mindanao. There is *ABSOLUTELY NO WAY* you should consider, as a foreigner, living in this area. ARMM is located in the Mindanao island group that is composed of predominantly Muslim provinces, Basilan (except Isabela City), Lanao del Sur, Maguindanao, Sulu and Tawi-Tawi. It is the only country that has its own government. (Source: **Wikipedia**.) It may only cost an average of 54,000 pesos a **YEAR** to live there, 1,285 US Dollars, but it is an extremely dangerous area for a foreigner to live in. Let's move on.

Zamboanga Peninsula comes in at 71,000 pesos, roughly 1,700 US Dollars, per year is also located in Mindanao. However, one of my American expat friends lived in one of the cities located there, Dipolog, and never experienced any personal safety issue there. He has since moved to Iloilo City because of the lack of amenities found there. Caraga's annual cost-of-living is 74,000 pesos a year and is also located in Mindanao.

Mimaropa, the Southern Tagalog Islands, is one of two regions of the Philippines having no land border with another region, Eastern Visayas being the other. This region consists of such provinces as Occidental, Mindoro, Oriental Mindoro, Marinduque, Romblonand and Palawan. (source: **Wikipedia**.) At 77,000 pesos, 1,800 US Dollars, for the annual cost-of-living, it's a good place to check out and offers some possibilities to live inexpensively.

Eastern Visayas rounds up the list of some of the more inexpensive places to live in the Philippines according to this study. We live in Western Visayas, which has the province of Iloilo, where we reside. Eastern Visayas is composed of six provinces: Biliran, Eastern Samar, Leyte, Northern Samar, Samar and Southern Leyte. Ormoc City, Baybay City, Maasin City, Calbayog City, Catablogan City, Borongan City and the highly-urbanized city of Tacloban are located in Eastern Visayas. (Source: **Wikipedia.**)

The graph pegs the Eastern Visayas Region's annual cost-of-living at 78,000 pesos making it another location where it might be possible to live on a "shoe string budget." The chart clearly shows that living expenses are much higher in the metropolitan regions such as NCR, the National Capital Region, which consists of the Metro Manila area. At an annual cost of 197,000 pesos, 4,700 US Dollars, this tops the list of the most expensive areas to live in the Philippines.

BEST BANKS IN THE PHILIPPINES

The Three Biggest Banks in the Philippines

Financial disasters are real as has been observed over the past several years with the global financial crisis of 2008 being the biggest. The fear of losing one's savings from a bank failure is understandable. Today, the Philippine Deposit Insurance Corporation (PDIC) insures up to only 500,000 pesos of anyone's total deposit in a single bank. But that does not ease the fear of many who saw how the victims of bank closures struggled to get back their deposits even with much lower amounts. The cases of Banco Filipino and Urban Bank's closure carry some weight to depositors who worry about the risks involved with banking institutions.

Big banks are not immune to the dangers associated with the financial sector. But a combination of their size, management and history are indications to the public of their respective reliability. This is reinforced by the fact that the two examples mentioned above both involve banks which are comparatively smaller than the top three banks. It can be argued that the biggest three banks in the Philippines are our best bet to trust our money with either for savings or wealth management. This would make us more conservative with our limited choice but it would surely still give us some options to choose a safe haven.

I have been banking with BPI (Bank of the Philippine Islands) for as long as I can remember. This did not come about from a reasonable assessment but rather from pure chance. My first job after after college used BPI for its payroll system. I was therefore using this particular account for more than six long years before I left the company. Subsequent employers also preferred BPI although they did not require it. If I had more experience with the other banks, I know I could have easily opted for either one of them. Even so I have friends and relatives using Metrobank and Banco de Oro. I believed then as I still do now that they are also as dependable as BPI, if not more so.

Bank of the Philippine Islands (BPI) is the third largest bank in the Philippines. It also happen to be the oldest being founded in 1851 and is now on its 161st year in existence. Its financial statement as of September 30, 2011 puts its total resources to 788 billion pesos. Customers are also assured of its management being an Ayala-owned company. The Ayalas are known for their aptitude in running businesses that are efficient and profitable or for turning a faltering endeavor into a good venture.

For ordinary working people, a bank's ubiquitous ATM's either in shopping malls or in numerous branches all over the country is an advantage that cannot be underestimated. This is the primary selling point of the largest bank in the Philippines, **Banco de Oro (BDO.)** Apart from having the most assets amounting to more than a trillion pesos as of September 30, 2011, the company is owned by SM which operates the largest and most popular mall chains in the country. BDO does not take its ties with the SM malls for granted. It has littered its sister company's malls with ATM's which are hard to miss given their prime location and number.

The only time I was able to open an account with BDO was when I decided to take a job with an insurance company as a part-time agent. That did not last too long and so did the account I opened. My experience with BDO was therefore limited to a few months but I have frequently transacted with their ATM's as an alternative to BPI even with the associated charges due to their convenient locations. I also remember applying for a business loan from them which I intended to use as capital for a franchise venture. They disapproved the loan because of an undisclosed reason and advised that I reapply after six months. I was displeased by their refusal but was satisfied looking back at their cautious assessment of loan applications.

Metrobank used to be the largest bank in the country until BDO merged with Equitable PCI bank which had the end result of subordinating Metrobank to second place from that point forward. As of September 30, 2011, its asset is declared to be in the neighborhood of 918 billion pesos. This places Metrobank at a comfortable second place only slightly behind BDO.

I have never had an account with Metrobank but have also transacted using their ATM's and did business with their asset management subsidiary First Metro Asset Management, Inc. (FAMI). In 2006, I was witness to the extraordinary performance of FAMI's equity mutula fund that I invested more than 100,000 pesos to it. But the ensuing financial crisis in 2008 wiped out all the gains I made in 2007. Still, I waited until the market recovered in 2009 before I withdrew my money because of necessity without any profit whatsoever. It was a learning experience that showed me how a professionally run investment arm of Metrobank reflects well to its mother company's   image.

It would be simplistic to argue that these are the only banks that one should trust his or her money with. There are thousands of banks in the Philippines counting commercial, universal, rural, cooperative, thrift and quasi-banks. Specific knowledge of a particular bank's history, performance and service is invaluable in choosing which bank is good for you. (Source: **perakoto.com**)

Finance Asia Names BDO, Citi as Best Banks in the Philippines

BDO Unibank Inc and Citi were cited as the best banks in the Philippines in the latest regional report by leading business publication FinanceAsia.

Hong Kong-based FinanceAsia's annual country awards for achievement recognized the banking institutions in each country in the region. "Our annual look at the best financial services firms in each country around the region has produced the list of top domestic and foreign houses," it said.

Sy-controlled BDO was named the best domestic bank as well as the best foreign exchange bank while Citi won in the foreign commercial bank category.

Adding to BDO's accolade is unit BDO Capital Corp., which earned the top rating for investment banking and bond issuance, while UBS bagged the award for best foreign investment bank.

Meanwhile, First Metro Investment Corp. (FMIC) of the Metrobank Group took the best equity house title while Maybank ATR KimEng was acknowledged the best broker.

BDO president and chief executive Nestor V. Tan earlier said they expect 2012 to be characterized by moderate loan growth but strong growth in deposits that will "feed our loans, sustain growth in fee-based income, and normalize provisioning levels."

The country's biggest bank posted a net income of P10.5 billion in 2011, up 19 percent from the P8.8 billion recorded in 2010. It remains the largest Philippine bank in terms of total resources at P1.1 trillion.

Its loan portfolio expanded 24 percent to P670 billion last year "by focusing on creditworthy borrowers in fast-growing industry sectors."

Meanwhile, US financial giant Citi was also named best foreign commercial bank in Thailand and Indonesia.

Bank Mandiri was best domestic bank and best foreign exchange bank while Mandiri Sekuritas was the best investment bank and best equity house. Credit Suisse was cited best foreign investment bank.

In Malaysia, FinanceAsia said CIMB was a runaway winner as it bagged the best investment bank, best bond house, best equity house, best broker and best foreign exchange bank awards. HSBC was named best foreign commercial bank while Goldman Sachs was best foreign investment bank.

Incidentally, CIMB recently acquired from the San Miguel Group a controlling stake in the Bank of Commerce.

The best local bank and the best foreign exchange bank title went to the Siam Commercial Bank in Thailand. Maybank KimEng was named best broker while Morgan Stanley was best foreign investment bank.

In Singapore, DBS Bank was named best bank, best investment bank, best bond house, best equity house and best foreign exchange bank.

Standard Chartered Bank was named best foreign commercial bank while Bank of America Merrill Lynch was best foreign investment bank. (Source: philSTAR.com)

BANKING IN THE PHILIPPINES

My wife and I have a peso savings account at BDO, Banco de Oro, in Iloilo City. Opening this account required a P5,000 deposit, almost 120 US Dollars. If we let our savings balance fall below 5,000 pesos, we are assessed a fee of P300, 7.15 US Dollars. That's a fairly hefty charge, but we don't dip into that account and primarily opened it since our debit card we had from our bank back in the States had expired.

We were told by bank personnel that we would be able to transfer our funds online between our back in America and our new BDO account. Didn't work out that way. I called our bank in the States. They informed me that such a transfer cannot be done online with them and would be considered a wire transfer.

I went back to BDO and explained the situation to another customer service representative. The young lady that had told us we *could* transfer funds online was herself transferred to another branch in Iloilo.

The company that handles our retirement account distribution back in the States cannot direct deposit funds to a foreign bank. We still needed an account in the Philippines so my sister-in-law working as a domestic helper in Kuwait could send remittances to our account. We take care of her 13-year-old son and 14-year-old niece.

So what was our solution? Well, we could write a check from our bank in America and deposit it with BDO but it would take 30 days for our check to clear. We do not have access to our IRA account fund; we have a T-72 fund which is locked in for five years in order to avoid taking a big hit on my lump sum retirement check from AT&T. We have less than two years to access that. Our monthly distribution from the IRA is fixed and cannot be changed until our five year term is up.

We opted to transfer our money from our US bank account using XOOM. Send up to $2,999 for only **$4.99.** We pick up our money in pesos at our local BDO branch in SM City. XOOM also makes additional money on the Philippine Peso to US Dollar exchange rate in addition to the fee, but so does Western Union and their rates are higher.

Since our international debit card fee was P200, 4.75 USD, for each P10,000, 240 USD withdrawal from the ATMs, we're charged about the same from XOOM. But it's much more convenient and safer going to the bank in one trip instead of making three trips to the ATMs on three consecutive days. Only allowed to take out P20,000 a day in P10,000 increments when we used the automatic tellers.

Here's a list of BDO requirements. I have expat friends that have peso and dollar accounts which require additional deposits. For now, we're just going with the Peso Savings Account. When I start receiving my Social Security pension from the States, we're going to reevaluate our banking needs and probably open an additional type of account.

BDO Requirements:

•Two (2) valid and recent identification cards (IDs) with your name and picture.
Accepted IDs: Passport, Driver's license, PRC, NBI clearance, GSIS e-Card, SSS ID, Philhealth card, Senior Citizen Card, Postal ID, Voter's ID, Police clearance, Barangay certification, OWWA ID, OFW ID, Seaman's Book, Alien Certification of Registration/Immigrant Certificate of Registration, and other government office IDs
•Two (2) photocopies of your IDs
•Two (2) copies 1×1 latest ID picture
•Original and 2 photocopies of Billing Statement (electric, water or telephone bill; credit card billing statement, etc.) for address verification.

Upon entering BDO, proceed to New Account desk and tell the in-charged your purpose and fill-up the forms.

ACR card is usually needed for foreigners.

Provide your initial deposit. The minimum initial deposit requirements for BDO Accounts are as follows:

Initial Deposit / Balance Requirement

Account Type	Minimum Initial Deposit	Minimum MADB* Requirement	Minimum Balance to Earn Interest	Checking and Savings Accounts falling below maintaining balance for two (2) consecutive months	Dormancy Fee
Regular Checking Account	Php 5,000.00	Php 5,000.00	N/A	Php 300.00	Php 300.00
Smart Checking - Personal	Php 15,000.00	Php 15,000.00	Php 15,000.00	Php 300.00	Php 300.00
Smart Checking - Commercial	Php 25,000.00	Php 25,000.00	Php 25,000.00	Php 300.00	Php 300.00
Super Checking	Php 100,000.00	Php 100,000.00	Php 100,000.00	Php 300.00	Php 300.00
Peso Checking Account Payroll	Php 100.00	Php 100.00	N/A	Php 300.00	Php 300.00
Automatic Transfer - Savings Account ATF Personal	Php 25,000.00	Php 25,000.00	Php 25,000.00	Php 500.00	Php 300.00
Checking Account ATF Personal	0.00	0.00	N/A	N/A	Php 300.00
ccount ATF Commercial	Php 50,000.00	Php 50,000.00	Php 50,000.00	Php 500.00	Php 300.00
Checking Account ATF Commercial	0.00	0.00	N/A	N/A	Php 300.00

*MADB (Monthly Average Daily Balance)

OWNING PROPERTY IN THE PHILIPPINES

As mentioned in an earlier section, for the most part foreigners are not allowed to own property in the Philippines, but there are some exceptions. The information on this topic from the *Real Estate Buying Guide in the Philippines for Foreigners* website explains further:

By law, foreigners don't have the right to acquire land in the Philippines. Only Filipino citizens can own land (there have been many proposals to amend this law but of this writing, the law remains unchanged.) The simplest way for a foreigner to acquire real estate properties is to have a Filipino spouse purchase a property in his/her name.

Exceptions:

Corporations or partnerships that is at least 60% Filipino owned are entitled to acquire land in the Philippines. An exception to this rule, is foreign acquisition of Philippine real estate in the following cases:

*Acquisition   before   the   1935   constitution.

Acquisition thru hereditary succession if the foreign acquire is a legal or natural heir. This means that when you are married to a Filipino citizen and your husband/wife dies, you as the natural heir will become the legal owner of his/her property. The same is true for the children. Every natural child (legitimate or illegitimate) can inherit the property of his/her Filipino father/mother even if he/she is not a Filipino citizen.

* Purchase of not more than 40% interest in a condominium project.

* Purchase by a former natural-born Filipino citizen subject to the limitations prescribed by law. (natural born Filipinos who acquired foreign citizenship is entitled to own up to 1,000 square meter of

residential land, and 1 hectare of agricultural or farm land)

* Filipinos who are married to aliens who retain their Filipino citizenship, unless by their act or omission they have renounced their Filipino   citizenship.

Owning of houses or buildings is legal as long as the foreigner does not own the land on which the house is build.

*Setting up a corporation with 40% of the stocks in the foreigner's name and 60% to Filipinos is a good alternative. There must be a minimum of 5 stockholders, and foreigner can have the Filipino stockholders sign blank transfer of the stocks for security.

HOSPITAL CARE AND EXPENSES IN THE PHILIPPINES

I was fortunate to retire from AT&T in America after almost thirty years of employment and only had to pay 28 US dollars a month for a Blue Cross/Blue Shield PPO Plan for my wife and myself during our first year in the Philippines but discovered, through a personal experience with a kidney stone attack in February 2010, to be virtually useless in the Philippines at the time of my attack. Before moving to the Philippines, I contacted Blue Cross/Blue Shield to see if my coverage would be good in the Philippines. They assured me it would be. I discovered differently one evening. Here's the story:

The Attack

I'm sitting in the emergency room at the hospital in San Miguel in Guimaras province racked with pain in my lower abdomen. The resident surgeon has just told me they are going to be transporting me via ambulance to the Jordan Wharf to board a specially reserved pump boat to the **Great Saviour International Hospital in Iloilo City.** All signs point to an appendectomy. My wife has returned home to pack a bag for the hospital visit. My sister-in-law Alida and my twin nieces April and Michelle are with me.

The pain is severe! I can't get any medication until I give a urine sample. They finally give me a larger specimen cup, but I still can't give them enough urine even though I just had drank a liter of water. Finally, my sister-in-law goes to the doctors and *insists* on some pain medication for me *NOW!* I have been suffering since 5 pm, and it was now 10 pm. The doctor gives Alida a prescription for one pill. She goes to the pharmacy and comes back with the pill. Five minutes later the pain is gone! To this day I do not know what that pill was since the prescription for it was lost in all the confusion of that evening.

An ambulance from the local provincial hospital in Guimaras takes us to the Jordan Wharf to board a special night-time pump boat to Iloilo for the emergency run. The pump boat cuts through the waves in the darkness of the Strait of Guimaras. I ask my doctor where he was trained. He went to a medical college in Iloilo. Says it is easy to become a doctor in the Philippines. That was *not* reassuring. This could be my first time under the knife. I might be putting my life in this man's hands.

Get to the hospital through some winding side streets of Iloilo via a speeding taxi. Not many ambulances available like back in the States. Get admitted within minutes of my arrival (and after a **MANDATORY** deposit of 10,000 pesos, over 200 USD, is made; didn't have that much cash on us when we arrived at the Guimaras emergency room, had to borrow from some relatives in Guimaras before we left for Iloilo.) Electrodes are hooked up to me for a ECG (not EKG as we call it in the States), and then I am taken to the ultrasound area. The technician scans me as my sister-in-law watches the monitor; my wife is in the admitting area talking to my surgeon. I'm then wheeled into a semi-private room (all that was available) without any knowledge of what the technician found in his probe. A young stabbing victim is my roommate. Thankfully the room has air con. I drift off to sleep around one am not knowing if I will be undergoing surgery or not.

Six am my doctor comes in. Results of the ultrasound: two kidney stones and a polyp on my upper abdomen. One of the kidney stones moved, lacerated my stomach, and caused some blood in my urine. That was the cause of my terrible pain. Fortunately the stones were small and could be treated with medication. (The stomach polyp is later found to be a polyp on my gall bladder, but I will address that later.)

The kidney stones did not cause me any more discomfort, and were evidently shrunk by the prescribed medication and passed. My bill **HAD** to paid in full before I was released from the hospital, and I **had** to present a paid receipt to armed guards at the hospital exit before I was allowed to leave.

Here is a detailed outline of the hospital bill from Great Saviour International Hospital (all amounts will be in approximate US Dollar figures):

ECG (cardiac test)	$8.37
Ultrasound (includes doctor's fee)	$59.33
Urinalysis	$2.55
Syringe charge (for three disposable syringes in the three failed attempts to draw blood from me	$1.75
Alcohol 250 ml.	$1.00
Digital thermometer	$4.84
Cotton balls	0.44
Initial Pharmacy Bill	$43.84

Emergency Room	$8.86
Central Service Fee	$7.88
Room Accommodations (one day)	$22.15
Surgeon Fee (this is the doctor's fee from the surgeon at Guimaras that accompanied my wife and I to the hospital at Iloilo.)	$99.25
Residing Physician's fee	$3.88 (not a misprint)

My wife and I both felt the surgeon had extremely overcharged me, though in the United States, the fee would be considered very small. However, it is our personal belief that I was singled out by the doctor because I was a "rich" American. Again, another example of the "skin tax," or "foreigner tax."

Perhaps the surgeon had included the fee for our special pump boat ride to Iloilo from Guimaras. The standard daytime fee to rent a pump boat for individual use is about ten USD or P450. (Costs just 32 cents to ride the pump boat with other passengers.)

I also had to purchase additional medicine to shrink my kidney stone which totaled to around 40 USD.

We did not have our current Blue Cross/Blue Shield cards at the time of my kidney stone attack. Blue Cross/Blue Shield *did* send our insurance cards to us via Federal Express later, but after talking to the Blue Cross coordinator at Great Saviour, I found out they could not cover the cost because my hospital stay was under 24 hours. If I had elected to stay longer, according to her, I would have had my expenses reimbursed.

I was concerned about the polyp found and knew I needed to go for another ultrasound, but since I was unhappy with the care I received at Great Saviour's (whose medical technicians and one doctor could not even get blood drawn from my arm), I researched online and was also aided by one of my faithful website readers, whose ex-girlfriend used to live in Iloilo, for help in finding a different hospital.

St. Paul's Hospital and Doctor's Hospital were recommended as the best hospitals to go in Iloilo City so I later went for an ultrasound at St. Paul's. Their ultrasound technician verified I did have a polyp on my **gall bladder**, *not* my abdomen, that was one centimeter long. I opted to *not* have surgery to remove that polyp since my online research indicated that gall bladder polyps one centimeter or less really did not require any surgery to have it removed, and I did not want to under undergo any surgery in the Philippines.

The Doc and the fish bone. Only in the Philippines.

"THE SINGLE GUY'S GUIDE TO THE PHILIPPINES."

A series of articles I did for my website, **PhilippinesPlus.com**, prompted the writing of this special section for those single guys wanting to meet the woman of their dreams in the Philippines.

The information contained in this guide will provide you with some useful information that will help you meet that special someone. You'll discover that you are a *celebrity* in this land of 7,107 islands. Sometimes you might even feel like a rock star.

But be forewarned, there are lots of scammers out there that you may have chatted with already online and plan to meet. You're going to encounter a lot of really friendly people in the Philippines and many of those will be beautiful Filipinas. But you'll also come into contact with pretty pinays that will want to drain you of every peso you have. And that's a fact. I've talked to some expats that have lost tens of thousands of dollars, *not* pesos, to women they have met here. Don't think it can happen to you? Think again, my friend.

Hopefully this guide will help you sort it all out. I *sincerely* want you to find the woman of your dreams in the Philippines. I met my "dream woman" over twelve years ago and I'm so thankful I did. My wife is patient, loving and beautiful and puts up with my grumpiness. At the age of 60, I believe I am headed for a starring role in *"Grumpy Old Men"* if they ever do a remake of it. Thank God, most Filipinas have plenty of patience.

THE FILIPINA SCAMMER

Let's cover some of the more popular online scams that Filipinas, lady boys or even male foreigners are using. But first, here's my **NUMBER ONE RULE** regarding scammers: **IF THEY ASK FOR MONEY, RUN! CUT OFF ALL COMMUNICATION FROM THAT POINT ON.** You are being scammed, my friend. Here's several of the more common lines you might hear:

- "But honey, I need money for a web cam so you can see me."
- "It's my birthday next week. Can you send me some money to buy a present?" (Some Filipinas have three to four "birthday's" a year.
- "The Internet cafes are very expensive. Can you send me money so we can chat." (Hourly rates for Internet cafes in the Philippines run from P15-P30 an hour, 36¢-72¢. Chances are they have a relative working abroad as an OFW, Overseas Filipino Worker, giving them money to go

online in the first place.)

- "I don't have a cell phone. Can you buy me one so we can talk?"
- "My lola (grandma) just passed away and we don't have money for the funeral."
- " My school tuition is due and I need money to continue my schooling." (Chances are she's not going to school anyway.)

- "My mother (father, brother, sister, grandma, grandpa, cousin, cat, dog, etc., etc.) is sick. Can you help me?"

MORE SCAMMER TIPS

Here are some very good tips from a forum at DragonLadies.org BBS. I make my own observations in parentheses after each tip.

Signs your girl may be playing you, or not serious in a relationship.

1. **She says "I love you" too fast and within the first few chats.** (Guys, look out for this. I've had some expat friends that have told me the girls they have met in person have told them this on the first date. Be careful and heed this advice. The girl knows there is a *LOT* of competition for you out there and might try to tug at your "heartstrings" from the very start and try to get you to commit.)

2. **She constantly reminds you of how poor her family is.** (Drum roll, please. Rest assured, this is a true mark of a scammer. You're going to be hit up for a "loan" or a "gift" very soon.)

3. **She uses emotional blackmail to get money or gifts, but does not make direct requests.** (Good point. She might try to lay a huge guilt trip on you, crying "boo hoo" over this and that. Think. Think. Think. But not with the wrong "head.")

4. **A fair amount of chat from her is centered around money or material things.** (Getting the point? I'm sure you are.)

5. **Her body language in cam suggests she is not really interested in you or bored.** (I never went on a cam before meeting my wife. She didn't have ready access to an internet cafe and I didn't own a cam anyway and still don't. We were pen pals. But this is a good tip. And if the girl you are chatting with doesn't what to go on cam, you have to wonder why? But if you chat with one of my 19-year-old twin nieces that live with us, they have a good excuse. I'm too cheap to buy one.)

6. **Something you buy her suddenly goes missing or is pawned?** (Another good one. One of my stories later in this guide tells of a girl that used the pawnshop excuse to get money from her expat boyfriend. He fell for it every time.)

7. **She continually adds male friends to her networking profiles like Friendster and Facebook.** (Another good warning sign.)

8. **What she tells you does not add up. If she says she is conservative, for example, why is she wearing a top that exposes cleavage?** (Excellent point! Have you ever seen the risque pictures some of these Filipinas post on the dating websites and Facebook?)

9. She makes promises but does not keep them. (I have had this happen to many of my expat friends. I was told by a Filipino gentleman that **"a Filipino promise is like an airplane that grows wings and then flies away."**

10. **She chats to others while you are chatting to her.** (I have an expat friend that took a young lady out to dinner. The whole time she was on her laptop chatting with other people online. Now that's just rude.)

11. **She has more than 4 email accounts.** (Another good indicator.)

12. **She often is late for your scheduled time for chat.** (But don't worry, she'll have a good excuse, plus you always have to factor in "Filipino Time."

13. **When you meet the family, they appear to milk you for money.** (I can speak from personal experience on this point. You would not believe the almost daily parade of relatives that would stop by our home when we lived in Guimaras looking for a "loan." Your wife will see relatives she had not seen in years once word gets out that she married a "rich" kano.)

14. **She rarely or does not talk about her future life in your country.** (If she was serious about you my friend, there would be some discussion about that. I have not talked to a Filipino yet that doesn't want to come to the United States or get out of the Philippines. But if she's chatting with a hundred or so other guys, how could she keep track of all of those "future plans" with each guy?)

HOW TO SPOT A FAKE SCAMMER PHOTO

Came across this website, **http://www.tineye.com/** , which can track the source of a picture's image. It's a reverse image search. Have doubts about that gorgeous Filipina picture profile on your favorite Filipina dating website? Try this image search tool out. Should help weed out some of the fake profiles out there. Here are the result of a couple of searches I did. The first image that shows "0" results is from DateinAsia. That would indicate the young lady's photo is an original since no other image sources can be found for her online.

The second image, a Flipina celebrity, Angel Locsin, drew eight hits from the website. And listen, don't think that some Filipina, lady boys or even foreigners aren't trying to use such a scam because they are. My wife recently spotted someone using a photo of Angel Locsin on a website one of my expat friends was using. I told him about it and the dating website promptly pulled the profile down. Check out what **TinEye** can do for you. It's free to use. Give it a test spin.

Filipina watching the waves come in at Raymen Beach in Guimaras

THE WINGMAN'S DATING TIPS

Getting to know a woman and dating is not easy in *any* country. Can I hear a **BIG "Amen"** from you guys out there? If you're from a Western nation such as the United States, Canada, Great Britain, Australia, etc., and have never been to the Philippines, you're in for a pleasant surprise. For the single guy, the Philippines is a dating paradise.

Dating a Filipina, or pinay, is easy if you follow some simple rules and learn some basic facts about the culture. As the "Wingman," let me take you under *my* wing and give you some dating tips. I've been married to a beautiful Filipina over 12 years and have lived in the Philippines for over three years.

Now that certainly does not qualify me as a expert, but it has given me enough knowledge and insight that I believe can help you. I *want* you to succeed. I *want* you to find your "dream girl" in the Philippines.

I was married to an American woman for nine months before she threw me out of the house. At least she had the courtesy to pack my clothes in cheap garbage bags she bought from an Aldi's Supermarket and toss them in the front yard. I did not abuse her nor did I cheat on her. But she did me a *huge favor.* I would have never met my Filipina wife years later and be retired and living in the Philippines if she would not have divorced me. Talk about your "blessings in disguise!"

The following dating tips will help you to become well informed before you even try to date a pretty pinay. By the way, "pinay" is slang for Pilipino (Filipino) female. You'll see the term "filipina" or "pinay" used throughout this guide.

DATING IN THE PHILIPPINES

Dating in the Philippines will certainly be quite different from dating in your home country. Many Filipinas see dating in a different manner due to certain traditions which you might not be accustomed to. Keep in mind that the vast majority of Filipinos are Catholic, around 84%. This fact will play a strong role in how you court your pretty pinay. If you've never visited the Philippines before, you're going to be in for some cultural challenges in the dating game.

First off, you should be aware that there are many types of Filipinas you can find in the country, and their personality traits and custom can vary from region to region. Since I married a young lady from Guimaras, a rural province in the Western Visayas region known for the sweetest mangoes in the world, I'm more familiar of course, with the local ladies who are called "Ilonggas."

Not meaning to offend anyone with a girlfriend in the Metro Manila or Mindanao region, but Ilonggas are noted for being some of the sweetest and loyal girls in the Philippines. You will find a *vast* difference between a city girl from Manila and a girl from the province, such as Iloilo where my wife and I reside.

If you have decided to move to the Philippines or you are on vacation, and are just looking for a girlfriend or someone to date, you've come to the right place. If you cannot find a girl to date in the Philippines, and I'm talking about some beautiful, drop-dead gorgeous women, there is something seriously wrong with you. Looks don't matter for the most part. Many Filipinas look for foreigners in this archipelago. Why? You're the ticket out of poverty for many of these girls and their families and they're looking for security.

To be seen with a foreigner is a status symbol for some of these ladies. But where can you find them? And I'm deliberately omitting any "gentleman's clubs" or KTV bars (strip bars.) Guys, there are plenty of young ladies wanting to meet you outside of these establishments. You really don't have to hang out at those places. But if you do, just be careful. I wouldn't recommend it personally but that decision is up to you.

WHERE TO MEET FILIPINAS

Here are some places, other than bars and strip clubs, to find women when you want to date in the Philippines:

1. **Mall stores or shops** that are frequented by tourists. SM (Shoemart) malls, one of the largest chain of shopping malls in the Philippines, are a good place to go. Talk to the sales associates at the stores. You'll generally find them very eager to talk to a foreigner. I've had more than one expat friend that has chatted with the local sales associates and later went out on a date with them. Just watch out for bar girls that might be hanging out at the malls trying to snag some "rich" kano, foreigner.

2. **Resorts/Grills/Restaurants.** Filipino hangouts are great places for a single guy to meet girls because they are usually there with their friends and family. The ladies are very approachable at these locations. Some of my single expat friends have met several ladies at outside grills or restaurants in Iloilo City where we live. Don't be surprised if they send one of their male friends over to invite you to their table because one of their "shy" Filipina friends would like to chat with you.

3. **Church.** Yes, church. You're sure to meet some good (and some bad) Catholic girls at Mass. No doubt you'll be the center of attention. But if you're searching for Filipinas with some good morals, this is the place for you. Sure, you'll feel awkward at first, but Mass usually only lasts an hour or so. You don't have to be Catholic to participate. I used to go to an English-speaking mass in the Philippines with my wife on Sundays. I just did what she did and followed what the congregation did. Hang out afterward and introduce yourself. Now's not the time to be shy.

4. **Jeepney Stands.** Check this meeting place out. It's almost like an audition. You can view the girls for several minutes while they wait for a jeepney. If you see one you like, strike up a conversation with her, a VERY gentle "hi miss" can start the conversation. Ask for advice on what jeepney you need to take to get to "such and such" location. Ask her where *she's* going. What have you got to lose? (The above photo is a cute jeepney girl sitting next to her lola, grandma, that my wife took.)

5. **Referrals and Blind Dates.** When somebody offers an introduction to their "beautiful" friend, be cautious. Sometimes there may be a little (or a lot of) exaggeration on their part. I've had some friends of mine that wanted to introduce their "beautiful" friend to a single expat buddy of mine. My friend *did* meet one of these ladies and while she was cute, she failed to mention she had two children in previous text messages she had sent to my amigo before they met. Their initial meeting did not evolve into any future dates. But it's another option to explore.

Sales Associates at SM City in Iloilo

6. **Factories and Mall Workers Entrances and Exits.** This suggestion (the factory reference) along with some of the above were suggested by the following website:http://www.cebu-nightlife.com/how-to-meet-your-next-girl-friend/ There are a generous supply of girls, primarily 18 to 22 years old, who work in these boring jobs that leave no room for excitement in their lives due to such long hours. When the doors open for break, lunch or between shifts, pretend you're lost and wander around. Ignore your male pride and ask for directions. You'll have a whole assortment of girls to choose from that are happy to help you. You'll also find a huge number of cute Filipinas during shift breaks at SM Malls throughout the Philippines. Just say "hi" to those that are going on lunch break. You might be surprised at the friendly response you could get.

When you check out the above suggested locations, you will soon notice that there are Filipinas checking *you* out. Get used to it. If you notice them still looking at you, go over and chat with them. Be respectful. Though they may be shy or think their English skills aren't that great, you'll find many of them receptive to going out on a date with you. Don't be surprised if they would like a chaperone to come with them on the first meeting, whether it be a close friend or relative such as a sister. That's very common in the Philippines.

WHERE TO TAKE YOUR DATE

So now that you have that first date set up, where do you go? My single expat friend that lives in Iloilo City often takes his date to the movies. It's a cheap date in the Philippines, only costs about P130 for a ticket, three bucks, and she probably won't mind if you buy her a small popcorn and soda to boot. The whole date for both of you shouldn't cost more than ten bucks. I'm a cheap guy. That's why I like to take my own asawa, seen in the picture below, to the movies in the Philippines.

If you like, you could take your date to the local mall. Stop by her favorite fast food restaurant, order some food and chat. For many Filipinos eating out is a luxury few can afford. Plus, she'll be "showing you off" to other shoppers

in the mall. A foreigner is a prize "catch" to many of the ladies here.

Don't be too aggressive that first date. I wouldn't even recommend a kiss goodbye when the date is over. Holding hands will do. Understand that many Filipinas are shy and do not often like public displays of affection.

Why not buy a small gift, or pasalubong, for her family when you bring her back home. You'll score some huge points with that gesture. It is said that in the Philippines, courting a Filipina means courting her family as well.

WHAT NEXT?

These have been just some basic dating Philippines tips you should know regarding where and how to find a Filipina girl and what to do on your dates together. If you decide you do not want to pursue the relationship any further, *be extremely* careful how you approach that subject.

Remember, you're in the Philippines now. If you piss off some girl by breaking up with her, there's a possibility you might piss off the family, too. You have to make sure that you tell her in a ***respectful manner*** or she may make life hard for you. And you really don't want that.

Filipina dating is not that difficult. There are thousands and thousands of pretty pinays that are waiting to meet you. However, when you wish to get into a serious relationship with a Filipina, you will have to go through a courting process you might find somewhat peculiar. Traditions here are likely to be different from yours.

But if you believe that she is the right girl for you and you want to take your relationship to the next level, here are some tips that should help you.

COURTING TIPS FROM A FILIPINA

I ran across this article on **how to court a Filipina** online on a "Hub Page" from <u>edenloibsalilig.</u> She has some **great advice** and it makes sense to include some input from a member of the opposite sex if you're publishing a single guy's guide to meeting girls in the Philippines. Here's her article:

"Filipina women are known to be one of the most beautiful women in the world bagging lots of international beauty pageant awards and winning the hearts of men with different nationalities. After all, it is home to most mixed races. You look at Filipina woman and you will see a woman who has a very rich ancestry. She can either be fully-Asian, or half Asian and half Caucasian. It doesn't matter as it all yields the same result, a beautiful woman. So how do you capture the heart of a Filipina? Follow the advice below and you might just get yourself a beautiful Filipina.

Filipina women are generally shy. This is rooted in their conservative upbringing. Unlike Western countries where being liberated is acceptable, in the Philippines, being conservative is highly encouraged. If you are going to court a Filipina woman then it's going to take a lot of time and effort. But don't worry as all hard work bears fruit and in this case, it's a Filipina woman's love.

Filipina women are not very particular with looks as they more focused on personality. It doesn't matter if you're a fellow Filipino or a foreigner. If you have the personal traits that a Filipina woman looks for then there's a big chance that you will win her heart. So what traits do Filipina women look for in men? Filipinas like men who are sincere and honest. That's why it takes longer to court a Filipina woman. The patience on the man's part determines whether he is sincere with his intentions for her or not. If you are just looking for a good time then don't bother courting a Filipina as your chances of being said yes to are very slim.

Another reason why Filipinas are very meticulous in choosing a boyfriend is because they don't like to be mistaken for being easy to get. That's why they take longer to please. Do not worry because a Filipina will tell you if you have a chance. If she allows you to continue courting her then it means that she might actually like you. If she tells you straight up that she doesn't want you to court her then don't fret. She cares enough to not let you waste your time on her. Move on and find another girl to court.

Another tip in courting a Filipina is to be consistent. Since it takes longer to court a Filipina, you should show your sincerity through your actions and not just words. Filipinas don't fall for flowery words very easily. It is shallow and it doesn't express sincerity. It has been a known tradition that one good way to court a Filipina is by visiting her in her home where you can meet her parents. This shows that you are serious enough to want to meet her family.

More ways you can show your sincerity is by being on time when planning to meet up with each other. Compliment her. Don't overdo it by telling her grandiose words. Only compliment her on something that's really special about her. Also, don't get too touchy with other girls as the Filipina woman is jealous. She is conservative so this means that she will take it seriously if you are doing something physical or intimate with somebody of the opposite sex.

All this may seem hard but if you have perseverance, it'll all be worth it in the end. Once you win the heart of a Filipina, you not only win a beautiful woman but also a woman who is loving, kind and understanding."

Here's some more courting advice from **"Got A Crush?"**

"To conquer the heart of Filipina Singles, you should be aware of some courtship traditions in the Philippines. Yes, the courtship methods in your country may work, but if you show her that you are willing to do anything for her, in this case court her traditionally, then she will be smitten by your actions. So let us start with a few Philippina dating traditions.

Court her Family
Firstly, you should also be courting her family. The practice in the Philippines is the suitor asking permission of the girl's parents for dating the girl. You could do things differently by visiting her parents or taking the whole family out for a fun day at the mall or at the beach. If they find you to be a perfect partner for their daughter, she will love you more.

Go to Church with your Filipina
Secondly, go to church with her. Filipina singles are religious by nature and those that are in relationships expect their man to hear mass with them. This simple gesture will show her that you are serious about her.

Be Fun and Outgoing
Thirdly, be more fun and outgoing. Philippina singles are known to be fun despite of the problems they face. They enjoy cracking jokes or talking about silly things. Being in a relationship should not deprive them of that. If you are into serious Filipina dating, then this is a must.

Be Affectionate
Fourth, Filipinas are very affectionate. Your Filipina lover needs constant communication and reassuring words from you. Hugs and kisses will make her day. Even a simple message such as asking how her day was can make her feel more comfortable around you.

Traditions play a Role for Philippina Singles
Fifth, respect her country and her traditions. The Philippines is not a first world country and you should keep that in mind. It is a country stricken by poverty and old-world traditions. If you really want to continue with serious Filipina dating, then you will have to respect where she comes from.

Love and Respect Her
Last and most importantly, shower her with the love and respect she deserves. Filipina dating is known to lead to finding the perfect wife for many men who are in search for a lasting loving companionship. You will be treated like a king by your Filipina wife and the least you could do is to love her faithfully and honestly in return."

My asawa with some "cowgirls" at SM City in Iloilo

3 Tips for Dating Filipino Women

Women from different countries have certain characteristics that are common to them. The Filipino expat woman is not an exception to this. There are so many common characteristics that define the Filipino woman and if you plan on getting serious with a true "Pinay," be prepared to learn a whole new world of rules on dating and culture.

Here are a few tips on dating for men specifically for those dating Filipino women:

Know her dating mindset and culture.
The Filipino expat woman is still deeply involved with her roots. Even if she has been working for a long time in another country, her values, beliefs, and traditions are deeply ingrained within her. When dating Filipino women, most

if not all, believe and expect that men should cover the cost of the date. At least for the time being (during the dating stage), be prepared to shell out some of your hard earned money when dating Filipino women. It's not at all that bad. Most Filipino women like simple things and are very understanding so if you don't have the budget for a particular date, just tell her and she can easily forgive you. Of course, do this with finesse and suave or else you might not see her again.

Respect her conventional ways.

If anything, Filipino women are still very conventional. It can take some time to get to know Filipino women because in her country, courting or courtship still exists. Know that she will not reveal everything to you right away so never rush her. This characteristic still holds true for the Filipino expat woman. This is not to say that she isn't open to doing a lot of things. In fact, in Asia, Filipino women can be considered as one of the most open amongst Asian women. This in part is due to the many cultures that she has been exposed to.

Get to know her family.

If you are in a serious relationship or considering dating Filipino women, you need to be open to getting to know her family. No matter how many years a Filipina stays abroad, the Filipina expat woman never forgets her family. Some even live with their families or support them financially. It is often said that when you marry a Filipina, you marry her family too. Don't be overwhelmed. Most Filipino families are welcoming and hospitable. The decision to be with you partly lies in what her family thinks of you so it's best to try to make her family to like you. If she sees that her family loves you, she will definitely love you more.

Dating Filipino women can open up a lot of new possibilities for you. Filipino women are generally warm, loyal, and caring. If you find yourself falling for one, use these tips and you will find her holding on to you instead.

You can get more information on multi-cultural relationships and finding true love by visiting **http://www.manifestingmydestiny.com**
Lori Abela, the author of the above article, *"3 Tips for Dating Filipino Women,"* is an expert on finding true love for expats. She has finally found

the love of her life in her 40s. She shares her secrets to finding true love with the readers of **http://www.manifestingmydestiny.com**. Lori is available for coaching, speaking engagements and consultancy.

Guide To Dating Filipino Women

from <u>Made Man</u> By: Jane Ellis

Need a guide to dating Filipino women? Maybe you've been lusting after a gorgeous, sultry Filipina, a Nicole Scherzinger look-a-like, but you just weren't sure how to approach her or what to expect. Don't just sit around wondering what it would be like to get to know her and take a chance, ask her out. But make sure to read this guide first. Remember, though, every woman is an individual and there are always going to be exceptions to these rules. Also, if a Filipina and her family have been in the United States for a long time, she will probably be fully Americanized and many cultural differences will be minimal.

1. **Filipino time**. Some countries are just not as clock-oriented as United States. On time for Filipinos means being about 30 minutes late. Even Filipino weddings don't start on time. Dating a Filipina means being patient and possibly telling her that events will start a half an hour earlier than they actually do. It's important to understand that her tardiness is not because she is trying to be rude. It's just that being somewhere at an exact time is not stressed in the Filipino culture.

2. **Family is important**. Filipinos are very family-oriented people and it is usually very important to a Filipina to have her family's approval of the person she is dating. Large family gatherings with lots of singing and eating are not uncommon. Don't be surprised if you are constantly meeting cousins as the extended family is also important to Filipinos.

3. **Education is important to Filipinos**. According to the Migration Policy Institute, 50 percent of Filipino immigrants over the age of 25 have at least a bachelor's degree. It is highly likely that the Filipina you are interested in has a college degree or is working towards one, as well. Don't be surprised if her parents are interested in your educational background and career.

4. **Inter-racial dating**. Although most Filipino families would probably prefer their daughters marry someone of the same race, inter-racial dating, especially with an American, is not a huge issue. It wouldn't hurt, though, to find out from the Filipina woman her family's views on inter-racial dating before meeting them just in case they do have an issue, so you can mentally prepare. If there are biases, hopefully, over time, you can charm them into forgetting about them.

5. **Be smart**. You can't charm people if you offend them. Until you get to know the Filipina and her family, it is wise not to make any Asian jokes, especially ones like, "This is my mail-order bride." You may think you're hysterical. She and her family, not so much.

6. **Don't mistake nice for pushover.** Many men are initially attracted to Filipinas because they are usually very nice and tend to smile easily. Do not, however, take their apparent easy-going and sweet nature as meaning a Filipina will be meek and subservient. Filipina women are usually pretty independent and self-sufficient. Many work, and of those who are employed, almost one-quarter are registered nurses.

7. **Be open to trying new things.** Filipino families will encourage you to try to eat traditional favorites like lumpia (which is actually very similar to egg rolls) and will probably encourage you to do Karaoke at a family gathering. Try to fit in at these large family gatherings and have fun.

For Filipina Dating Success – Here Are The Top 5 Tips

If there's one thing that should be said about Filipina dating, it is that <u>Filipino women</u> are famous for being "great wife material", which says about their level of flexibility when it comes to love and men.

In the Philippines, it is common to see Filipino women with black men, Filipino women with older men, Filipino women with overweight men. The kind of interracial Filipino couples you can see in the Philippines are, in all probability, as many as the number nationalities on earth.

However, just because Filipino women are known to be open to everyone, it doesn't mean they're easy, quite the contrary. So, if you really want to date a Filipino woman and be successful at it, read up and learn.

As with any other nationality, if you are keen on marrying a Filipino woman, be sure to know and understand dating customs in the Philippines, as your success will mainly depend upon it.

1. Feed her a full meal

You should know that Filipinos like to eat. During your first date with a Filipino woman, ensure you feed her well with a full meal. The typical Filipino woman loves meat dishes like crispy pata or lechon (so-called inasalin Cebuano). Wine is not necessary on your first date, however, make sure you have a glass of coke with plenty of ice on the table.

Other than that, read below for a few dating tips and insights:

2. Pay for everything

This is specially true on first dates and may even carry on no matter if you are already a couple. Never commit the gaffe of having a Filipino woman pay for her share of the dinner, except if you do not want to meet her again. Paying for everything might seem expensive but it really isn't, even if you are having a date at an expensive restaurant in the Philippines.

3. Don't be too aggressive

In the old days, if a man is caught holding hands with a Filipino woman, he had to marry her or else. Of course, right now things have evolved and Filipino parents don't anymore expect their children to be virgins on their wedding day. Nonetheless, Filipino women continue to be old-fashioned compared to Western women.

A decent Filipino woman is not into one-night stands. You need to be her boyfriend to get into bed with her. When she's ready, she will sleep with you, but until that happens, be a gentleman or else she might run and hide from you.

4. If you are serious, meet her parents

Nearly all Filipino women live with their parents until they got married, and generally find it hard to stand up to the parents if they do not approve of the man she is with. With that being said, if you're truly serious about a Filipino woman, your first order for the day is to win her parents over to your side.

Visit her house and bring some little gifts for her mom and dad. If she's got siblings, it is best to bring some small gifts for them too.

5. Understand that Filipino women have very close family ties, even after marriage.

The bonds between Filipino women and her family extend well beyond marriage, and depending on her family's financial situation, she may be inclined to help her family financially even when she's already married to you.

If you understand this part of Filipino culture because it is part of your own, good for you. At least, that's one issue out of the way. However, if you find it strange, you should talk it over with your Filipina girlfriend BEFORE getting married.

That's it. Keep these **Filipina dating** tips in your mind and you'll discover that dating Filipino woman is the best thing that ever happened for you.

(Source: <u>Cherry Blossoms</u>)

If you move to the Philippines with the intention of meeting that special someone to spend the rest of your life with, or if you are looking for a girlfriend, then the Philippines is an *excellent place* to do that. Many Filipinas consider having a foreign husband or boyfriend to be something special.

Here's a true story about someone I fear is involved with a scammer. It's a cautionary tale I call:

The Trouble with Malcom

I have received a steady stream of daily emails recently from a reader I'll call **"Malcom."** "Malcom", and let's just say he's from Australia, though he could be from anywhere actually. He has sold all of his furniture, most of his worldly possessions, given up his job and his home to move to the Philippines. He's in love with a Filipina.

Malcom has no retirement income or pension. No savings once he arrives. He's spending everything on his move. He will have absolutely no income once he arrives in the Philippines but is assured by his fiancee that he will be able to get a job at the call center she works at. If not, his future wife's relatives assure him he can sell "a special breed of pigs" for P3,000 and sell them for P9,000 in just two-three months. By the way, the relatives are the ones that want to sell him these prized porkers.

Malcom has been chatting with his "true love" online for three years now. Let's call her "Jenny." He has never met her. Jenny has three children but has never been married, but her pastor assures Malcom that she is a "good Christian girl." Well, people make mistakes. Lord knows I've made more than my share.

"Jenny" assures Malcom that they can live on just P12,000 a month. To rent a place in their area only costs P3,000 a month. So if the call center job doesn't pan out, she maintains that, even with three children in the family, all five of them can live on that sum of money. In Malcom's budget he had allotted P6,000 for food.

Really? I asked my Filipina wife who literally grew up in the middle of a jungle with no electricity and no running water and lived in a dirt floor nipa hut if that was possible. **"Yes,"** she said, **"*IF* everyone only eats just fish and rice. Some days everyone will not have a meal, however."** I then told her that the P12,000 amount includes P3,000 for rent. She just shook her head.

But Malcom's budget does not contain any money for visa fees. Until he is married and can have his wife sponsor him for a 13(a) Permanent Resident Visa he will need to cough up about 6,000 pesos every two months to get his visa extended. He told me that if need be, he will stay in the Philippines *illegally* to be with the one he loves. Sigh! I'm afraid his plan is not looking very good to me at this point.

He then sends an email wondering if he ran out of money and spent the visa money he had set aside and had to go to the Australian Embassy to ask for help. Would the embassy send him back to Australia or report him to the Philippine Bureau of Immigration where he could be locked up in a Third World prison?

Why in the world would you want to get yourself in such a position in the first place? It's beyond my comprehension. Remember what I reprinted from the US Embassy website earlier about US citizens that needed financial assistance? I don't know if Malcom would be able to get much help, either, at his embassy.

But Malcom sent me an email to inform me he was finally able to convince his future wife to let her father live with them and some other relatives till they can get on their feet. Awfully generous of his future father-in-law considering Malcom sent him P15,000 last year to pay off his taxes. P15,000? My wife's property bill is around P1,000 a year.

So Malcom has violated one of my **MAJOR** rules whenever communicating with a Filipina online. **IF THEY ASK FOR MONEY, RUN! DROP THEM. QUIT COMMUNICATIONS WITH THEM. MOVE ON. MOVE ON, MOVE ON.** Please do not end up like some expats that did not heed my advice in advance and tell me: **'DAVE, I WISH I WOULD HAVE LISTENED TO YOU!"** Let me assure you, my own wife has NEVER said that to me in over 12 years of marriage, but I've heard that from too many expats lately.

Another email Malcom sent me raised my suspicions about his future bride even more. "Jenny" does not want to move to Australia with Malcom once they are married. I have never met a Filipina, or Filipino for that matter, that did not want to move out of the Philippines and live in another country which they might perceive as "rich" and offering more opportunities than what they can find in the Philippines. Why doesn't she want to move? Is she married and thus, would not be able to get through the immigration process? What about the **CENOMAR**?

A CENOMAR, Certificate of No Marriage Record from the National Statistics Office (NSO) is simply what its name implies. It is a certification by the NSO stating that a person has not contracted any marriage. Also called a certificate of No Record of Marriage or Certificate of Singleness.

Malcom claims Jenny has a genuine CENOMAR. Really? How has he seen it since he has never visited her yet? And did you know there are no privacy laws in the Philippines which prevents someone else from obtaining a CENOMAR and claiming it as their own? (Want more info on the CENOMAR? Just click this **LINK**.)

And the following email from my Aussie friend just poured *more* gasoline on the fire. Jenny showed up one day at the Internet cafe cam sporting a ring on her wedding finger. She claims it was her Mother's ring and she just happened to wear it that day and had no idea that the finger she put it on was the wedding finger. But Malcom is convinced that Jenny is the "real deal." I emailed him back telling him I hope that he is right, and that he has his

mind made up. Nothing more I could tell him at that point, and I've since no longer been in communication with him. Maybe I will be proven wrong, and he's found the "girl of his dreams." Won't be the first time. Won't be the last.

THE REAL DEAL

Enough about the scammers. You'll be glad to know that the majority of Filipinas are loyal, honest and sincere ladies. In fact, once you arrive in the Philippines and go to any mall, you will be *amazed* by the looks you will receive from countless Filipina salesgirls that work at the malls. Sometimes you will hear them say *"gwapo"* as you pass by, meaning **"handsome."**

I've heard that many times since I've been in the Philippines. While it a nice ego boost, I'm reminded by what I've often stated on my website, some Filipinas think a foreign guy that has a face like a dog's rear end will think you are a good-looking guy. Maybe it's just because we are different. I also realize that part of that attraction is that some of the people here think we **all** are *"rich Americans"* or *"rich foreigners."* In comparison to the majority of people here, I suppose we **are** rich. So I am sure that the illusion that most foreigners have money contributes to our appeal towards the ladies.

But if you plan to settle in the Philippines or spend a vacation, and if you aren't planning to meet anyone you may have been chatting with online, then how do you meet some beautiful Filipinas? Simple. Go the your nearest mall, and in my case, my wife and I frequent SM Malls in Iloilo City which are found throughout the Philippines, and talk to any salesgirls I just mentioned.

Most of the ladies at the SM Department Stores I have met through out the Philippines are glad to talk to a foreigner and are very friendly. Some may be somewhat shy or not sure of their English skills, but you single guys out there should just strike up a conversation with some. They are eager to hear about your home country, in my case, America, and if you are a single man, they might be open to having a soda or coffee on their break time to talk with you further. You might get some envious looks from their female co-workers, but go out on a limb, and start a conversation.

Talk to the Dunkin Donuts girl that has a kiosk in the mall. I often chat with the salesgirls, tell them I am married, and have had many instances (that I have reported to my wife) when they are visibly dismayed and vocalize their disappointment when they learn that I am married. I tell them my asawa has many friends back in America that are married to Americans. Their eyes brighten when they hear that and always tell me how they would love to meet some Americans. Oftentimes they want me to introduce them to my American friends.

So just be yourself. Be honest. Be respectful. You will be surprised how attentive the ladies will be. I have had groups of six or seven or more Filipinas gather around me when I am talking. They are eager to hear what you have to say. Here's a tongue-in-cheek post from my website **"PhilippinesPlus.com"** that I'll close out this dating tips guide with.

I'm a Stud in the Philippines!

"Now before some of my regular commentators on **PhilippinesPlus.com"** leave a disparaging remark that this post title *should* read **"I'm a *DUD* in the Philippines!,"** let me assure you, oh, intelligent and *obviously* gifted reader (since you're visiting this website) that the title is **no** misprint at all. Many times I have remarked that a poor sap can have a **face like a dog's butt** and still seem attractive to many of the cute Filipinas residing in the Philippines. As **Lance the Canadian (the handsomest man in the North)** recently remarked, Filipinas living in Canada and the United States *might not* necessarily feel that way. All the more reason for you guys with a face only your mother would love, to come over and visit the Philippines.

Why, at the meal held after **Tita's funeral** the other day, a young Filipino lad of around 11 even kept staring at me. He continued to look at me, obviously in awe of the **gwapo (handsome) kano** he saw. My Filipina wife spoke to him in the local language, and it seems the young man was in awe of my **"long nose."**

But despite the Pinoy's observation of my nose, I can tell you that heads will turn when you walk into the local SM City Malls like my wife and I shop at in Iloilo. Cute Filipinas will greet you with a huge smile and a cheerful **"Good Morning, Sir!"** even if it is three in the afternoon. Sometimes you will even hear a salesgirl say to a nearby associate: **"Ang** *gwapo noh***?" (Isn't he handsome?)**

Oh, sure, there's been some cases where it *was* possible that the cute Filipina just might have thought I was a rich kano and wanted me to **buy her a laptop.** And there's been that recent **Filipina Facebook friend** asking for money, but for the most part the pretty Pinays think we kanos are good looking guys.

But *why* do some gorgeous Filipinas think that? I'm sure part of it is the fact that we are just *DIFFERENT LOOKING.* Ask the average cute girl from the Philippines if she thinks she is beautiful, and she will say **"no."** Many times they will just say they are average. But many guys from other countries will confess that Filipinas are some of the **most beautiful women** they have ever seen (I agree, I married one.) They are exotic and different looking from what we might be accustomed to.

So I can't help it if I'm a stud in the Philippines. It's a curse sometimes, but I'm blessed with a wonderful Filipina wife and a home where I'm treated like a celebrity wherever I go. Again, if you've never visited the Philippines, what are you waiting for? Who knows? You might even find the love of your life on one of these 7,107 islands that makes up this archipelago called the Philippines. And you can even have a face like a dog's butt!"

CLOSING THOUGHTS

I hope you have found "The Philippines Expat Advisor" to be a source of useful information, and it is my *sincere desire* that it has helped you in some way in planning your move to the Philippines and given you a glimpse of what to expect.

I cannot adequately put into words all the emotions I felt when moving here after living 57 years in the United States. Living in the Philippines is *not* for everyone. Sometimes it can be difficult. But then again, life in the States was difficult at times, also. With a positive attitude and some planning on your part (such as reading this book and doing a lot of research online), I think anyone can make a move to the Philippines and experience their own little slice of paradise. I sincerely thank you for purchasing this book, and again, hope it's contents will prove beneficial to you.

Dave DeWall

Iloilo in Western Visayas

The Philippines

A Lizard Poop Production

Made in the USA
Lexington, KY
26 June 2014